S0-CCV-687

ACHIEVING
ECO-NOMIC SECURITY*
ON SPACESHIP EARTH

By

Jim Bell

This book is dedicated to the children of all life, those living in the present and those who will share our planet in the future.

*ECO-NOMIC SECURITY -- The condition in which all economic activities, individually and in concert, are conducted in ways that preserve the social and ecological foundation upon which they ultimately rest.

The term Eco-nomic Security is more or less interchangeable with the term Eco-nomic Sustainability.

An ELSI Publication --- San Diego, California

A NOTE TO THE DEVELOPING WORLD

Although this book uses many developed world examples to illustrate ideas and strategies, the principles behind these examples can be used anywhere on our planet.

Ultimately, this book is about conducting a survey of the resources and hazards in your region or country, and learning how to use your resources in ways that protect genetic diversity, soil fertility, and that maintain an ample mineral reserve.

It is also about working out trade agreements that are consistent with these goals.

If these conditions are maintained, the potential for a people to prosper anywhere on our planet is virtually unlimited.

If you would like to reproduce any portion of this book, permission can be obtained by writing to Jim Bell at the Ecological Life Systems Institute (ELSI), 2923 East Spruce Street, San Diego, California 92104, USA, or call (619) 281-1447.

Copyright Jim Bell 1994. This book was first published in April 1994 in the United States of America by ELSI. Second Edition - December 1995, ISBN # 0-915841-19-3.

The cover of this book is printed on 50% total recovered fiber, 10% post consumer recycled paper. The text is printed on 100% total recovered fiber, 50% post consumer with soy based ink. This was the best we could come up with in our area at the time of printing.

Cover design - Robert Ocegueda

TABLE OF CONTENTS

ABOUT THE AUTHOR

Jim Bell is an internationally recognized expert on ecologically sustainable development. As an ecological designer, Jim works with developers, business, and various public and private agencies.

As of this publication Jim's is working on a number of fronts, including teaching classes and working on starting a weekly radio program which he would host. The program's working title is COMMON SENSE. The focus of the classes and the radio show, when it happens, is to help create a new constituency of voters who understand that to have a prosperous future we must develop an economy that is ecologically and economically sustainable --- and to encourage members of that constituency to run for local office. Jim is also working as a Design Consultant for the DeAnza Group and is directing the design and construction of an ecologically designed food cooperative community center. He also worked as a Co-Project Director for Eco-Parque, a prototype wastewater recycling plant in Tijuana, Mexico, until that projects was completed and he has also worked as a consultant for the Otay Ranch Joint Planning Project, the East Lake Development Company, and was the director of the San Diego Center for Appropriate Technology for 7 years.

Each year, Jim speaks to as many as 100 groups, ranging from third grade classes to graduate student seminars, business groups, and environmental organizations. Jim's lecture audiences have included the Society for International Development's 1994 World Conference in Mexico City, the American Institute of Architecture's California conference in Santa Barbara, and an International Audubon conference in Austin Texas. Jim is frequently interviewed by members of the television, radio, and print media, and was a guest on National Public Radio's "TALK OF THE NATION."

Jim also works with and serves on the Board of Directors of numerous eco-nomically oriented organizations.

THE AUTHOR ABOUT THE AUTHOR

I'm just a person who's trying to make things better. I work through ecology because ecology encompasses everything. If we don't figure out how to live and make a living on our planet, in ways that are eco-nomically sustainable, anything else we may accomplish will at best be temporary. I'm not saying that we will necessarily go extinct as a species, though that is a possibility. But if we don't rectify the basic conflict between how we currently satisfy our needs and desires, and the damage that these methods cause to our planet's life support system, we are clearly in for some hard times.

I don't happen to think that this is in inevitable. I believe that if conscious people work together, our present situation can be turned around. I believe we have the capability to turn our world into a virtual planetary Garden of Eden -- that we are ultimately intelligent enough to use the many strategies and technologies available today, and those yet to be discovered, to live quite comfortably on our planet, until the sun burns out some 5 billion years from now.

Helping this to happen is basically what I'm about, but as my friends will tell you I also like to party, especially when the music is good.

ACKNOWLEDGMENTS

Although I take full responsibility for any errors, faulty logic, or incorrect premises put forward in this book, many people have contributed to making it a reality. The following is only a partial list of those who have helped. To those whose names I've missed, please accept my apology and gratitude for your support.

Gretchen Lemke . Larry Fishbain . Sheryl Sheperio . Estelle Rubenstein . Jim Neshiem . Dave Neptune . Johanna Argoud . Mike and Pat McCoy . Watie Alberity . Jennifer Andersen . Fred Cagle . Marjorie Fox . The Lenny Cooper Foundation . Leone Hays . Lyn Snow . Gary Flo . Bianca Molinari . Forest Marshall . Natori Moore . Dave Burnite . Deborah Johnson . Bernie Kirby . Rebecca Margolis . Roberta Golliher . Kate Crawford . Norris Clement . Keith Mescher . Eugene Ray . Bill Rolie . Lynne Bayless . Karie Kios . Luis Sanchez . Howard Wilcox . Alice Barns . Heather Bell . Derek Eder . Michael Gelfand . Joy Billings . Martha Fort . Pat Dintino . Mark Overby . Russ Ives . August West . Lynn Scholl . Brian Parker . Ann Parker . Anne Colloredo Mansfeld . Donna Vary . Bill Bardallis . Angelica Castrellon . John Bowling . Doug Stewart . Susan & Pat Wallace . Wadad Dubbelday . Colleen Dietzel . Charles St. Hill . Keith Pazolie . Steve Scheck . John Cenzano . Romeo Carumbus . Nadia Amer . Chris Allen . Laura Dunbar . Gene Troxel.

Special thanks to Sharon Hudnall, Jean Courtney, Hilda Bejarano, Pat Parris, and Carolyn O'Patry who contributed greatly to getting the first edition of this book together in the final month of its production.

Another special thank you goes to Mary Clark who helped on the first edition and who sent my her througly edited copy of the book's first edition which was very helpful in putting this new edition together. Also thanks to Robert Ocegueda and Richard Carter who helped design this second edition and to Jim Danielson and Walter Venable who checked my math in the new final chapter.

A very special thanks goes to Marti Goethe who helped on the book in many ways and kept other projects moving while I took the time to get the book ready for this its second publication.

Finally, I thank my mother and father who always encouraged me to follow my heart.

We Are Everything

We are one substance.
Matter and energy,
Differing forms of the same thing.

We are one age.
Out of the substance of the universe
We are formed anew from what has existed
Since the beginning of time.

We are star children.
The literal transformation of light
Into thoughts, feelings and physical form.

We are one life.
Plants and animals, we are part of and dependent
Upon the total that we are.

We are one people.
Though we may differ in culture and color,
In the core of our being we are all the same.

We are part of the process
Of the universe knowing itself.
We are the light of stars looking back at ourselves
As we ponder the future it is our destiny to
Create.

Jim Bell
(6/7/91)

We Did Not Create Ourselves

We did not create ourselves.
If we are less than perfect,
it is not our fault.

But, once we make this realization,
it is our fault if we don't become
a little more perfect than we are now.

Consciousness is not something mystical and mysterious,
it's simply the process of becoming less of a jerk.

A process of becoming more helpful and less hurtful
and trying to be fairer and kinder in our dealings with each other,
and the world of life we are part of and dependent on.

Jim Bell
(2/3/95)

PREFACE

How This Book Is Organized

Part One is a short description of our situation, as a species, on our planet. It also suggests an encompassing goal to guide us in the creation of a more eco-nomically secure future.

Part Two explains why the ecology or life-support system of our planet is the foundation upon which all our actions as a species rest. It also shows that if we use eco-nomically sustainable methods to supply ourselves, as a species, with the things we need and want, it will strengthen our economies, aid in bringing population growth under control, and make us less vulnerable to natural phenomenon like earthquakes, floods, fires, diseases, etc. and to intentional human acts of destruction.

Part Three is about Eco-nomically Integrated Planning (EIP). EIP is a method of land use planning aimed at achieving eco-nomic sustainability on our planet. Part Three also describes how to develop and use the tools needed in this effort.

Part Four is the how to part of the book. The primary aim of this section is to focus on how we can maximize our energy, water, and food security in ways that are eco-nomically sustainable. Part Four also shows why our present strategies for getting and using energy, water, food, and the products of industry are not in our short or long term interests.

Part Five offers some suggestions on what we can do as individuals, families, business people, as artists and scientists, through our educational institutions, governments, religious and philosophic organizations, and the media to help ourselves on the path to achieving eco-nomic sustainability. Part five also includes the book's new chapter --- Achieving Eco-nomic Security, The San Diego/Tijuana Region, A Case Study. This chapter shows how this particular region, given its particular vulnerabilities, can gracefully evolve from its present non-sustainable economy to an economy that is completely sustainable, and in ways that are cost-effective.

INTRODUCTION

This book is about answering a very simple yet profound question: How can we, as individuals and as a species, do the things that we need and want to do, on all levels, in ways that are economically viable and ecologically sustainable? Put another way, if we are doing things in ways that damage our planet's life support system, how can we do them differently to avoid these problems?

This book is also about critical thinking. About analyzing the solutions presented in this book and elsewhere from the perspective of their potential to be truly sustainable. In other words, if several billion people use a particular technology or group of technologies, are the impacts associated with that use truly eco-nomically sustainable?

As an ecological designer, it is my belief that solar energy, in its various forms, is the best source of energy available to meet the world's energy needs. But from the perspective of eco-nomical sustainability, not all solar energy collection systems make sense. Even if a solar collector is extremely efficient at converting sunlight into work, its creation, use, and disposal may not represent an ecological plus.

For example, if the collector is made of copper or some other metal, what kind of damage was caused when that metal was mined and smelted? What will it cost in time, energy, and money to repair the damage that was caused? When the collector was fabricated, what kind of solders, adhesives, plastics, insulation, etc. were used in the process? What impact does their creation and use have on the environment? How are the people who work with these materials affected by them? If their health is affected, how much will it cost to take care of them?

When the collector is used, what kind of contaminants might it contribute to the environment? With a solar waterheater, for example, contaminants can be picked up by the water that passes through it. If lead-based solder is used in the collector, a person taking a shower may be breathing lead laced steam and bathing in lead contaminated water. What effects will this have on the bather's health? What will these health problems cost the individual and society?

Finally, is the collector and its components designed to be easily reused and recycled? If not, in part or whole, the collector will take up space in a landfill. In addition to the damage to the environment that landfills cause, they also cost money for the land they occupy and perhaps the eventual cost of cleaning up the groundwater storage basins which underlie them or receive leachate from them.

If, on the other hand, the collector is designed to be easily recycled, the cost of land filling and potential groundwater pollution is avoided. Additionally, the negative impacts associated with mining and processing metals and other materials to make a new collector or other product are largely eliminated. It takes a relatively small amount of energy to melt and reform a refined metal, compared with what it takes to produce it from virgin ore. The pollution generated by recycling a metal is also much easier to control and greatly reduced in volume, compared with getting the same amount of metal by mining and processing virgin ore.

The issues raised in the solar collector example just discussed are almost never considered when we unleash products on the world. This is because there is a general lack of knowledge about how the ecology of our planet works and how what we do affects it. This lack of ecological savvy has led us to accept half-solutions in dealing with human caused ecological problems. Even solar energy, if not thoughtfully implemented, can be ecologically destructive.

Another example relates to how we have approached the global carbon dioxide-greenhouse warming issue. In proposing solutions to this problem, a number of scientist have called for growing various plants, from algae to trees, as a way to reduce the amount of CO_2 in our atmosphere. While there are many good reasons for growing plants and particularly trees, a permanent reduction in atmospheric CO_2 may not be not one of them.

If we stopped using fossil fuels today and millions of young trees were planted, the amount of CO_2 in our planet's atmosphere would be reduced, at least temporarily. As they grow, trees and other plants extract and embody carbon from the atmosphere and thus reduce the amount of CO_2 in the atmosphere. But when plants die and decay or burn, the carbon they have embodied is recombined with oxygen and released into the atmosphere as CO_2. A large percentage of atmospheric CO_2 cycles through the biosphere once every 20 to 30 years. [1]

Thus, if forests and other vegetation communities are expanded permanently, a permanent reduction of atmospheric CO_2 would occur, but only if the combustion of fossil fuels ends. As plant communities become larger, they can store more carbon. This storage can be more or less permanent since the CO_2 released by burning or decaying plants will be absorbed by new growth. However, if the use of fossil fuels continues, the only way plants can be used to reduce the buildup of CO_2 in the atmosphere would be to harvest them and store them in a place where they could not decay or burn.

While photosynthesis is only one aspect of the carbon cycle, it does illustrate the need to think through natural processes. If we do this, we can better understand whether a perceived solution is really going to be effective or if we need a more comprehensive approach, based on how our planet's life support system actually works.

---

[1]   *Clark, Mary. Contemporary Biology. Second Edition, W.B. Saunders Company, Philadelphia, London, Toronto, (1979): p. 528.*

Another way that this lack of whole planet or biospheric analysis manifests is in how we focus on a problem. Take the issue of increasing levels of atmospheric methane. The media has made much of the fact that cattle and other domestic ruminants are collectively releasing large amounts of methane gas into the atmosphere as part of their digestive processes. Molecule for molecule methane gas is 20 to 30 times more effective at trapping atmospheric heat as is CO_2. [2]

Along with reducing their contribution to atmospheric methane, there are many good reasons to reduce the number of domestic ruminant animals that live on our planet at any one time. (**See index for soil erosion for details.**) But the focus on the methane contributed by such animals distracts us from the methane releases that human activities are causing. While "livestock account for 15-20 percent of global methane emissions", it is at least equaled by our own activities. [3] Currently, our use of fossil fuels contributes 20% of the methane that is being released into the atmosphere. [4] At least half of this 20% results from the release of methane gas related to mining coal. [5]

As stated in the first paragraph of this introduction, this book is about solutions. Solutions that are not only consistent with principles of ecological sustainability but those that can be successfully applied on a scale that can sustainably support a global population of 7 billion or more individuals who increasingly live in urban areas. It is also about developing a planning strategy that will help us in this effort.

It is my belief that the recommendations presented in this book are workable and cost effective, even within the narrow confines of how we currently measure material wealth. But, I also see these recommendations as only a starting place. We are just beginning to understand how the life support system on our planet works.

Indeed, we have not even named all the organisms that share this planet with us. Our relationship to them, as interdependent elements in the web of life, is even more of a mystery.

As our knowledge grows, new insights and ideas about how we can live and make livings sustainably on our planet are sure to evolve. To people of the future, the ideas I have presented here will, undoubtedly, seem as crude and quaint as the technologies of the distant past seem to us today.

[2]   Schneider, Stephen H. _Global Warming_. Sierra Club Books, San Francisco, (1989): p. 20, (Taken from the uncorrected proof).

[3]   Brown, Lester R. _State of the World 1992_. Worldwatch Institute, W.W. Norton and Company, New York, London, (1992): p. 74.

[4]   Ibid. pp. 37-38.

[5]   Ibid.

PART ONE

OUR PRESENT PREDICAMENT

Chapter I

DECIDING ON A GOAL

With all the drama we manage to create as a species, it's easy to lose sight of the fact that we are, like other life forms, part of and totally dependent on our planet's ecology for our survival. Arguments about how much abuse our planet's ecology can sustain before a major collapse ensues may be interesting, but isn't it a little crazy to cause unnecessary damage to the only life support system that we have?

The human species is endowed with unbounded cleverness. Unfortunately, this cleverness is poorly balanced with wisdom. Nowhere is this imbalance more graphically illustrated than in the contradiction between how we as individuals, nations, and as a global community, go about satisfying our needs and desires, and the negative effect these activities have on our planetary life support system. Daily, the media bombards us with information chronicling the results of our assaults on nature. But, even as our awareness and concern are increasing, we still respond to this information as though hearing reports of some distant battle in which we are not personally involved.

Deep down, any thinking person knows that this is not the case. Yet, day to day, we are carried along by the momentum of practices and attitudes that no longer correspond to the current eco-nomic situation on our planet.

To date, we do not yet know how to live on our planet in ways that are **eco-nomically sustainable**, even though most of the technologies needed to do so have already been developed. Yet, if we don't learn soon how to do this, any success toward solving other human problems will, at best, be temporary.

I therefore submit that the underlying goal that will allow us to achieve whatever else we set our sights on as a species is:

> To learn how to live and make a living on our planet in ways that are **eco-nomically sustainable** and to teach that knowledge to our children.

To achieve this goal, we must answer two basic questions:

1. On the surface of our planet, "WHERE is it appropriate for humans to do WHAT?"

If our goal is to live on our planet in ways that maximize **eco-nomic sustainability**, how do we decide where it is most appropriate to site our cities, what areas should we set aside for agriculture, for wildlife habitat and so forth? If we have made land use mistakes in the past, how can we evolve gracefully into a more **eco-nomically secure** land use pattern?

2. Once we have resolved the "Where" issues, we must determine "HOW should we do the WHAT?"

How do we design our cities, and the buildings and infrastructures that make them up, so that they operate in ways that are eco-nomically sustainable? How do we grow and use food, timber, and other plant materials in ways that protect genetic diversity, build soils, and eliminate pollution? How do we mine and use our planet's mineral wealth in the same way?

The chapters that follow attempt to answer these and related questions as a guide toward learning how to live in ways that are more eco-nomically secure.

PART TWO

SEEING FAMILIAR THINGS IN A DIFFERENT LIGHT

Chapter II

SPACESHIP EARTH

Synopsis

Essentially our situation on planet earth is that of 5.6 billion astronauts living on a spaceship. Like any well designed spaceship, ours has a life support system (solar powered) that directly and indirectly supplies us with all the necessities of life, including the conditions that make life as we know it possible. The more we understand about how our life support system works, the better we can meet human needs in ways that make us more eco-nomically secure.

---

* (Teacher)   # (Students)

Scene: Children in classroom giving answers to questions about recycling. Questioning shifts from recycling to a broader perspective.

*	How many of you ever have thought about being an astronaut?
#	Children raise hands.
*	Have you ever thought that you are already an astronaut?
#	Children look puzzled.
*	Let's imagine that we are going on a long space journey. What do we need to take with us to make our journey possible?
#	Food!
*	Yes, we certainly need food.
#	Water!
*	Good.
#	Air!
*	Excellent, but there's another problem. We are going so far that we can't carry enough food, water, and air on our spaceship to get us to where we are going.
*	What should we do?
#	We need plants!
*	That's good. How do the plants help us?
#	Plants recycle the air.
*	That's right, plants use the carbon in the carbon dioxide we breathe out to grow and release the oxygen we need to breathe. What else?
#	Plants give us food.
*	Let's see if I've got this right. Plants provide us with oxygen and food. O.K., If we drink water and eat the food the plants provide us, eventually we have to go to the bathroom. What do we do with the waste that we flush down the toilet?
#	UGH, we'll flush it out into space. (laughter)
*	But wait a minute, where did this waste come from?
#	It came from us.
*	Where did it come from before that?
#	It came from the plants we ate.
*	Where did the plants get it from?
#	They got it from the soil and water the plants grew in and the carbon dioxide we breathe out.
*	Well, if we flush our toilet wastes out into space what will eventually happen?
#	We'll run out of the soil, water, carbon dioxide and oxygen resources that we and the plants

       need to live and grow.
*   So what do we have to do?
\#   We have to recycle!!!!

In the 1960's and 70's, the architect and technologist Buckminster Fuller and others popularized the phrase "SPACESHIP EARTH". They recognized that just like any well designed spaceship, the earth has a life support system that supplies us, its astronauts, with everything we need, and will continue to do so indefinitely, as long as we don't damage it too seriously.

Our planet's life support system is actually a sophisticated recycling system. In this system the sun provides the energy to recycle the air, water, and nutrients essential to life as we know it.

In a seemingly endless cycle, solar energy lifts water from our planet's surface into the atmosphere where it condenses as rain, snow, fog, and dew and returns to the earth to replenish the soil, waterways, and groundwater basins.

The sun also provides the energy needed to recycle the air we breathe and the nutrients necessary for life. Through solar-powered photosynthesis plants grow by absorbing nutrients and water from the soil and carbon from the air. In the process, plants release oxygen and provide food and materials.

Because humans and other animals eat plants directly or eat animals that eat plants, we are also part of this solar-powered recycling system.

Through this recycling process every atom in our bodies has been recycled thousands or even millions of times through other life forms that lived in the past. When we eliminate waste from our bodies or when we die, decomposing organisms break down our bodies and wastes into materials that can be used by plants, thus beginning the cycle of life once again.

Indeed, even as we live, 98% of the atoms in our body are replaced or, more correctly, recycled each year. [1] Minute by minute we extract new atoms from the food we eat, the water we drink, and the air we breathe, to replace the atoms we lose through our bowels, from our hair and skin, and when we perspire and exhale.

Unfortunately, all is not well with our solar-powered life support system. And though people are becoming increasingly aware of the problem, there is a lot of confusion concerning what to do about it.

Part of this confusion stems from our failure to make some basic connections between how the life support system or the ecology of our planet functions and how this relates to our individual and societal well-being and security. The material that follows in **PART TWO** is an attempt to clear up some of this confusion.

---

[1]   *Chopra, Deepak. Quantum Healing: Exploring the Frontiers of Mind/Body Medicine.*
    Bantam Books, New York, (1989): pp. 48-49.

_____

CHAPTER III

ECO-NOMICS: EXPOSING THE MYTH OF ECONOMY VS. ECOLOGY

Synopsis

The ecology of our planet is the foundation of everything we do, including what we do under the heading of economy. When we damage the ecology through inappropriate economic activities, we undercut the potential for economic activities in the future. Today, very little of what we do economically actually increases our energy and material wealth. This is because almost everything we do, and more precisely, HOW we are doing it, depends on the use of non-renewable resources and the procurement and use of potentially renewal resources in ways that are not ecologically sustainable.

"True cost pricing" or "full cost pricing" is a free-market strategy aimed at integrating the principles of ecological sustainability with economically sound business practices. The basic idea behind the concept is to insure that the consumers of economically harmful products and services are those who pay for any damage those commodities cause. Currently, the public, through taxes, health costs, etc. pays most of the environmental and social costs associated with ecologically damaging products. By paying these costs, the public is caught in the ironic position of actually subsidizing the very products and processes that are causing them harm. Even worse, these subsidies retard the development of technologies that are ecologically benign, by reducing the market-place-cost of ecologically and socially damaging technologies. With true cost pricing, these costs would be included in the market price of ecologically damaging products and services.

Including these costs up-front would cause the consumer price of such commodities to rise. This would unleash pent up entrepreneurial or competitive energy toward the development of ecologically friendly products and services that would avoid such costs and thus be less expensive than their damaging counterparts.

As technologies become more ecologically sophisticated there is no reason for commonly used products to be any more expensive to purchase than they are now. But even if they did end up costing more at the point of purchase, under true cost pricing they would still be more cost effective to society. It's less expensive to prevent ecological and social problems, than to attempt to fix them after they have been created.

Adding the eco-nomic or true cost to products and their packaging would also eliminate most of our solid waste disposal problems. With true cost pricing everything sold in the marketplace would be designed to be reused or at least recycled or composted. When all costs are included, this is the most cost effective thing to do.

There is a general view that the free enterprise system is the antithesis of a healthy environment. With true cost pricing, however, free market forces can be powerful tools toward creating an eco-nomically secure future.

Ecology Vs. Economy?

Probably the most misunderstood connection between ecology and our day-to-day lives is the relationship between ecology and the economy. By now most people are beginning to sense that major changes are needed to protect our ecological security. A New York Times poll in 1990 found that "74 percent (U.S. citizens) said that protecting the environment is so important that requirements and standards cannot be too high, and environment improvements must be made regardless of cost." [2] In a more recent Wall Street Journal/NBC News Poll it was "revealed that eight in ten Americans call themselves 'environmentalists.'" [3]

Globally, the sentiment seems to be much the same. "In a Gallup poll of 22,000 people in 22 nations, a majority in 20 rich and poor countries - from the U.S. and Japan to Russia and Brazil - favored a green emphasis. In the other two, India and Turkey, 43% supported the environment. In 16 of the countries, most respondents said they would accept higher prices so industry could pay for environmental measures." [4]

BUT -- lurking in the back of many of our minds is the idea that if we don't give industry and its products the freedom to damage and pollute the environment, the economy will be hurt and people will lose their sources of income. If this notion is true at all, it is valid only from a very narrow perspective. Obviously, if we damage our planet's ecology beyond its point of recovery or turn-around, the economy will collapse and most of the ways that we currently earn income, as that term is used in the modern world, will cease to exist.

Ecology: The Foundation Of The Economy

At the most fundamental level, the ecology or life support system of our planet is the foundation of everything we do. It provides us with the air we breathe, the water we drink, and the food we eat. It also, directly or indirectly, provides us with the wherewithal to get everything else we need and want to keep ourselves comfortable and stimulated.

As such the ecology of our planet is the foundation upon which all our eco-nomic activities rest. When money is made in ways that unduly damage the life support system of our planet, the foundation of our economy is being undermined as well.

In economic terms the ecology of our planet is like the money or capital in a bank account. The productive potential of the ecology is the interest generated by that capital. Presently, most of our activities affect our planet's ecology in ways that reduce both its capital and productive potential. Instead of increasing our ecological wealth, we are spending it.

Agricultural and forestry practices worldwide are characterized by the loss of topsoil and soil fertility to erosion. Similarly, our methods of obtaining, using, and disposing of the earth's mineral resources are reducing the capital in our ecological account. As ecological capital is reduced, the amount of interest or income it can sustainably produce is reduced as well.

If we protect our planet's ecological capital, we can live off the interest it generates forever. This idea is similar to economist Herman Daly's concept of "no net loss of natural capital". [5] By using some of this interest wisely, we can actually <u>increase</u> our planet's ecological capital and thereby increase the sustainable interest or income that it generates. If we grow food and manage our forests in ways that enrich the soil, we are increasing the earth's ecological capital, or the earth's potential to produce more food or forest products on a given piece of land. If we use sustainable methods to obtain, use, reuse, and recycle the earth's mineral resources, we are preserving the eco-

---

[2] Ladd, Everett Carll. "How Americans View the Environment". <u>Christian Science Monitor</u>. (April 20, 1990): p. 19.

[3] Miller, John. "The Wrong Shade of Green", <u>Dollars & Sense</u>. No. 185, (April 1993): p. 6.

[4] Holman, Richard L.. "World Wire: Environment Wins Over Economy". <u>The Wall Street Journal</u>. Eastern Edition, New York, New York, (May 6, 1992): p. A-11.

[5] John Miller. "The Wrong Shade of Green," <u>Dollars & Sense</u>. No. 185, (April 1993): p. 9.

nomic foundation that allows us to benefit from these resources indefinitely.

When all costs are considered, there is no conflict between ecological health and economic vitality. They only appear to be at odds because many of the environmental and social costs associated with creation, use, and disposal of products offered in the marketplace <u>are not included</u> in price that is paid for them. Instead, these costs, which in effect subsidize the product or service they are attached to, are paid for by everyone.

Even if we do not use or benefit from an ecologically damaging product or service, we pay for the impacts they create. In other words, we pay a hidden subsidy to cover any costs associated with a product or service that is not covered by its retail price.

This is especially true in the energy sector of our economy. For example, as consumers we do not pay additional money up front for cars and trucks or the fuel we burn to run them to cover the health costs that result from breathing or being exposed to the pollution that comes out of their exhausts, crank cases, breaks, etc. Even if only exhaust related air pollution is considered, studies sponsored by American Lung Association came up with air pollution related health costs for the U.S. ranging from "$4.43 billion to $84.99 billion" in 1985. [6]

Similarly, as consumers we do not pay the true cost for electricity to cover the health costs to society caused when fossil fuels containing sulfur and other harmful chemicals are burned to generate it. A Pace University study estimated that each ton of sulfur dioxide emitted into the atmosphere "costs society $3,500 in health-related damage alone -- and in 1988 the United States emitted 22.8 million tons of sulfur dioxide." [7] If Pace University's estimates are correct, the health costs caused by sulfur dioxide emissions in 1988 were just under $80 billion. [8]

Hidden costs related to fossil fuel use also show up in crop damage. Experiments by the University of California show that ozone levels, "half those (typically found) in Southern California-reduce yields of cotton by 20%, table grapes by 25% and Valencia oranges by 25%. [9]

Even though they are not commercially traded and therefore not easily quantified, there are a number of other hidden costs related to fossil fuel use. They include:

☐ the disfigurement of historical monuments which are eroded by acid deposition and discolored by fossil fuel particulates;

☐ damaged watershed function and wildlife which are harmed by ground level ozone (smog), acid deposition, and particulate materials; and

☐ visibility which affects mental health and productivity, traffic safety, tourism, property values, and our general quality-of-life.

Even if we only consider the two obvious health-related costs discussed above, the hidden

---

[6] Cannon, James S.. *The Health Costs Of Air Pollution*. (Pre-published Edition), American Lung Association, Washington D.C., (1990): p.49.

[7] Wager, Janet S. "How Much Are Fossil Fuels Really Costing You?". *Nucleus*. Vol. 15, No. 2, (Summer 1993): p. 7.

[8] Author's calculations.

[9] Pasternak, Judy. "Pollution Is Choking Farm Belt." *Los Angeles Times*. (April 22, 1991): p. A-1.

health cost related to air pollution is somewhere between 84 and 165 billion dollars a year. [10]

A 1988 German study on the true cost of energy, titled the "Social Costs of Energy Consumption," uncovered similar costs. Hohmeyer, the author of the study, "concluded that the direct social costs attributable to electric generation in Germany is about $.03/kwhr (more than is actually paid for it). This accounts for medical expenses, loss of pay due to sickness, repairs required to buildings, loss of forest revenues, etc. but little or nothing for pain and suffering, bereavement, loss of scenic tourist attractions, etc." [11]

Also not included in Hohmeyer's analysis are the health costs associated with carbon monoxide emissions, or the potential cost of building locks and dams to hold the sea at bay if global warming caused by greenhouse gases cause ocean levels to rise as the polar ice cap and glaciers melt. If these costs are included, some experts have pegged the cost of mitigating the negative impacts of fossil fuel use at $.07 per kwhr for coal and $.04 per kwhr for natural gas above what we currently pay for them. [12]

Presently, the United States uses about 7.6 quads or around 2.25 trillion kwhrs of electricity each year. If 3, 4, or 7 cents were added to the cost of each kwhr of electricity used in the U.S. we would be paying an additional $66, $89, and $155 billion respectively for electricity each year. [13]

Even these higher estimates do not include everything. Not included are the social or ecological costs associated with exploring for oil and natural gas, the installation of pipelines, the occasional natural gas explosion and tanker oil spill. Nor do they include the even more serious costs related to strip mining coal. [14]

Just considering health costs alone, whatever their exact cost turns out to be, the payments to cover them are made on many levels. Some payments go directly to our personal doctors to cover the care for illnesses that are caused or aggravated by air pollution. Some come out of tax revenues to pay for the health care of people who cannot afford it. Others come in the form of lost productivity that results in higher costs for general goods and services. Air pollution both aggravates and prolongs respiratory illnesses. People thus affected are less productive when they work and they are off the job more often. Because more people are sick more often, we also pay higher premiums for health and life insurance. And these costs are paid by everyone, whether they drive a car or truck, ride a bus, or use electricity produced by burning high sulfur fossil fuels. [15]

Hidden subsidies in other economic sectors include costs like cleaning up water polluted during mining and smelting operations. They also include the cost of replacing eroded topsoil when

---

[10]   *Author's calculations based on the figures taken from: Cannon, James S.* The Health Costs Of Air Pollution. *(Pre-published Edition), American Lung Association, Washington D.C., (1990): p.49, and Wager, Janet S. "How Much Are Fossil Fuels Really Costing You?".* Nucleus. *Vol. 15, No. 2, (Summer 1993): p. 7.*

[11]   *Quoted by Lorin L. Vant-Hull. "Solar Thermal Central Receivers".* Solar Today. *Vol. 6, No 6, (Nov./Dec. 1992): p. 15.*

[12]   *Ibid, p. 16.*

[13]   *Author's calculations.*

[14]   *Vant-Hull, Lorin L. "Solar Thermal Central Receivers".* Solar Today. *Vol. 6, No 6, (Nov./Dec. 1992): p. 16.*

[15]   *See index for more entries.*

forests are clear cut or when land is improperly farmed. The pollution caused by using poorly designed products and the cost of land filling packaging and product residues are additional costs borne by the taxpayer. More detailed examination of these and other hidden costs associated with how we currently do things will be covered in the chapters to follow.

Direct Subsidies

In addition to hidden subsidies, there are also a number of direct subsidies that taxpayers pay to keep the retail price of non-renewable energy resources artificially low. Resource depletion allowances, for example, permit resource extractors to write off some of the taxes they would otherwise have had to pay on their profits. In other words, resource extractors pay less taxes on their profits than do other businesses.

To foster and protect its subsidies, the oil industry supports its own lobby. "The largest lobby in Washington is the American Petroleum Institute, with over 500 employees." To keep its employees busy, the American Petroleum Institute "spent $50 million" in 1988. [16] What does the oil industry get for its money? Oil companies "receive massive government subsidies" -- $8.5 billion in 1984 for example. [17] For comparison, Exxon had $7 billion in sales in 1990. [18]

Another way the taxpayer subsidizes the non-renewable energy industry is by paying for research and development. Compared with other energy sources, nuclear energy has consumed the lion's share of public research funding related to energy. Since 1948 "65% of all federal energy research dollars --- has gone to nuclear fission and fusion." [19]

As a whole, the energy industry receives direct subsidies in the form of federal tax credits and research funding to the tune of "roughly $50 billion per year". Twenty-six billion dollars of this amount goes into supporting fossil fuels and $19 billion to support the nuclear industry. [20] By comparison, "energy savings received less than $1 billion (in subsidies), and returned 185 times as much in savings per Federal dollar invested than a dollar invested in nuclear power." [21] And as if current direct subsidies were not enough, the U.S. Government is offering Texaco, Chevron, and other U.S. companies involved in exploring oil fields in the former Soviet states full protection from commercial risk. [22]

---

[16]   *Russell, Dick. "Empires of Black Gold". New Internationalist. N. 206, (April 1990): p. 12.*

[17]   *Ibid.*

[18]   *Ibid.*

[19]   *Magavern, Bill. "A prescription for Fiscal and Environmental Health". Critical Mass. Vol. 3, No. 1, (May 1993): p. 1.*

[20]   *Hubbard, Harold R. "The Real Cost of Energy". Scientific American. Vol. 264, No. 4, (April 1991): p. 37. Also see Lovins, Hunter et al. Changing America: Blueprints for a New Democracy. (Reprint), Rocky Mountain Institute, Old Snowmass, Colorado, (1992): p. 7.*

[21]   *Lovins, Hunter et al. Changing America: Blueprints for a New Democracy. (Reprint), Rocky Mountain Institute, Old Snowmass, Colorado, (1992): p. 7.*

[22]   *"Eximbank Signs Historic U.S.-Russia Oil and Gas Agreement", BISNIS BULLETIN, U.S. Department of Commerce International Trade Administration, September 1993, page 1 - 3.* "All trade and investment-related U.S. Government agencies, including the Overseas Private Investment Corporation (OPIC), the Export-Import Bank of the United States, and the Departments of State, Treasury, and Energy participate in the U.S.-Russia Business Development Committee. . . . OPIC announced it will provide guarantee and insurance support for Texaco's oil well restoration project in Western Siberia.*

In total, the net value of all the subsidies, hidden and direct, that benefit the conventional energy industry "range between $100 billion and $300 billion per year" in the United States alone. [23]

Our dependence on imported oil also costs us economically by amplifying our nation's trade imbalance. Depending on the level of economic activity, oil imports have accounted for as much as 92 percent of the U.S. trade deficit. [24] When we import oil we export money.

We can avoid this capital drain from our local and national economy by investing the money we now export in becoming more energy efficient and switching to renewable energy resources. Not only would this help protect the environment from damage and help our national trade imbalance, it would also help the economy by turning jobless people in the U.S. into tax paying workers.

The Mining Industry

In addition to benefiting non-renewable energy systems, direct subsidies like resource depletion allowances also benefit the mining industry. According to the Federal Office of Management and Budget (OMB), most of the mining industry's $505 million 1991 tax windfall came in the form of resource depletion allowances. [25]

Other subsidies enjoyed by the mining industry include the General Mining Act of 1872. This 122 year old act allows mining interests to purchase publicly owned land at $5 per acre or less if they discover hard-rock (gold, silver, lead, iron, and copper) mineral deposits on it. Additionally, no matter how much a particular mineral deposit is ultimately worth, the public is not entitled to a royalty. This is because the land containing the deposit is sold outright to the mining company. [26]

Beyond the overt subsidies discussed above, the mining industry also benefits from hidden subsidies. These subsidies are the result of environmental laws which exempt mining interests from clean-up responsibilities. Mining wastes constitute the "single largest category of wastes produced" in the U.S. Yet the Federal Resource Conservation and Recovery Act of 1976 "specifically exempted mining wastes from regulation as a hazardous waste." [27]

Although it is not required by law to do so, Kennecott Copper, which operates the Bingham Canyon copper mine in Utah, reported its cumulative toxic chemical release in 1987. "Out of the 18,000 industrial facilities reporting nationwide that year, the Bingham Canyon mine came in fourth in total toxic release and first in metal." [28] As large as Kennecott's contribution to toxic waste is, it should be borne in mind that the Bingham mine is only one of many copper mining operations. Further, copper is only one of the many resources that are mined.

---

[23] Hubbard, Harold R. *"The Real Cost of Energy"*. <u>Scientific American</u>. *Vol. 264, No. 4, (April 1991): p. 36. (See index for more entries.)*

[24] Banks, Howard. Editor, *"What's Ahead For Business"*, <u>Forbes</u>. *Vol. 149, No. 5, (March 2, 1992): p. 37.*

[25] Young, John E. *"Free-Loding Off Uncle Sam"*. <u>World Watch</u>. *Vol. 5, No. 1, (Jan./Feb. 1992): p. 34.*

[26] Ibid.

[27] Ibid.

[28] Ibid.

Subsidies and Their Effect On Reuse And Recycling

One of the worst results of the subsidies just described is that they hamper reuse and recycling by artificially reducing the true price of virgin materials. Mining, harvesting, and processing virgin materials requires far more energy and causes far more ecological damage than does reusing or recycling the same materials. If these costs were included in the consumer price of virgin materials, industries would design more products for reuse and purchase recycled materials when reuse was not practical. More costly virgin materials would only be purchased as a last resort.

The benefits of reuse and recycling would be further enhanced if the cost of landfilling poorly designed products and packaging were included in their price. If this happened, the least-cost strategy for manufacturers would be to design products and packaging to be reusable and/or easily recycled.

If products and their packaging were designed to be reusable, recyclable or compostable, landfills could be transformed into Resource Recovery Centers. At these centers, reusable products would be put back into circulation and worn out objects would be sorted and returned to industry to be made into new products in a perpetually sustainable cycle. Resource Recovery Centers would also recycle organic materials not suitable for direct reuse or recycling by composting them. Once composted these materials would be returned proportionally to the forests and fields where they originated.

Even without considering the broader costs involved, some municipalities are finding that composting is already a cost effective way to process organic wastes. Fairfield, Connecticut has instituted a composting operation that combines sewage sludge with yard wastes to produce compost. "Richard White, supervisor of Fairfield's wastewater treatment facility, which produces sewage sludge for the composting facility, figures the town is saving at least $100,000 in its first year of composting. He hopes to increase those savings by marketing the compost to local landscapers, and by charging nearby companies to compost spoiled food and other organic materials." Odors from the operation have not been a problem. Even though the Fairfield facility is located in a residential neighborhood where some houses cost $500,000 there have been no complaints. This is probably because "the Fairfield facility smells no worse than wet leaves" from a few yards away. [29]

In general, direct and hidden subsidies give ecologically damaging products and practices an economic edge over practices and products that are more ecologically benign. As presently structured, these subsidies take up the economic slack for polluters which, in effect, penalize companies that operate in ways that are more ecologically benign. For its part, the taxpaying public is caught in the ironic situation of subsidizing the very industrial and commercial practices that they are threatened by and end up paying for to correct.

True-Cost-Pricing

The answer to this dilemma is embodied in a concept called true-cost-pricing. True-cost-pricing is a two step process through which the free-market can be used to stimulate economic activity while protecting the ecological foundation that supports it.

Step one requires a thorough ecological and social accounting to determine what things are really costing us. What would a styrofoam cup really cost if we include all the costs associated with its creation, use, and disposal in its point-of-sale price? Consider just one of the impacts of using styrofoam: one hundred percent of the human tissue samples analyzed by the Environmental Protection Agency's National Human Adipose (fatty) Tissue Survey contained styrene. Although the final cost of treating people who become ill from such exposure is unknown, styrene contamination

---

[29] Simon, Ruth. *"The Whole Earth Compost Pile?"*. <u>Forbes</u>. *(May 28, 1990): p. 136.]*

has been linked to "neurotoxic, hematological, cytogenetic, and carcinogenic effects". [30]

Or, what is the true cost of the pesticides we use in our homes and gardens or eat with our food? A 1987 National Cancer Institute study revealed that children in households where parents used home or garden pesticides "are six times more likely to develop some forms of childhood leukemia." [31] Beyond the tragedy this finding portends, what costs should be added to the price of pesticides to cover the children who contract leukemia from pesticide exposure? A vigorous accounting would bring these costs to light.

Step two involves the adoption of State and/or Federal legislation to insure that all or at least most of the costs associated with a particular product or service be included in the end-use price of the product or service in question.

Implementing True-Cost-Pricing

The implementation of true-cost-pricing could take place in a number of ways. One possibility would be to require companies to pay a specified amount of money into an escrow fund for each product they produce. The amount of money deposited for each product would be based on a true-cost-pricing audit that would target the ecological and social costs that a particular product's creation, use, and disposal would incur.

The deposit for styrofoam products, for example, would include:

◻   Health and ecological costs related to the extraction and use of the petroleum that went into making them. (Styrene is an oil-based product.)

◻   Health and ecological costs associated with the creation, use, and landfill disposal costs of styrofoam products. (Currently, very little styrofoam is recycled and when recycled, it is made into products like plastic lumber and outdoor carpet that will be landfilled when these products wear out.)

◻   Any extenuating environmental costs related to landfilling styrofoam, like groundwater contamination.

◻   Other costs, like the public cost of litter cleanup for improperly discarded styrofoam. These costs could be based on historic information, such as the historic percentage that styrofoam has contributed to total litter over the 5 preceding years, divided into the total cost of litter abatement.

To facilitate recycling, some items like flashlight batteries would include a returnable deposit of perhaps $.50 each to ensure they would be recycled instead of thrown away when exhausted. When batteries were returned, the $.50 deposit would be redeemed or carried over to the purchase of new batteries. Such deposits would ensure that valuable resources like those found in flashlight batteries would be returned to the industrial sector for reuse instead of being landfilled or discarded in the general environment. Currently, most flashlight type batteries are disposed of in ways that

---

[30]   *"Styrene: Health Effects Of Low-Level Exposure."* FASE Reports. *Foundation For Advancements In Science And Education, Vol. 7, No. 2, Winter (1988), p. 2.*

[31]   *Bashin, Brian Jay. "Bug Bomb Fallout".* Harrowsmith. *Vol. IV, No. 21, (May/June 1989), p. 44. Also see Ruzicka, Angie. "Is Spraying Pesticides Around Home Worth the Risk of Childhood Leukemia?,"* The Journal of Pesticide Reform. *Vol. 7, No. 3, (Fall 1987): p. 23.]*

contaminate surface and groundwater with toxic liquids and heavy metals. [32]

True-cost-pricing is already having an impact on price in the energy sector. The state of Wisconsin "considers either conservation or non-fossil fuel-generating capacity economically comparable to a conventional (energy production) system even if it costs 15 percent more." [33] Wisconsin's "public service commission also requires utilities to include the future cost of mitigating air-quality problems in proposals to renovate existing power plants." [34]

New York's approach is to add "a certain amount per kilowatt-hour based on air and water pollution and land degradation to the expected price of electricity from each source." [35]

An even more complex and comprehensive way to calculate the hidden costs related to energy is being considered by California, Oregon, Wisconsin, Colorado, and New Jersey. This method, developed at the Bonneville Power Administration by a team led by Shapard C. Buchanan, is "based on the total cost per kilowatt-hour produced or saved over the lifetime of a power generating or conservation resource." [36] The costs targeted in Buchanan's method include "the capital cost of building a plant or purchasing conservation equipment, the incremental costs of generating or saving each kilowatt-hour and various identifiable environmental and social costs." [37] "Conservation receives an additional 10 percentage bonus because of its many unqualified environmental benefits." [38]

Using market mechanisms to achieve ecological goals is even picking up support in the corporate world. "Last October, (1992) Frank Popoff, chairman and CEO of the Dow Chemical Company, suggested that the pricing system for chemicals should be changed so that individual products directly reflect their environmental costs." [39]

The Effect Of True-Cost-Pricing

The primary effect of true-cost-pricing would be to level the economic playing field. One result of this leveling process would be to stimulate a pent up reservoir of entrepreneurial energy toward the development of more ecologically benign products and services. To some extent this is already happening even though the market is currently skewed against it. By releasing entrepreneurial energy, leveling the economic playing field would also lead to the creation of new ecologically sustainable jobs. Currently, entrepreneurial activity in this area is being stifled by the direct and hidden subsidies discussed previously.

Another result would be to insure that the people who purchase ecologically harmful and non-recyclable products would pay for any health, clean up, or repair costs related to their creation,

---

[32]   Ranber, Paul. *"Mercury Madness."* <u>Sierra</u>. *Vol. 77, No. 6, (Nov./Dec. 1992): p. 38.*

[33]   Hubbard, Harold R. *"The Real Cost of Energy".* <u>Scientific American</u>. *Vol. 264, No. 4, (April 1991): p. 42.*

[34]   *Ibid.*

[35]   *Ibid.*

[36]   *Ibid.*

[37]   *Ibid.*

[38]   *Ibid.*

[39]   Flavin, Christopher and John E. Young. *"Will Clinton Give Industry A Green Edge",* <u>World Watch</u>. *Vol. 6, No. 1, (Jan./Feb. 1993): p. 30.*

use, and disposal. Since consumers purchase such products for their own benefit, it is only fair that the purchaser pay any external costs associated with them. This would relieve this burden from the shoulders of more ecologically conscious consumers and the public at large.

In general, the effect of true-cost-pricing would be to stimulate manufacturers and service providers to provide products and services that are as ecologically sustainable and socially beneficial as possible. When all costs are included, this is the most cost effective and therefore profitable thing for them to do.

Eco-nomic Success Stories

Even without true-cost-pricing, some well known companies are finding that being more eco-nomically responsible is the most cost effective way to operate. The April 1988 issue of Technology Review reported that the 3M Corporation has eliminated 50% of its toxic wastes, and greatly reduced the pollution it formerly released into the environment. During the ten year process from 1975 to 1985, 3M has saved around $300 million on disposal costs and through more efficient resource use, and increased energy efficiency. [40] Duphar, a large chemical concern in the Netherlands, has done even better. Duphar "adopted a new manufacturing process that decreased by 95% the amount of waste created in making pesticide." [41]

Like 3M, other U.S. corporations are benefiting from waste reduction as well. "According to a recent EPA study of 28 firms that have undertaken waste-reduction measures, 54 percent found that their investment paid for itself in less than a year, 21 percent found that it took one to two years, and only 7 percent found it took more than four." [42] With true-cost-pricing, this industrial clean up process would be greatly accelerated. [43]

Some companies have found ways to get the job done without using toxic chemicals at all. Perchloroethylene or PERC is the solvent of choice in most dry cleaning operations. It is also a toxic material that has been associated with a variety of health and environmental problems. These problems range from "central nervous system depression and liver damage" to being listed as a "hazardous waste under the 1984 Resource Conservation and Recovery Act (RCRA)". [44]

"Ecoclean", a dry cleaning method that has been in use in London, England since 1920 avoids the use of solvents altogether. The process was developed by the grandfather of Richard Simon who now runs the family business. Although the "sponge and press" method developed by his grandfather is practiced in much the same way as it was over 70 years ago, Richard Simon has added a number of innovations. These include the use of an environmentally safe soap called Aveda produced in Minneapolis and "the use of returnable wooden hangers" and cover bags to minimize waste. [45]

If Simon has his way the "Ecoclean" process will soon be available in the United States. "In

---

[40]   *Hirschhorn, Joel S. "Cutting Production of Hazardous Waste". Technology Review. Vol. 91, No. 3, (April 1988): p. 55.*

[41]   *Langone, John. "A Stinking Mess". Time. Vol. 133, No. 1, (Jan. 2, 1989): p. 45.*

[42]   *Ibid.*

[43]   *See Index for more entries.*

[44]   *Cohn, Linc and Mary O'Connell. "Dry Cleaning Without Chemicals" In Business. Vol. 15, No. 2, (March/April 1993): p. 39.*

[45]   *Ibid. p. 38.*

December, 1992 the EPA conducted a month-long economic feasibility study and preliminary performance test of Ecoclean techniques in collaboration with the Neighborhood Cleaning Association in Manhattan and two dry cleaners in Washington D.C." In the study "Federal and New York State employees were invited to drop their clothes off at designated points to be cleaned using the Ecoclean Methods. As part of the study, manufacturers donated 13 kinds of garments which were worn by volunteers over a four week period, and cleaned once a week, half using Ecoclean." [46] As of this writing, the test results are not in, but considering that the Ecoclean process has been competing successfully in England with solvent based cleaning processes for over 70 years, the outcome should be a foregone conclusion.

The 91,000 acre Collins Almanor Forestry operation is another eco-nomic success story. Recently, the media has made much out of the apparent conflict between saving the forest from clearcutting and preserving jobs for loggers. Meanwhile, the Collins Almanor foresters continue to quietly harvest timber sustainably and profitably as they have for the past 50-plus years.

When Collins Almanor began harvesting the forest in 1941, estimates indicated it contained 1.5 billion board feet of lumber. A board foot of lumber is 12 inches by 12 inches and one inch thick. Since 1941, 1.7 billion board feet of lumber have been harvested from the forest -- approximately 34 million board feet per year, with 1.5 billion board feet of unharvested timber still remaining. Over the 50 year-plus harvest period "only a few trees were snaked out of the woods at a time", matching the forest's natural rate of growth and renewal. [47] This approach has made it possible to harvest the forest profitably while "wildlife, clear water, and recreational possibilities abound, even on land that has just been cut." [48] To increase the forest's value as a wildlife habitat the Collins Almanor foresters leave some potentially harvestable trees in the forest to die. When the crowns of these trees break off they become snags which provide nesting habitats for birds like woodpeckers and the spotted owl. [49]

Creating Wealth Vs. The Illusion Of Wealth

> On a fundamental level true-cost-pricing is about developing an economy
> that creates real wealth as opposed to the illusion of wealth.

The difference between real wealth and illusionary wealth can be illustrated by comparing houses "A" and "B" which are identical in size and appearance. To the uneducated observer each house would appear to represent the same amount of wealth. But looking below the surface we can see that one house represents the creation of wealth whereas building the other house creates little if any wealth, and may actually result in a net loss of wealth.

Here is how Houses "A" and "B" differ.

House "A" is made of materials that were mined, harvested, and processed in ways that sustain the ecological foundation from which they were drawn. Toxic materials, which might cause its occupants to become ill were not used in house "A".

These issues were not considered in the construction of house "B".

House "A" is very energy and water efficient. It is well insulated and is equipped with a

---

[46] *Ibid, p. 39.*

[47] *Zuckerman, Seth. "Old Forestry". Sierra. Vol. 77, No. 2, (March/April, 1992), p. 44.*

[48] *Ibid.*

[49] *See index for more entries.*

ventilating system that saves energy by using heat, extracted from exhausted stale air, to warm up the fresh air replacing it. Energy efficient lighting and appliances are also incorporated in house "A". Additionally, house "A" features low flow showerheads and water efficient toilets.

In house "B" these amenities are either not included or minimally included.

Where appropriate, house "A" is designed to collect rainwater from its roof and store it in an underground cistern. It is also equipped with graywater (bath, sink, and wash water) recycling for landscape irrigation and uses a state-of-the-art water efficient irrigation system. House "A" also features a landscape design that is consistent with the rainfall and weather conditions of its location.

House "B" does not include these amenities and features a water intensive landscape design.

House "A" also incorporates construction strategies that stress durability and minimize the cost of and need for maintenance. It is also designed to minimize the threat of fire and avoids the use of materials that would produce harmful toxins if ignited.

In the construction of house "B" these issues are only minimally considered.

Finally, house "A" is constructed on land that is reasonably geologically stable and not subject to flooding.

House "B" is built on geologically hazardous alluvial deposits, within the boundary of a 100 year frequency flood plain.

Clearly the construction of house "A" represents the creation of real wealth. With house "B" this is probably not true or at least far less wealth has been created through its construction. When all the peripheral or "true" costs associated with house "B" are tallied, it may even represent a net wealth loss.

Unfortunately we currently have a house "B" economy. Even when we grow food, wealth is more often lost than created. In the U.S., 8 to 20 units of non-renewable energy are consumed for every unit of food energy delivered to our tables. [50]

In addition to the non-renewable energy it consumes, agriculture as it is commonly practiced, causes some of our most valuable topsoil to erode away more rapidly than nature can replace it. "The USDA estimates that some 23 percent of U.S. cropland suffers erosion rates greater than is considered 'tolerable'. [51] Globally, "an area the size of China and India combined has suffered moderate to extreme soil degradation caused mainly by agricultural activities, deforestation, and over grazing in the past 45 years". [52]

Since 1972 "the world's farmers lost about 480 billion tons of topsoil, roughly equal to that

---

[50]   *Portola Institute. Energy Primer. Portola Institute, Menlo Park, California, (1974): pp. 115-116. Also see Gever, John et al. Beyond Oil. A Project of Carrying Capacity Inc. Ballinger Publishing Company, Cambridge, Massachusetts, (1986): p. 28.*

[51]   *Gever, John et al. Beyond Oil. A Project of Carrying Capacity Inc. Ballinger Publishing Company, Cambridge, Massachusetts, (1986): p. 164.*

[52]   *World Resources 1992 - 93. The World Resources Institute, The United Nations Environmental Programme, and The United Nations Development Programme. Oxford Press, New York, (1992): pp. 111-12.*

which covers the agricultural land of India and France." [53] These losses of wealth (topsoil and non-renewable energy) are less apparent to us in the western world because they are masked by large inputs of non-renewable energy. Inputs which make our present agricultural system appear to be productive, but which is only kept afloat by subsidized, non-renewable energy consumption that lets us:

■ Mine and manufacture nutrients and other additives to replace those that are lost to erosion and through other avenues;

■ Divert rivers into deserts; and

■ Pump water out of aquifers at rates that exceed their recharge. [54]

The recent damage from Hurricane Andrew offers us another look at the wealth question. Well-built homes, constructed above high water lines, can withstand the onslaught of the fiercest hurricane and suffer only minimal damage. Even well-designed mobile homes can survive hurricanes if they are properly anchored. In other words, with a bit more care in construction and siting, much of the damage (loss of wealth) caused by Andrew could have been avoided.

Ironically, as reconstruction of the damaged area commenced, the enormous costs of the rebuilding activity showed up as a plus in our nation's Gross National Product (GNP) or measure of economic health. In reality, rebuilding the area will probably end up being a drain on our national resource wealth base unless the area is rebuilt in a more eco-nomically responsible way.

Or as economist Robert Repetto put it, "A country could exhaust its mineral resources, cut down its forests, erode its soils, pollute its aquifers, and hunt its wildlife and fisheries to extinction, but measured income would not be affected as these assets disappeared." [55] Once these resources are gone, however, the economy based on their use will obviously collapse.

Fortunately, this kind of outcome is not inevitable. If the true-cost-pricing measures illustrated in the example of house "A" were applied, rebuilding Florida and our use of resources in general would be wealth producing and our nation and the world would be more eco-nomically secure for it.

Some Thoughts On Trade

Recently, a flurry of regional and global trade agreements have been proposed, hammered out, or adopted. [56] The reason given for these high priority government and commercial efforts is to spur economic activity and therefore create jobs, profits, and expanded consumer choice. While this view may hold true in the short term for some people, it will not be true for most of us for long.

Why? Because the underlying economies of the countries that mine, grow, harvest, and manufacture the goods they seek to trade are not eco-nomically sustainable. Almost without

---

[53]   Brown, Lester R.. *Saving The Planet*. W.W. Norton & Company, New York, London, (1991): p. 20.

[54]   See index for more entries.

[55]   Repetto, Robert et al. *Wasting Assets*. Washington D.C.: World Resources Institute, (June 1989): p. 2.

[56]   Specifically, the North American Free Trade Agreement (NAFTA) and General Agreement on Trade and Tariffs (GATT).

exception, the world's economies are close to being totally dependent on non-renewable energy resources and the procurement of other resources in ways that are not eco-nomically sustainable, even if energy issue, just discussed did not exist.

In other words:

> As long as our underlying economies are not eco-nomically sustainable, spurring them along by accelerating trade and consumption will only hasten their decline.

This is not to say we should eliminate trade. If our economies were ecologically sustainable, their stimulation through trade would be positive. The real issue is not trade at all, but the need to develop local, national, and global economies that are eco-nomically secure. In other words, we need economies that create real wealth instead of its illusion. If we achieve this goal, the foundation of our economy will be strong and resilient in the present and far into the foreseeable future.

Chapter IV

ECO-NOMIC SECURITY AND POPULATION

Synopsis

Up to the present, the issue of population growth has primarily focused on the developing world. From the perspective of global sustainability, however, the smaller developed world population causes far more damage. At 1970 per capita pollution levels, "an increase of 75 million Americans (U.S.) would be the equivalent to adding 3.7 billion Indians to the world population." [57] This is not to say we should slow our efforts to stabilize and eventually reduce our global population. (Even if we do everything right ecologically, our planet can only support so many people sustainably, at a given average standard of living.) But considering the ecological damage that the developed nations are causing, reducing the environmental impact per capita in these nations is perhaps the more immediate issue at hand.

The challenge for the developed world then is to demonstrate how people can live comfortably on our planet in ways that are ecologically sustainable. As this is accomplished, the technological know-how proven in this effort can be transferred to the developing world. With such technologies, people living in the developing world can raise their own standard of living in ecologically benign ways. Historically, as standards of living have risen, the rate of population growth has tended to fall.

Population Numbers Vs. Negative Impact Per Capita

The connection between increasing world population and its impact on ecological security is another area of public misunderstanding. By now most people are aware that increasing human population is causing ecological problems. Currently, the most dramatic increases in world populations are occurring in the developing nations. Given this fact, people in the "developed world" tend to focus their concerns on the impact of increasing population in those areas. The prevalent view in the developed world goes something like this, "I wish that people in the developing world would quit having so many children because they're messing up the environment."

If we look at population from the perspective of ecological damage per-capita, however, we see a different picture. This is because most of our planet's ecological problems result from "how" we procure, process, and transport our planet's resources and "how" we use and dispose of the things we make from them. Since people in the developed world use far more resources per capita than do their less affluent developing world neighbors, their negative ecological impact is far greater. The operative word in the previous discussion is "how".

IF

- ecologically sustainable methods are used to procure and process raw materials,
- and the products made from them can be used in environmentally benign ways,
- and they are designed to be easily reused or recycled,

THEN

an ecologically sustainable, materially secure standard of living can be maintained by a large number of people.

---

[57]   Thompson, David. *The Economics of Environmental Protection*. Winthrop Publishers Inc., Cambridge, Massachusetts, (1973): p. 5.

It should be noted that even if we develop ways to extract, process, use, and "recycle" (replaces "dispose") the material wealth that our planet offers, in ways that maximize eco-nomic sustainability, population will still be a limiting factor. Even if we do everything correctly, we still can only support a given number of people at an average given material standard of living, sustainably. As population grows, the average standard of living has to go down if eco-nomic sustainability is to be maintained on a finite planet.

Based on contemporary levels of consumption and waste, the average person in the U.S. has 20 to 100 times more negative impact on the world's ecology than the average person living in a developing country. The "average U.S. citizen consumes 50 times more steel, 56 times more energy, 170 times more synthetic rubber and newsprint, 250 times more motor fuel, and 300 times more plastic than the average citizen of India." [58]

In spite of their considerably smaller populations, people living in the developed world have a far greater negative impact on our planet's ecology than do people living in developing nations.

The per capita contribution to pollution in the developed world is also greater than the per capita pollution generated in the developing world. At 1970 pollution levels, "an increase of 75 million Americans (U.S.) would be equivalent to adding 3.7 billion Indians to the world population." [59] This puts the pollution contribution of the average U.S. citizen at almost 50 times greater than that contributed by the average Indian. [60]

In terms of mineral and fuel consumption, "75 million Americans (U.S.) are the equivalent of 2 billion Colombians, 10 billion Nigerians, or 22 billion Indonesians." [61] Even if we assume that the negative ecological impact of the average U.S. citizen is only 20 times the per capita impact of the average third world resident, the U.S. population alone has almost twice the negative ecological impact as all the people living in the developing world combined. If we assume the ratio of 100 to one, the ecological damage caused by 250 million U.S. citizens is almost 10 times greater than the combined impact of all the people living in the developing world. [62]

Even though the average U.S. citizen consumes more resources than the average citizen elsewhere, the rest of the developed world comes in a close second. "The world's wealthiest nations, which have 25% of the world's population, consume 70% of its resources." [63] "The industrial world accounts for up to 90% of the carbon dioxide (CO_2) (mainly from fossil fuel burning) that has so far accumulated in the earth's atmosphere." [64]

---

[58] Miller, G. Tyler. *Environmental Science, an Introduction.* 2nd Edition, Wadsworth Publishing Co., Belmont, California, (1988): pp. 7-8, Also see David Dickson's, *The Politics of Alternative Technology.* Universe Books, New York, (1975): p. 19. Also see Myers, Norman. "The Big Squeeze". *EarthWatch.* Vol. XII, No. VII, (Nov./Dec.): p. 27.

[59] Thompson, Donald N. *The Economics of Environmental Protection.* Winthrop Publishers Inc., Cambridge, Mass. (1973): p. 5.

[60] Author's calculations. Also see Horton, Paul B. et al. *The Sociology of Social Problems,* Eighth Edition. Prentice Hall Inc., Englewood Cliffs, New Jersey, (1985): p. 412.

[61] Thompson, David. *The Economics of Environmental Protection.* Winthrop Publishers Inc., Cambridge, Massachusetts, (1973): p. 19.

[62] Author's calculations.

[63] Miller, John. "The Wrong Shade of Green". *Dollars & Sense.* No. 185, (April 1993): p. 7.

[64] Ibid. Also see Udal, James B. "Turning Down The Heat". *Sierra.* Vol. 74, No. 4, (July/August 1989): p. 30.

Additionally, many of the negative impacts that occur in developing nations can be directly attributed to the consumption patterns of people living in the United States, Europe, and Japan. [65] For example, the consumption of beef imported from developing nations hastens rain forest destruction by providing ranching interests in rain forest countries the economic incentive to clear forests and convert them into grazing land.

This is not to say that overpopulation is not a problem. Slowing population growth and eventually reducing the number of people that live on our planet at any given time is something we should all work toward. Even if we do everything else perfectly from an ecological perspective, our planet's ecology can only support a finite number of people sustainably -- even at a very low level of consumption per-capita.

Doing Our Part In The Developed World

Considering our impact on eco-nomic sustainability, the most immediate thing we can do, in the developed world, is to reduce our per capita impact. Doing this will reduce and eventually eliminate the damage our current ways of doing things are causing while demonstrating that the developed world's commitment to eco-nomic sustainability is legitimate. Our present focus on raw population numbers instead of negative ecological impacts per-capita gives people living in developing countries cause to question our concern for the preservation of "their" environments. As numerous people from developing countries have observed, the developed countries use most of the world's resources in ways that are not ecologically sustainable, then admonish developing countries when they try to emulate us.

Additionally, by focusing on reducing our own negative impacts, we will be developing the strategies and technologies needed to live and make livings in ways that are eco-nomically sustainable -- the very strategies and technologies that developing nations need to improve their own living standards in ways that avoid the ecological damage that the developed world has caused, up to now, in the same pursuit.

This in itself can be a powerful tool in curbing population growth in the developing world. Historically, a rise in living standards has tended to reduce the rate of population growth.

Indeed, the development and transfer of ecologically sustainable strategies and technologies, coupled with promotion of equal rights for women may prove to be the best way the developed world can contribute to the stabilization of our species' global population.

---

[65] Miller, G. Tyler. *Environmental Science, an Introduction*. 2nd Edition, Wadsworth Publishing Co., Belmont, California, (1988): pp. 7-8.

Chapter V

ECO-NOMIC SECURITY AND NATIONAL DEFENSE

Synopsis

Blind spots in security planning leave us increasingly vulnerable to natural phenomenon like earthquakes, floods, and fires and to terrorism and other intentional human acts. Eco-nomically based security planning, however, can reduce our vulnerability to both intentional human acts and natural phenomena.

If human settlements are designed to be resource efficient, whatever supplies they have stored locally will last longer should imported resources be cut off.

Local security can be enhanced by using locally available resources in ways that are eco-nomically sustainable, i.e., wealth producing. Not only does this reduce a region's vulnerability to cutoffs, it also creates jobs and reduces the flow of cash away from local economies to pay for imports. For example, solar cells or solar water heaters can be installed on roof tops instead of importing oil. Sewage water can be recycled and used to grow food, wood and fiber, and energy crops.

Ecology and Security: Making the Connection

A major concern for most nations and their citizenry is national defense. But even in this time of heightened environmental concern, the connection between national defense and eco-nomic health is not often made. Some issues, like military generated toxic waste and war-related environmental damage, have received attention, but the dependency of military security on eco-nomic sustainability has been barely explored.

Around the globe, national defense consumes inordinate amounts of resources and scientific talent. All costs considered, more money is spent on national defense than for any other single item. [66] Worldwide, "$15 to $20 of every $100 spent by central governments now goes to military purposes, triple their budgets for education, eight times their budgets for housing." [67]

In the United States, "over 52 cents of each income tax dollar goes to the military", for a total of $589 billion during the 1991 fiscal year. Of this amount $287 billion was spent to maintain current military programs. The remaining $302 billion was spent on military related costs like the research and development and the construction of nuclear weapons through the Department of Energy. Also included in this $302 billion are veterans' benefits, and the interest on the war-related portion of our national debt. [68]

By 1990 Americans were "spending twice as much each year on the military as we were in 1980." [69] "Over the last decade the United States government has spent almost $3 trillion of federal tax money in the military, or $45,000 for each U.S. family." [70]

There are a lot of complicated reasons why nations feel inclined to spend so much on defense. But underlying all these reasons is the feeling shared by many that some other nation will

---

[66] Sivard, Ruth Leger, et. al. *World Military and Social Expenditures 1991.* 14th Edition, World Priorities, Washington D.C. (1991) p. 10.

[67] Ibid. p. 26.

[68] Midgley, Jane. *The Women's Budget.* October 1991 Edition, Women's International League for Peace and Freedom. Philadelphia, PA., p. 8.

[69] Ibid.

[70] Ibid.

take advantage of them if their military is unprepared.

Hopefully, in the not too distant future, feelings like this can be eased through the process of building trust. But until the trust between nations becomes more universal, defense spending will continue to be a high priority. Yet, even in the context of the present world tension, does our desire for a strong defense necessarily conflict with our need for eco-nomic security?

A brief analysis of the recent events in the Middle East and other related issues will illustrate that this is certainly not the case.

During the period preceding U.S. involvement in the Persian Gulf War, much of the debate centered around sending troops or using economic sanctions to get Iraq to withdraw from Kuwait. What was not discussed, however, was that the conflict could have been avoided altogether if the U.S. had spent the 15 to 20 years before the war becoming more energy efficient, and switching to renewable energy resources.

The aggressive pursuit of efficiency and renewables in the U.S. during these decades would have driven world oil prices down to $5 per barrel or less. In fact, over-production by OPEC and minor efficiency improvements in the West drove world oil prices down to $8.50 per barrel in 1986. [71]

Even if oil prices had stayed at $8.50, much less $5, Saddam Hussein's ability to purchase weapons and support his army would have certainly been limited. Indeed, most of the weaponry now present in the Middle East would not be there at all if the U.S. had aggressively pursued an efficiency and renewable energy strategy in the past.

In response to the fear that OPEC's lack of unity on production quotas would drive oil prices down to $5-a-barrel, "intense pressure (to cut production) was put on the Saudis by Iran, anxious to boost oil revenues to pay for its treasury-busting war against Iraq. Gholamreza Agazadeh, Iran's Oil Minister, declared the prospect of $5-a-barrel oil 'simply unbelievable.'" [72] Iraq was also hurt by low oil prices "and was clearly seeking a higher oil price to meet its financial needs than the $21 per barrel agreed upon at OPEC's July (1990) meeting." [73] Iraq's charge that Kuwait, through over-production, was driving oil prices down was one reason Iraq gave for its invasion of Kuwait. [74] Even though oil prices hovered around the $10 per barrel mark for only a few months, the ability to wage war throughout the Middle East was affected.

Note: Although the OPEC Cartel can affect the price of oil by reducing production, the impact of trimming production on oil prices is limited. As is discussed in the chapters on energy, the U.S. has the potential to eliminate its need, not only for imported oil, but for non-renewable energy resources all together. If either of these things happened, Opec's ability to manipulate oil prices would be greatly reduced if not completely eliminated.

Even a much less aggressive move toward efficiency could have removed the issue of foreign oil dependence from the U.S. rationale for intervention in the Iraq war. According to Amory and Hunter Lovins of the Rocky Mountain Institute, the U.S. "wouldn't have needed any oil from the Persian Gulf after 1985 if we'd simply kept on saving oil as quickly as we did for the previous nine

---

[71]   Copeland, Jeff and Penelope Wang. "Too Much Oil, Too Little Unity." *Newsweek*. Vol. 108, (October 27, 1986): p. 88. Also see Karmin, Monroe W. et al. "OPEC Searches for Those Good Old Days." *U.S. News & World Report*. Vol. 101, (August 18, 1986): p. 35.

[72]   Karmin, Monroe W. et al. "OPEC Searches for Those Good Old Days." *U.S. News & World Report*. Vol. 101, (August 18, 1986): p. 35.

[73]   Kohl, Wilfrid L., Editor. *After the Oil Price Collapse*. The Johns Hopkins University Press, Baltimore, Maryland, (1991): p. 207.

[74]   Ibid.

years." [75] Just an improvement in U.S. domestic car efficiency from the current average of 19 MPG to 22 MPG "would replace U.S. imports of oil from Iraq and Kuwait." [76] Raising the average fuel efficiency to 31 MPG would eliminate the "need for any oil from the Persian Gulf" altogether. [77]

Military Action And Energy Use

Mobilizing the military to keep imported oil supplies flowing is a very costly and energy consuming activity. "Counting military costs, Gulf oil in late 1990 cost over $100 a barrel." [78] "In 1989 the U.S. Department of Defense spent more than $15 billion -- as much as $54 billion according to some estimates -- to safeguard oil supplies in the Persian Gulf." [79] In the same year, about 38 percent of the oil imported from Saudi Arabia by the U.S. was used by the Pentagon. [80] During wars it was estimated that the oil consumed by the Pentagon would double or triple this amount. [81] "An M-1 tank gets 0.58 miles to the gallon. An oil fired aircraft carrier gets 17 feet per gallon." [82]

In short, the aggressive pursuit of energy efficiency and renewables would drastically reduce the ability of Middle Eastern countries to maintain large armies and purchase costly high tech weapons. It also would benefit the U.S. by reducing the need for the United States to maintain a costly military presence in the Persian Gulf to safeguard access to foreign oil fields. Further, independence from oil would reduce the amount of U.S. financial aid needed by Israel to maintain a military balance in the Gulf Region.

On the home front, becoming more energy efficient and switching to renewables would increase eco-nomic security by creating millions of new jobs. "A study by Steve Colt of the University of Alaska at Anchorage found that state spending on weatherization creates more jobs per dollar of outlays (sic) than any other type of capital project-almost three times as many direct jobs as highway construction". [83]

A study prepared by Leon Rodberg for the Joint Economic Committee of the U.S. Congress in 1979 confirms these findings. "Assuming an annual investment of $115 billion (in 1989 dollars), Rodberg found that more than 2 million jobs might have been created in 10 years -- a quarter of them in conservation and the rest in solar energy." [84]

On the down side, the performance of these 2 million jobs would cause the gradual loss of one million jobs in the non-renewable energy sector. "But re-spending the associated savings in energy outlays elsewhere would have brought additional employment gains for a net increase of

---

[75] Lovins, Amory and Hunter Lovins. "Winning The Peace". RMI Newsletter. Vol. VII, No. 1, (Spring 1991): p. 1.

[76] Ibid.

[77] Ibid.

[78] Ibid, page 3.

[79] Hubbard, Harold M. "The Real Cost of Energy". Scientific American. Vol. 264, No. 4, (April 1991): p. 36.

[80] Lovins, Amory and Hunter Lovins. "Winning The Peace". Rocky Mountain Institute Newsletter. Vol. VII, No. 1, (Spring 1991): p. 3.

[81] Ibid.

[82] Ibid.

[83] Brown, Lester R. et. al.. State of the World 1992. Worldwatch Institute, W.W. Norton and Company, New York, London, (1992): p. 144.

[84] Ibid, page 145.

almost 3 million jobs as a whole." [85]

Switching to energy efficiency and renewables would have a similar positive impact on the job picture in other countries as well. A 1985 study prepared for the Commission of the European Community (EC) bears this out. The study which "analyzed the employment potential of six energy conservation and renewable energy technologies in Denmark, France, the United Kingdom, and West Germany ... found that some 34 million tons of oil equivalent could be saved and an average of 142,000 job-years gained by the year 2000," if the measures studied were implemented. [86] Further, the study's authors "suggested that a full-fledged conservation and renewables program could yield a minimum of 530,000 job-years for the EC (all 12 countries) as a whole, or on average 3,800 jobs per million tons of primary (non-renewable) energy saved." [87]

Studies in Canada and Oregon comparing the job creation potential of investing in other economic sectors instead of the energy industry show similar gains in employment. For every $1 million invested in Alberta Canada's oil and gas industries, 1.4 jobs are generated. If the same amount of money is invested in manufacturing, 9 jobs are created. [88] An Oregon study "revealed that spending $1 million in the utility industry generates roughly 12 jobs, while $1 million spent throughout the state produces 35 jobs." [89]

A study in the United States which compares the job creation potential for investing in efficiency, as opposed to the energy sector, shows comparable job creation potential. In the U.S., electric utility and petroleum industries "typically produce about five jobs per million dollars of investment. Weatherization of buildings, by contrast, produces 50 jobs for the same investment." [90] Because the performance of these jobs would reduce energy consumption, energy related pollution would be cut accordingly.

Notwithstanding investments in other sectors, investing in the civilian economy provides many more jobs than spending money on military build-up. "According to a study by Employment Research Associates, if the money spent on the military build-up between 1981 and 1985 had been spent on civilian economic activities, 1,146,000 more jobs would have been generated." [91]

In addition to creating jobs, becoming more energy efficient has other eco-nomically related security benefits. It has been estimated that 80 to 90 percent of the money spent on energy by a typical community leaves it to pay for energy imports. [92] Investing in efficiency halts this dollar export because investing in efficiency and renewables pays for itself by reducing or eliminating the need to purchase imported energy. It also creates local jobs. And as the money saved through efficiency accumulates, the wealth gained can be reinvested to create even more jobs.

---

[85] *Ibid.*

[86] *Ibid.*

[87] *Ibid.*

[88] Romm, Joseph J.. *The Once and Future Superpower*. William Morrow and Company, (1992): p. 135.

[89] *Ibid.*

[90] Totten, Michael, et al. *The Road to Trillion Dollar Energy Savings*. Public Citizen, Washington D.C., (1984): p. 14.

[91] Midgley, Jane. *The Women's Budget*. October 1, 1991 Edition, Women's International League for Peace and Freedom. Philadelphia, PA., p. 19.

[92] Totten, Michael, et al. *The Road to Trillion Dollar Energy Savings*. Public Citizen, Washington D.C., (1984): p. 14.

This would further strengthen the U.S economy by putting the money we now export to purchase imported energy in the pockets of the people whose work reduces our energy dependency -- people who get paychecks, pay local and national taxes, and spend their money in local businesses. When we export money to pay for imported energy, that money is lost to our local economies and, more often than not, our national economy as well.

The U.S. Infrastructure - Vulnerability by Design?

Another security issue brought to light during the war with Iraq was the United States' vulnerability to terrorism. During the conflict, the threat of terrorism was considered very real. As the media played it, the aim of invading terrorists would be to smuggle explosives on to airliners, and blow them up.

Thankfully this didn't happen. But as tragic as it would have been, losing lives and airplanes would be minor compared to the loss of life and the chaos that would have occurred if a terrorist group had materialized and attacked the U.S. infrastructure. A country's infrastructure consists of the power lines, pipelines, roads, aqueducts, communication systems, etc. and the activities they link together.

Like other infrastructural elements, our energy delivery and supply infrastructure is quite vulnerable. A few determined people with nothing more sophisticated than hunting rifles with scopes could shoot down key power lines and black out our whole country in a matter of seconds. If such an attack was well planned, it could take weeks or longer to repair the damage. As one Department of the Interior expert put it, "a relatively small group of dedicated, knowledgeable individuals . . . could bring down (the power grid supply in) almost any section of the country," or could black out "a widespread network" if more widely coordinated. [93] In the introduction to the book Brittle Power, Admiral Thomas Moorer, Chairman of the Joint Chiefs of Staff under President Nixon, and R. James Woolsey, Undersecretary of the Navy under President Carter, wrote that, ". . . the vulnerabilities are so numerous -- to weather, to accidents arising from complexity, to a handful of terrorists, . . . that denying the plausibility of such threats is unlikely to prove persuasive". [94]

Natural gas pipelines are similarly vulnerable to attack. In a lecture given at Orange Coast College in California, Amory Lovins (founder of the Rocky Mountain Institute) stated that terrorists could cut most of the natural gas supply to the eastern seaboard without ever leaving Louisiana. This is not surprising since "eighty-four percent of all interstate (natural) gas either is from Louisiana wells", . . . "or flows from Texas, mostly via Louisiana". [95]

Oil pipelines are equally vulnerable. "Damage to key facilities on just a few pipeline systems could greatly reduce domestic shipments, causing an energy shortage exceeding that of the 1973 Arab Oil embargo." [96]

Terrorism within our own borders is not the only threat to energy security. Our dependence on oil imports from abroad extends our infrastructure all the way to the oil fields of the Middle East. Saudi Arabia, the world's premier oil exporter, has "more than 700 producing wells, generally 1,000 to 3,000 meters apart, over an area of more than 10,000 square miles. Nearly 100 of these wells

---

[93] Lovins, Amory B. and L. Hunter Lovins. *Brittle Power: Energy Strategies for National Security*. Brick House Publishing Co., Andover, Mass. (1982): p. 129.

[94] Totten, Michael, et al. *The Road to Trillion Dollar Energy Savings: A Safe Energy Platform*. Public Citizen, Washington D.C. (1984): p. 6.

[95] *Brittle Power: Energy Strategies for National Security*. p. 112.

[96] *Ibid.*

are offshore rigs -- and all are vulnerable to attack." [97] In short, "the numerous and widely dispersed oil fields in Saudi Arabia and elsewhere in the Persian Gulf are extraordinarily vulnerable to Iraqi (or other) saboteurs, experts said yesterday. Moreover, if more than a dozen targets were hit at once, the world's limited oil industry fire fighting resources would be overwhelmed." [98]

Like oil and gas pipelines, water pipe networks, aqueducts, and pumping stations could be laid to waste with nothing more powerful than explosives, commonly used in mining and construction.

Freeway overpasses, tunnels, and railroad trestles are similarly vulnerable. The loss of just a few key overpasses, bridges, and tunnels would greatly limit the delivery of food to most urban areas. "A study for the U.S. Department of Defense estimated that the average molecule of processed food in this country travels 1,300 miles before it is eaten." [99] This means that the delivery of food supplies to any particular area could be interrupted by intentional or accidental acts by humans or by natural phenomena that occur in locations distant from where people live.

The loss of overpasses, bridges, and tunnels would also disrupt the delivery of energy sources like coal and gasoline. The loss of escape routes coupled with fuel shortages would also reduce the possibility for people to transport themselves to where food and energy might be available. Although only one major freeway collapsed during the 1990 earthquake in the San Francisco Bay region, its loss had a dramatic effect on all transportation-related activities around the bay area. [100] The loss of just a few overpasses during the recent Los Angeles earthquake caused even greater disruptions in auto transportation. One can only imagine the kinds of problems that could be caused if a terrorist group attacked a typical urban infrastructure at its most critical and hard-to-repair junctures.

Eco-nomic Design Vs. Natural Disasters and Terrorism

Obviously, this picture of infrastructure vulnerability has alarming implications. But how can becoming more eco-nomically secure make us less vulnerable to terrorism or natural calamities?

An important way to increase both military and ecological security is to become more energy efficient and to switch to renewable energy resources. Militarily, becoming more efficient and switching to renewables would extend the useful life of locally stored energy supplies in the event that imported resources were cut off. [101] This is on top of the other security benefits discussed earlier, such as reducing the amount of cash available in the Middle East to purchase arms and reducing the amount of aid needed by Israel to maintain a military balance with her neighbors.

Ecologically, this strategy would greatly reduce the creation of non-renewable energy related pollution, and reduce the United States' contribution to global warming. Becoming more energy efficient and switching to renewables improves our energy security in another way.

Renewable energy resources are, by nature, diffuse. The places where solar or wind energy can be collected are spread out. In other words, the nature of renewable energy sources is that they lend themselves to the development of a more decentralized energy production and delivery system

---

[97]   *Knight-Ridder Newspapers. "Gulf Oil Said Vulnerable to Saboteurs". The San Diego Union. North County Edition, (Tuesday, September 25, 1990): p. A - 6.*

[98]   *Ibid. p. A -1.*

[99]   *Empty Breadbasket? The Coming Challenge to America's Food Supply and What We Can Do About It. A Study of the U.S. Food System by The Cornucopia Project of Rodale Press, Emmaus Pennsylvania, (1980): p. 5.*

[100]   *Author's personal experience.*

[101]   *See index for more entries.*

than we currently have.

Present centralized power production systems use coal, oil, natural gas, or processed nuclear fuel rods in centralized power plants. From a military perspective such systems are inherently fragile. If one large plant is knocked off-line a large number of people are affected. Plus, as previously discussed, the infrastructure (wires, pipes, and roads) needed to get the energy source from the place of extraction to these centralized plants, and from them to the end users, is vulnerable to disruption on many levels. A decentralized solar based system largely avoids such problems.

In the sun belt, for example, solar cells on roof tops could supply all the energy needed by homes and for many businesses directly or from storage when the sun isn't shining. If such a system was in place, the only way for terrorists to cut off power would be to go house to house and business to business. In less sunny areas wind power and biomass crops (fast growing trees and other plants) can be used to decentralize power supplies. [102]

If energy is used efficiently, developing renewable energy powered decentralizing energy supply systems becomes easier. A typical home, incorporating state-of-the-art energy efficient features, could be energy independent in the sunniest half of the U.S. with a 100 to 200 square foot, roof-top mounted photovoltaic panel. [103]

Eco-nomic planning strategies can also reduce the vulnerability of our water delivery infrastructures. Using water more efficiently, recycling water after use, and better water storage systems make us less vulnerable to intentional water supply disruptions. These measures also reduce the threat to water supplies from natural phenomenon like earthquakes.

If water supplies from distant sources are cut off, efficient water use helps to extend the life of whatever locally stored supplies are available. Water recycling further extends local supplies by allowing the water to be used more than once. In dry urban areas with low rainfall, underground water storage cisterns can be used to meet local water needs if imported water supplies are disrupted and until repairs to conveyance systems can be made. Underground tank storage would also eliminate losses to evaporation. In semi-arid regions, losses to evaporation in open reservoirs can exceed 10 feet of water per year from reservoir surfaces. [104]

Even in urban areas with sufficient local water resources, a dispersed covered tank storage system would be easier to protect from contamination than open reservoirs. Open reservoirs can be contaminated directly or indirectly via the watersheds that drain into them. Since it would take a large number of tanks to hold the same amount of water contained by one large reservoir, many tanks would have to be contaminated to cause a serious impact on the whole system. It would take a squad of terrorists to contaminate or damage a dispersed network of covered storage tanks, whereas only one terrorist might be able to contaminate or damage a single large reservoir.

In addition to making our water system less vulnerable to sabotage or earthquakes, the strategies described above also save money and protect the environment. By minimizing the need to dam more rivers and build new aqueducts, the costs and ecological trauma associated with such

---

[102] *It can be argued that natural gas, oil, and to a certain extent coal would be just as easy to use as fuels in a decentralized power system as biomass where they are locally available. But unlike biomass, which in the process of growing absorbs the CO_2 released from prior burnings, fossil fuels are nonrenewable and their combustion adds CO_2 to the atmosphere.*

[103] *Author's calculations - based on a 10 percent efficiency of converting sunlight into electricity, the equivalent of 275 sunny days per year and a daily consumption of 5 to 10 kwhrs respective of a 100 square foot solar array or a 200 square foot array. (See index for more entries.)*

[104] *State of California, Department of Water Resources. Evaporation From Water Surfaces. Bulletin No. 73-1, State of California, (May 1974): pp. 26-170.*

activities can be avoided.

Military and eco-nomic security can be improved in urban areas by producing a higher percentage of the food consumed in them locally. Ecologically, this would save energy and reduce energy-related pollution by shortening the travel distance between where food is grown and processed and where it is consumed. Growing food locally would also provide a productive use for recycled sewage water and composted sludge which urban dwellers generate.

Local food production, especially if coupled with local food storage banks, would also enhance military security. If imported food supplies are disrupted by damaged overpasses and railway trestles, food banks could provide civilian populations with a secure food supply until road and railway repairs were made. As a security precaution, each urban area should have at least a one-year supply of nonperishable food in storage at all times. Food storage, coupled with local food production would make urban areas much less vulnerable to the intentional cut off of food shipped in from distant locations or the disruption of normal distribution networks by earthquakes, hurricanes, or other natural phenomenon.

More details on the recommendations just discussed will come in later chapters but the main point is that all the measures just discussed would make us more secure ecologically as well as from a national security perspective. They also would make us less vulnerable to natural phenomena like earthquakes, hurricanes and the like.

Considering the clear linkages between military and ecological security, it would seem prudent to spend at least as much money on making our national and regional infrastructures less vulnerable as we spend on "smart weapons". This is especially true considering that high-tech (smart) weaponry can do little, if anything, to protect us from the kind of threats our present infrastructure is vulnerable to.

PART THREE

ECO-NOMICALLY INTEGRATED PLANNING

Chapter VI

ON OUR FINITE PLANET
WHERE IS IT APPROPRIATE TO DO "WHAT?"

Synopsis

One of the most important aspects of eco-nomic security lies in how we answer the question, "Where is it appropriate to do What" on our planet? Where are the best places to site our cities? What land should we set aside for agriculture, for wildlife habitat? What hazards, like flood plains and geologically unstable areas, should we avoid?

Eco-nomically Integrated Planning (EIP) Maps are designed to make it easier to answer such questions. Preparing EIP Maps involves the development of a set of maps for your region or country based on the watersheds which lie within its boundaries or flow into it or through it. As land forms that direct the flow of water, watersheds are nature's planning units. In addition to directing the flow of water, the plant and animal communities that inhabit watersheds protect us from floods and soil erosion. These natural communities have also created all the organic materials in our soils and play a vital role in groundwater recharge.

EIP maps consist of a set of base watershed maps and corresponding sets of transparent overlay maps. Each transparent overlay map highlights a particular resource like agricultural soils, groundwater storage, and wildlife habitat or hazards like unstable geological formations or floodplains. Because EIP Maps allow us to see the synergy between the various resources and hazards in an area, the question, "where is it appropriate to do what" in that area can be readily answered. If our goal is eco-nomic security, it is obviously better to have intense human settlement sited in locations that are not subject to flooding, or that do not use up prime agricultural soils or irreplaceable habitat.

EIP Maps can be used on two levels. They can be used to determine the best locations for new developments. They can also aid in the relocation of existing developments or other improperly sited activities to more eco-nomically productive areas.

This second use would allow for the reclamation of resources, like prime agricultural soils, that have been used improperly in the past. For example, floodplains have been developed world wide. In addition to being subject to flooding, floodplains often overlie alluvial deposits, which are subject to liquefaction (to liquify) during earthquakes.

On the positive side, many floodplains are covered by prime agricultural soils as well as providing valuable wildlife habitats. Obviously floodplains are dangerous places to develop. They are also costly places to repair when floods or earthquakes occur. It therefore makes sense to prohibit further flood plain development and hope that a major flood or earthquake does not occur until we have had the time to relocate the development that has already been built on them.

Developing A Plan

Understanding how national defense, population, and the economy are connected to our planet's ecology is clearly important to our goal of creating an eco-nomically sustainable future. But in order to make the most productive use of this and other information, it is necessary to develop a unifying planning process.

To get a clearer picture of what this planning process would look like, let's imagine that we are the crew of the Starship Enterprise and we've just received a distress call from the people inhabiting earth. The message from earth is that human activities are threatening to cause a planet-wide ecological collapse and that our help is needed to avoid the disaster.

Our mission then is to develop a habitation plan for the earth that would allow 8 billion inhabitants to live and make livings in ways that are ecologically sustainable. Eight billion is the approximate number of people that are expected to be living on earth by the year 2020 if our present rate of population growth continues. [105]

Eco-nomically Integrated Planning

Whether we are the crew of the Enterprise or planners here on earth our first logical step would be to develop a planning strategy that is consistent with our goal of supporting 8 billion people in ways that are economically and ecologically sustainable. Let's call this planning strategy ECO-NOMICALLY INTEGRATED PLANNING or EIP for short.

The goal of EIP is to help us to do two basic things. One, decide "where to do what" on our planet. In other words, where are the most suitable locations for intense human activity? What lands should be set aside for growing food and for wildlife habitat? Where are the hazards like flood plains and unsafe geological deposits that we should avoid developing? For example, it makes more sense to grow food where the soils are fertile and to build cities where they are not.

Once we have answered the "where" question, the next goal of EIP is to illustrate how to build and maintain cities and practice agriculture and industry in ways that are truly eco-nomically sustainable.

EIP Mapping Tools

Ok, that's the general idea. But in order to fulfill our first task of deciding "where to do what", we are going to have to develop some EIP mapping tools, using advanced Geographical Information Systems (GIS) to help us locate and organize the resources we need to protect and the hazards we should avoid. For example, we need to know where our best agricultural soils and groundwater deposits are located. We also need to know the location of the most valuable plant and animal habitats and where hazards like flood plains, steep slopes, and earthquake faults are located.

Ultimately, to meet our goal of sustainability, this and similar information should be developed into a set of maps for our whole planet. But since we wouldn't be able to see much detail if we looked at the whole planet at once, smaller land areas would be mapped in more detail for actual planning.

The first step in developing a set of EIP maps is to develop a base map. The borders of a base map are determined by assessing the density and distribution of a region's or country's population and delineating the watershed boundaries in which that population resides.

Watersheds and Their Importance

The focus on watersheds as planning units is very important to the EIP process. Watersheds determine the flow of water and to some extent the flow of air that passes through them. Also, any heavier than air material, such as a pollutant, that is released into a watershed will eventually impact its lower elevations. For example, a heavy gas like clorine will tend to flow to lower elevations until it is disapated by winds. Even solids will be carried to lower elevations and

---

[105] *Author calculation assuming an annual population growth of 92 million people per year, based on material taken from Brown, Lester R. et al. State of the World 1992. W.W. Norton & Company, New York/London, (1992): p. 3.*

eventually to the ocean by flowing water. These are important considerations when deciding where to locate an activity (industrial or otherwise) that may release toxic materials or other pollutants into the environment.

Watersheds are also important as planning units because they form semi-autonomous biological units. Though there is considerable interaction between the biologies of adjacent and even distant watersheds, (birds and other animals that migrate long distances), each basin functions as a somewhat autonomous mutually inter-dependent, self-perpetuating plant and animal community.

Although natural watershed communities are inherently valuable as unique examples of life's complexity and vitality, they are also resources that benefit humans in a number of profound and practical ways. For example, watershed communities create soil. All the organic materials found in the soils on our planet today were created by watershed communities. When plants and animals die or when animals eliminate wastes or plants lose their leaves, soil organisms convert them into soil.

Watershed communities also protect the watersheds from soil erosion and the loss of nutrients. They also help watersheds to store water. Plant foliage and dead plant debris protect the soil from pounding rain. Root systems in concert with tunneling soil organisms, make it easier for water to be absorbed into the soil. In the soil this water is used by plants or becomes groundwater that emerges at springs or is stored in groundwater storage basins. By absorbing rainwater and snow melt runoff, healthy watershed communities help minimize downstream flooding.[106]

In addition to base watershed maps, a set of map transparencies will need to be developed for each watershed. These transparencies will be used as overlays on the base map with which they are associated. These transparencies will use color and patterns to delineate the various resources and hazards in a region.

To make them more manageable, map transparencies are divided into four categories; ecological resources, human support resources, potential hazards, and the human constructed environment. Ecological resource maps focus on environmental features. These would include resources like wetlands, and other wildlife habitats. If the area being mapped has a coastal zone, map transparencies would also include features like kelp beds and estuaries. Though they are closely related to the ecological resources listed above, the human support resources are listed in a separate category. The maps in this category include agricultural soils, forest lands, rivers and streams, groundwater recharge areas, and groundwater storage basins. Since not all agricultural soils are equally fertile the maps representing them will feature several colors to differentiate between the various levels of fertility. A third category includes maps showing potential hazards. These maps would highlight areas susceptible to earthquake damage and other features like steep slopes and flood plains. Finally, the human infrastructure maps focus on zoning and the location of existing and proposed developments.

Using EIP Maps

By laying map transparencies over the base map, one at a time or in combination, or through computer manipulation, the synergy between different resources and hazards and their relationships to existing and proposed development can be readily seen. When maps are used in combination, it becomes relatively easy to determine whether a particular area should be left natural or used for agriculture or intense urban activity. It is obviously less desirable to develop where it would cause valuable resources to be damaged or where hazardous conditions are present. This is especially true where more than one resource and/or hazard are located in the same area.

---

[106] Pereira, H. C. *Land Use and Water Resources in Temperate and Tropical Climates*. *University Press, Cambridge England, (1973): p. 25. (See index - water security for more details.)*

In most areas flood plains, agricultural soils, and valuable plant and animal habitats frequently occur in the same areas. In addition to the risk of flooding, such areas often lie over alluvial deposits. Structures built on alluvial deposits are subject to earthquake damage due to liquefaction. During severe earthquakes alluvial deposits literally liquify and will not support structures.

On the other hand, it makes sense to locate development on sites where such resources and hazards are absent or marginal. It may even make sense to develop marginally productive soils, if the tradeoff is preserving soil with more agricultural potential. Similarly, it is better to develop an area with marginal habitat value if doing so would facilitate the preservation of environmentally rich habitats.

PART FOUR

ECOLOGICAL SUSTAINABILITY AND THE HUMAN CREATED ENVIRONMENT

Chapter VII

EFFICIENT ENERGY USE

Synopsis

Almost without exception, most countries have the potential to completely free themselves from their dependence on non-renewable energy resources. Key to accomplishing this goal is more efficient energy use. When compared with the option of producing energy, becoming more energy efficient is also very cost-effective. Because it reduces energy demand, becoming more energy efficient makes it easier for a country or region to switch over to renewable energy. By reducing demand, efficient energy use reduces the amount of collector area needed by solar collectors, windmills, biomass, etc. to meet a country's or region's energy needs.

Studies discussed later in this chapter indicate that even highly industrialized, relatively cold, and densely populated countries like Japan could achieve energy self-sufficiency through increased energy efficiency coupled with the development of renewable resources. Even if a country has sufficient domestic supplies of non-renewable energy resources, efficiency and renewables are desirable. In addition to being relatively benign ecologically, their use enables a country to save its non-renewable energy reserves indefinitely.

Introduction

With EIP mapping tools to help us decide "where it is appropriate to do what" on our planet, our next charge is to determine how to do the "what", i.e., the things we need and want to do in ways that are eco-nomically sustainable. In other words, how do we provide ourselves with energy, water, food, clothing, shelter, and the other needs and pleasures we want in ways that are both economically viable and ecologically sustainable?

Given the myriad of environmental problems facing us, we have to date done a poor job in this area. Nevertheless, the chapters to follow will show that most of the strategies and technologies needed to live eco-nomically on our planet already exist. This is not to say that the examples discussed in this book, as currently practiced, are totally ecologically sustainable. But the contradictions in how they currently manifest can be resolved with a little attention to details.

Developing Eco-momic Security Through Efficient Energy Use

One of the most ecologically damaging aspects of our present way of doing things is connected to "how we do what" as it relates to energy. With the exception of solar energy in its various forms, i.e., direct solar, hydro-power, wind, biomass (plants grown for energy), solar electric, etc., the non-renewable energy resources we primarily depend on are both finite and polluting. Even hydro-power, as it is presently utilized, is not renewable because the reservoirs it depends on are destined to fill up with silt. [107]

---

[107] Reisner, Mark. <u>Cadillac Desert</u>. Penguin Books, New York, New York, (1987): pp. 490-494. (See index for Water Security for more details.)

Fossil Fuel's Hidden Costs

In addition to being finite, our use of non-renewable energy resources causes a myriad of other problems. Pollution from fossil fuels, which account for around 93% of current U.S. energy use, include: [108]

1. Acid deposition in the form of rain, fog, snow, and dry deposition.

    Acid deposition or acid fallout is harmful to all air breathing organisms. It also retards the growth of plants or kills them outright and can cause lakes and other waterways to become so acidic that the aquatic organisms living there cannot survive. Each year fossil fuel-powered electric generating plants in the U.S. "discharge 24 million tons of sulphur-dioxide (SO_2) and 20 million tons of nitrogen-oxide (NOx)". [109]

    When these compounds combine with water they form sulfuric acid and nitric acid, respectively. In Europe, "thousands of lakes are now lifeless and 22 percent of the forests are now showing signs of damage from air pollution". [110] Additionally, "Tens of thousands of U.S. and Canadian lakes are being sterilized" by acid deposits. [111] As of 1990, 4 percent of the lakes in the Eastern U.S. are too acidic for most aquatic life. [112] Acid laced water is also "leaching heavy metals from the soil into the water system, where more toxic metals accumulate as this highly acidic water eats away the metal pipes that bring water to consumers." [113]

2. Smokestack particulates like soot, ash, and heavy metals.

    Particulates are harmful to air-breathing organisms and often carry deposits of acid and other pollutants. Heavy metals are toxic and can concentrate in food chains. Increasing scientific evidence "suggests that thousands of respiratory-related deaths are occurring because human lungs have no choice but to serve as 'stack scrubbers.'" [114]

3. Acids and heavy metals that leach from coal mines and mine tailings into our waterways. [115]

4. Drilling mud and other residues associated with drilling for oil and natural gas.

5. Methane gas (natural gas) leaks related to coal mining and natural gas drilling and distribution.

---

[108] Stobaugh, Robert and Daniel Yergin. *Energy Future*. Random House, New York, New York, (1979): p. 15.

[109] Totten, Michael, et al. *The Road to Trillion Dollar Energy Savings*. Public Citizen, Washington D.C., (1984): p. 16.

[110] Young, John E. "Acid Rains, Acid Waters". *World Watch*. Vol. 1, No. 5, (Sept./Oct. 1988): p. 9.

[111] Totten, Michael, et al. *The Road to Trillion Dollar Energy Savings*. Public Citizen, Washington D.C., (1984): p. 16.

[112] Easterbrook, Gregg. "Everything You Know About The Environment Is Wrong." *The New Republic*. (April 30, 1990): p. 14.

[113] Totten, Michael, et al. *The Road to Trillion Dollar Energy Savings*. Public Citizen, Washington D.C., (1984): p. 16.

[114] Ibid.

[115] Ibid. pp. 16-17.

Molecule for molecule, methane gas is 20 to 30 times more potent as a greenhouse gas than CO_2. [116] Because of methane's potential impact, it has been estimated that the amount of methane gas released during its transmission through pipelines, around 5 percent, has as much impact on global warming as the CO_2 that is produced when the gas that is not lost is burned. And a 5 percent transmission loss may be low. One study, which looked only at San Diego County, pegged local gas losses at 4.6 percent. [117] If 4.6 percent is a typical regional loss, it seems likely that with a more lenththy distrubution system, the national loss could easily exceed 5 percent.

Added to transmission losses, coal mining also releases large quantities of methane gas into the atmosphere. Methane gas is often released when oil is extracted and it is also released at natural gas well heads. Because the combustion of natural gas is rarely 100 percent, additional gas is released when it is burned to heat homes, cook food, etc.

6.   Oil spills related to normal tanker operations and accidental spills.

In addition to the impact they have on the aquatic environment, the accidental or intentional release of oil into the ocean has other costs. The clean-up costs associated with the 1989 EXXON Valdez oil spill in Alaska are as high as $20 Billion dollars. [118] While the EXXON spill was dramatic, an equivalent amount of oil is dumped into the ocean each year just during normal ocean going vessel operations. [119]

7.   Land damaged by mining coal and strip mining coal. [120]

8.   Toxic sludge which is collected by scrubbers designed to remove toxic ash from the exhaust stacks of coal fired power plants.

Each year a 1,000 megawatt coal-fired power plant produces one million metric tons of ash sludge which requires 1.5 square kilometers of land for disposal. [121] Beyond the land used up for disposal, "Scientists warn that it is inevitable that these toxic wastes will leach into the soil, potentially migrating to aquifers and contaminating water supplies." [122]

9.   Finally, the use of all fossil fuels also contributes to global warming by releasing CO2 into the atmosphere when they are burned.

Even though carbon dioxide is not a pollutant, it is a "greenhouse gas." Although not all climate specialists agree about the ultimate effect of adding greenhouse gases like CO2 to our atmosphere, the six warmest years in the last hundred occurred from 1983 to 1988. [123]

---

[116]   Schneider, Stephen H.. *Global Warming*. Sierra Club Books, San Francisco, Ca. (1989): p. 20.

[117]   San Diego Gas and Electric. *San Diego Regional Energy Plan (Draft)*. (8/27/93): extrapolated from the flow chart on p. 3.

[118]   Newscast, National Public Radio.

[119]   Ibid.

[120]   Brown, Lester R. et al. *Saving The Planet*. W. W. Norton & Company, New York, London, (1991): p. 60.

[121]   Totten, Michael, et al. *The Road to Trillion Dollar Energy Savings*. Public Citizen, Washington D.C., (1984): p. 16.

[122]   Ibid. pp. 16-17.

[123]   Udal, James B. "Turning Down The Heat". *Sierra*. Vol. 74, No. 4, (July/August 1989): p. 26.]

Nuclear Power's Hidden Costs

Pollution related to the nuclear power industry includes:

1. Radioactive residues borne by wind and water from uranium mines and mine tailings.

    Rain water runoff from uranium mines and their tailings causes harmful pollutants to be distributed far beyond mining sites. Land is also required for uranium processing facilities and for the storage of radioactive wastes. In some areas, radioactive residues from mining are scattered so extensively that the public is at risk. The Grants Mineral Belt, a large area in West-central New Mexico, is so contaminated from mining and milling operations "that scientists have recommended that human habitation of the area be permanently prohibited." [124]

    An associated cost connected with mine residues is the illnesses, primarily cancer, that uranium miners have experienced. To address this problem, Congress passed a bill which will pay 300 to 500 miners or their survivors $100,000 each in compensation. [125] Although no amount of money can make up for the tragedy of cancer, this compensation package equals $30 to $50 million.

2. The release of radioactive materials during fuel enrichment processes and when the enriched fuel is loaded into reactors. [126]

3. The release of radioactive materials as part of normal reactor operation and during nuclear plant accidents. [127]

4. Contamination of the environment with radioactive materials at nuclear waste storage facilities. [128]

    In recent years nuclear power has been touted as a way to reduce CO_2 emissions. Even if this is true, investing in efficiency reduces CO_2 emissions for a lot less money. A study by the Rocky Mountain Institute concluded that "every dollar invested in energy efficiency displaces nearly seven times more carbon dioxide than the same investment in nuclear power." [129]

    In general, investing in efficiency will displace more carbon dioxide than investing in nuclear power or any other power production system. Investing in efficiency also makes better economic sense. In 1991 a Lawrence Livermore Laboratory analysis revealed that a government investment

---

[124] Shuey, Chris. "Uranium Mines and Their Problems". The Workbook. Southwest Research and Information Center, Vol. X, No. 3, (July/Sept. 1985): p. 113.

[125] Houston, Paul. "Compensation for Radiation Victims OKd". Los Angeles Times.(September 28, 1990): p. A-1.] This represents a total payout of $30 to $50 million.

[126] Gyorgy, Anna et al. No Nukes South End Press, Boston Mass., (1979): p. 103.

[127] Ibid. p. 106.

[128] Ibid. p. 45-70.

[129] Hall, Stephen. "Back From the Grave". New Internationalist. No. 206, (April 1990): p. 14. Also see Udal, James B. "Turning Down The Heat". Sierra. Vol. 74, No. 4, (July/August 1989): p. 26.

of $6 million in three projects to improve the performance of compact florescent lights, high-performance windows, and low-energy heat pumps, water heaters, and air conditioners had "already realized savings of $5 billion and will eventually generate savings of $82 billion -- a return on taxpayer investment of 14,000 to 1".[130] Just the $3 million dollars spent on the development of high performance windows "will eventually save as much energy as the Interior Department believes could be found from drilling in the Arctic National Wildlife Refuge."[131]

According to one study, nuclear power may actually be a net CO_2 producer. According to Gene Tyner Sr. of the Oklahoma Institute for a Viable Future, Robert Costanza of the Coastal Ecology Institute, Center for Wetland Resources, Louisiana State University, and Richard G. Fowler of the University of Oklahoma, nuclear power is probably not even a net energy producer. In their view, nuclear power, even without including past or future accidents, "is at best a re-embodiment of the fossil energies by which it was set in place."[132]

In other words, if all the energy inputs necessary to mine and process uranium for use in reactors, to build and operate a reactor, and to decommission it and store the wastes it produces are added together, they are greater than the amount of energy a reactor produces over its lifetime. If this is true, less CO_2 would have been released to produce the same amount of energy if the fossil fuels used up to create the nuclear industry had been burned directly to make electricity instead.

Even if nuclear power proves to be a net energy plus, it "cannot compete (economically) with either efficiency or renewables."[133] To date, nuclear power has "cost the United States about $200 billion in public and private investment -- by one government estimate over a trillion dollars if all the tax-payer provided R&D (research and development) is included."[134] That is more money than what was spent on "the Vietnam War and the Space Program combined, to deliver to the U.S. just over half as much energy as wood."[135]

In all, the health and environmental costs of our current energy direction are very high. If these costs are added to the tax subsidies enjoyed by the conventional energy industry, the cost to society is even higher. "Estimates for the U.S. alone range between $100 billion and $300 billion per year."[136]

An exhaustive study in 1985 identified federal subsidies for non-renewable energy sources, (nuclear, oil, natural gas, and coal) in excess of 30 billion dollars per year.[137] A number of other sources put the figure at around $50 billion per year.

In addition to government subsidies, there are a host of other costs associated with the use

---

[130] Romm, Joseph J. *The Once and Future Superpower*. William Morrow and Company, *(1992): p. 139.*

[131] *Ibid. p. 140.*

[132] Tyner Sr.; Gene. et al. "The Net-Energy Yield of Nuclear Power". Pergamon Journals Ltd. *Vol. 13, No. 1, (1988): p. 73.*

[133] Lovins, Hunter et al. Changing America: Blueprints for a New Democracy. (Reprint) *Rocky Mountain Institute, Old Snowmass, Colorado, (1992): 12. Also see: Romm, Joseph J.. The Once and Future Superpower. William Morrow and Company, (1992): p. 137.*

[134] *Ibid.*

[135] *Ibid.*

[136] Hubbard, Harold M. "The Real Cost of Energy. "Scientific American. *Vol. 264, No. 4, (April 1991): p. 36.*

[137] Romm, Joseph J. *The Once and Future Superpower*. William Morrow and Company, *(1992): p. 147.*

of non-renewable energy resources. A 1991 Scientific American article analyzed the true-cost of our present energy production and use direction, from the perspective of societal burden. In the article, our yearly energy production and consumption liabilities were listed as follows: [138]

Corrosion	$2	to	-	billion
Health Impacts	$12	to	82	billion
Crop Losses	$3	to	8	billion
Radioactive Waste	$4	to	31	billion
Military	$15	to	54	billion
Employment	$30	to	-	billion
Subsidies	$43	to	55	billion
Total Yearly Burden	$109	to	262	billion

Imported Non-renewable Oil: A Special Case

Added to the societal costs, our mainly fossil-fuel energy base creates other political and economic costs related to our dependency on imported oil and how that "addiction" provides people like Saddam Hussein with the money to purchase arms. The drain on U.S. tax revenues to maintain an American military presence in the Middle East is another factor. "According to the U.S. Congressional Research Service, the military cost of securing peacetime oil transport routes is estimated to be between $1 billion and $70 billion per year. [139] By eliminating our dependency on imported oil, much of this cost could be reduced. It would also eliminate the regular shock waves that hit our economy whenever political disturbances in the Middle East erupt or OPEC moves to increase prices by cutting oil production.

During the recent conflict with Iraq, speculation in the world oil market came close to doubling the per barrel price of oil. This happened even though there never was a real shortage of oil, only the fear that there might be a shortage in the future. [140]

Another liability connected to our dependency on imported oil is its negative effect on our international trade balance. Depending on the general level of economic activity, a high percentage of the U.S. trade deficit can be attributed to imported oil. During the 1991 economic slow down, the purchase of imported oil accounted for 92 percent of the U.S. trade deficit for the year. In other words, if we had not purchased imported oil, the $65 billion 1991 trade deficit would have been reduced to $5 billion or around 8 percent of what it was. [141] Unless efficiency begins to play a considerably larger role in the U.S. energy strategy, "our trade deficit in petroleum alone" could reach "$80 billion a year in the year 2000." [142]

The trade deficit we incur by importing oil causes other economic problems. When we import oil we export dollars. Since not many people working for OPEC are likely to spend the money we export to them in America's local businesses, this money is lost to our local economies. When

---

[138]   *Ibid. p. 148.*

[139]   *Wager, Janet S. "How Much Are Fossil Fuels Really Costing You". Nucleus. Vol. 15, No. 2, (Summer 1993): p. 7.*

[140]   *Bradsher, Keith. "Iraqi Moves Lift Crude To $38.25". The New York Times. (September 25, 1990): p. D-1.*

[141]   *Banks, Howard. Editor, "What's Ahead For Business", Forbes. Vol. 149, No. 5, (March 2, 1992): p. 37.*

[142]   *Romm, Joseph J. The Once And Future Superpower. William Morrow and Company, Inc. New York, (1992): p. 119.*

money leaves our local economies, it is not available to hire people to work in local businesses -- people who would earn paychecks, pay taxes, make financial investments, and spend most of their money locally.

When we invest in energy efficiency, we eliminate the need to import energy and thereby avoid the export of dollars from our local and often national economies to purchase it. Even if we only used energy as efficiently "as the Japanese and Western Europeans, we would save close to $200 billion a year in energy costs." [143] In other words, we would have an extra $200 billion per year to invest in other sectors of our economy.

Efficient Energy Use:
How Much Energy Can We Save and What Are The Benefits?

If energy efficiency was aggressively pursued, the amount of energy needed to run our country could be greatly reduced. A Solar Energy Research Institute (SERI) study "showed that pursuing cost-effective efficiency investments over the next two decades, in the residential, commercial, industrial and transportation sectors would cut in half American (U.S.) dependency upon depletable resources." [144]

A study by the Rocky Mountain Institute "projects that the United States could save about 70 percent of the electricity it uses, at an average cost of 1.0 cent for every kilowatt-hour saved." [145] The average cost per kilowatt-hour nationally is around 7 cents. Though their projection is less optimistic, the industry-supported Electric Power Research Institute estimates that about 38 percent of the electricity used in the U.S. could be eliminated at a cost of 2.5 to 3.0 cents per kilowatt-hour saved. [146] An analysis by The Solar Energy Research Institute's (SERI) falls between these two estimates.

Energy efficiency experts in Sweden "have calculated that Sweden could save 50 percent of its electricity at an average cost of 1.2 cents per kilowatt-hour (saved)." [147] This estimate from Sweden is almost twice as optimistic as that put forward by the Rocky Mountain Institute. Sweden has on average a colder climate than the U.S. and is already roughly twice as energy efficient. In general, the more efficient a country becomes, the more costly it becomes to improve efficiency even further. Given the difference in climate and efficiency, it should be roughly twice as expensive for Sweden to reduce its use of electricity by 50 percent than it would be to reduce the use of electricity by that much in the U.S. Put another way, if Sweden can cut the use of electricity by 50 percent for 1.2 cents per kwhr., the U.S. should be able to cut its use by 50 percent for .6 cents per kwhr or less.

Efficient energy use has the additional benefit of paying for itself. Money saved by not purchasing energy will usually pay back the money invested in saving it quite rapidly. Additionally, all the people employed in the "several million jobs" created would be paying taxes on the money they earned instead of needing or being in danger of needing public assistance. [148]

---

[143] *Ibid. p. 117.*

[144] *Totten, Michael, et al. The Road to Trillion Dollar Energy Savings. Public Citizen, Washington D.C., (1984): p. 2.*

[145] *Romm, Joseph J. The Once And Future Superpower. William Morrow and Company, Inc. New York, (1992): p. 122.*

[146] *Ibid.*

[147] *Ibid.*

[148] *Totten, Michael, et al. The Road to Trillion Dollar Energy Savings. Public Citizen, Washington D.C., (1984): p. 2.*

Becoming more energy efficient can also be "immensely profitable". [149] If aggressively pursued globally, energy efficiency "can save the world upwards of a trillion dollars per year -- as much as the global military budget." [150]   The Solar Energy Research Institute concurs. Implementing cost-effective energy efficiency measures throughout the U.S. economy "would achieve net energy savings of several trillion dollars, making the energy sector an exporter of capital to other parts of the economy." [151]

Though they were slow to recognize that it is less costly to invest money in saving energy than it is to build and operate power plants, many utilities are now embracing the idea through Demand Side Management (DSM). DSM is. the process of reducing the demand for energy by providing the energy service, like lighting, more efficiently. In 1989 U.S. utilities spent $900 million on DSM. By 1992 this figure had grown to $2.3 billion -- a 250 percent increase in just three years. [152]

Although most utility DSM programs focus on giving equipment like screw-in fluorescent light bulbs to customers or offering discounts or rebates for efficient lighting systems or appliances, some are more aggressive. Boston Edison, for example, helps businesses become more efficient by paying consultants and financing the efficiency changes they recommend. [153] In addition to saving energy, this also "helps local industry to modernize, preserves jobs, and . . . keeps paying electricity customers from fleeing to other parts of the globe." [154]

Sacramento Municipal Utility District (SMUD) in California has been credited with having one of the most aggressive DSM programs. SMUD's program has included "planting over 100,000 shade trees near homes and offices (often cutting air conditioning use by 30 percent)" and installing solar panels on roof tops for water and space heating. [155] Unfortunately, unlike SMUD, most utilities would pass on funding such projects even though they are more cost effective than building new power plants. [156]

Energy Use In Buildings

If we incorporate the best energy efficiency strategies in the design of new buildings and retro-fit older ones, our national energy budget could be reduced by as much as 25 percent. [157] Under presently accepted standards, the one-time cost of designing and constructing a building "represents only about one fifth of the (building's) total life cycle cost". [158]   The remaining 80 percent are consumed by maintenance and building operations. [159]   This includes repairs, cleaning, grounds-keeping, building administration, and meeting the building's energy requirements

---

[149] Lovins, Amory. "Abating Global Warming--At A Profit". Rocky Mt. Inst. Newsletter. Vol. V, No. 3, (Fall 1989): p. 1.

[150] Ibid.

[151] Totten, Michael, et al. The Road to Trillion Dollar Energy Savings. Public Citizen, Washington D.C., (1984): p. 2.

[152] Roodman, David Malin. "Power Brokers: Managing Demand for Electricity". World Watch. Vol. 6, No. 6, (November/December 1993): p. 26.

[153] Ibid.

[154] Ibid.

[155] Ibid. p. 29.

[156] Ibid.

[157] Author's calculations based on figures cited in the text that follows.

[158] Kreider, Jan F. and Ari Rabl. Heating and Cooling Design for Efficiency. McGraw Hill, p. 3.

[159] Ibid.

over the life span of the structure. [160]

Of these costs, energy use is by far the largest. Under present construction standards, almost 40 percent of the cost of operating a building during its life span can be attributed to heating, cooling/ventilation, and lighting. In total, the energy used to run a building during its lifetime, amounts to twice the cost of designing and constructing the typical building in the first place, assuming that the value of money remains constant. [161] With inflation the dollar cost for energy could be even 3 or 4 times the cost of designing and constructing the original building.

The poor efficiency standard used in designing buildings today is all the more puzzling considering the cost effectiveness of efficiency improvements. In new construction the payback on investing in efficiency is very lucrative. The payback on thick or superinsulation, efficient windows, systems for heating incoming cold air with out-going warm stale air, insulating shades, vapor barriers and passive solar design can be five years or less. If used as part of an integrated design such measures can reduce energy consumption in a building "by a factor of 10 to 100." [162] The payback for retrofitting existing buildings is usually longer but it can result in energy savings of 80 to 90 percent. [163]

Efficient Lighting and Day Lighting

Energy use in buildings can be substantially reduced by combining more efficient lighting technologies with the use of daylighting. Daylighting is the use of strategically placed windows and skylights to reduce the need to use electric lighting during daylight hours.

The So-Luminaire Corporation, based in the Los Angeles area, has come up with an active daylighting technology. This technology consists of a set of mirrors that track the sun and collect sunlight which is reflected through a skylight. Once in the skylight, light passes through diffuser lenses down to a semi-translucent fixture or box. The box extends below the ceiling one foot or more depending on the application and light enters the room on all four sides of the box and through its bottom. In addition to providing natural light for most of the day the So-Luminare system saves energy on lighting and air conditioning. This is because the amount of heat per quantity of light delivered by the So-Luminare system is considerably less than that delivered by electric lighting, even fluorescent. Only 25 to 30 percent of the electricity used by a fluorescent fixture is converted into light, the rest is given off as heat. [164]

The So-Luminaire system also saves money on electric lighting systems. With daylighting, electricity powered lighting systems work less often and therefore last longer. This saves on the purchase of new bulbs and the labor to install them. [165] Cam Potter, Safeway's Construction Manager, is so pleased with the system he plans to use it in other stores. [166] The energy savings can be especially dramatic in large facilities. The Solid Waste Management Facility being constructed in southwest Phoenix anticipates the So-Luminaire system will save around $50,000 per

---

[160] *Ibid.*

[161] *Author's calculations based on Figure 1.1 of Kreider, Jan F. and Ari Rabl. Heating and Cooling Design for Efficiency. McGraw-Hill, p. 4.*

[162] *Totten, Michael, et al. The Road to Trillion Dollar Energy Savings. Public Citizen, Washington D.C., (1984): pp. 48-49.*

[163] *Ibid. p. 49. Also see Scholand, Michael. "Building for the Future". World Watch. Vol. 6, No. 6, (November/December 1993): p. 36.*

[164] *"Recycling the Sun". Southwest Contractor. (Sept. 1992): p. 31.*

[165] *"Safeway Dims Lighting Costs". Chain Store Age Executive. (Sept. 1986): p. 220.*

[166] *Ibid.*

year on air conditioning alone for every 100,000 square feet of facility. [167]

Even without daylighting, the energy consumption for illumination in buildings can be reduced by 75 percent or more through comprehensive lighting system retrofits. If daylighting is included the savings can be even greater. A study by the Rocky Mountain Institute, projected that "at least 92% of all the electricity currently used to light American homes, offices, and factories can be saved without sacrificing quality or convenience." [168]

In April 1992, the EPA reported that "lighting electricity could be cut cost-effectively by up to 80 percent". [169] Also, according to Dr. Calvin A. Kent, of the Department of Energy's Energy Information Administration (DOE/EIA), "if the lighting equipment in all commercial buildings were changed to the best equipment, the potential savings for lighting could range up to 72 percent". [170] This estimate is quite remarkable since most commercial buildings already use fluorescent lighting. Even older, less efficient, fluorescent lights are considerably more efficient than incandescent lights. Additionally, efficiency estimates from the Department of Energy tend to be conservative.

Investing in efficient lighting also makes good economic sense, since such changes are often "better than free". This is because the monthly savings on electricity would more than make the monthly payments on the new equipment and its installation. [171] And once the equipment is paid for, the savings continue.

Actually the savings potential goes far beyond just saving energy. In addition to being 60 to 75 percent more efficient, fluorescent lights last ten times longer than incandescent bulbs. Not only does this save money in replacement costs, it also saves in labor costs to replace burnt out lights. [172] Fluorescent lights also produce less heat per unit of light than do incandescent lights or older fluorescents, thus reducing the air conditioning load for a given amount of light.

Recognizing the savings potential of installing efficient lighting, "Southern California Edison gave away over half a million . . . super-efficient lights to their low-income customers because it was cheaper to do that than to operate existing power plants." [173]

Although the retrofit program developed through a partnership between environmental groups and Northeast Utilities goes beyond just lighting, it serves to illustrate the economic advantage of efficiency over supplying energy. In addition to lighting, Northeast Utilities is including more efficient appliances, insulation, and even the redesign of industrial processes. Taking this tack, the utility projects that the demand for electricity in its service areas will "decline by at least half, at an average cost of just 6 cents for each kilowatt-hour saved." [174] This is substantially less than

[167]   *"Recycling the Sun". Southwest Contractor. (Sept. 1992): p. 31.*

[168]   *Flanigan, Ted, Amory Lovins, et.al. "U.S. Could Cut Light Bill by 92%." RMI Newsletter. (May 1988): p. 8.*

[169]   *Romm, Joseph J.. The Once and Future Superpower. William Morrow and Company, (1992): p. 124.*

[170]   *"Big Energy Savings Possible in Commercial Buildings". Energy Information Administration New Releases. Department of Energy, (March - April 1992, Issued: May 1992): p. 1.*

[171]   *Flanigan, Ted, Amory Lovins, et. al. "U.S. Could Cut Light Bill by 92%." RMI Newsletter. (May 1988): p. 8.*

[172]   *Romm, Joseph J. The Once and Future Superpower. William Morrow and Company, (1992): p. 123.*

[173]   *Hall, Stephen. "Back From the Grave". New Internationalist. No. 206, (April 1990): p. 15.*

[174]   *Flavin, Christopher. "Yankee Utilities Learn to Love Efficiency". World Watch. Vol. 3, No. 2, (March/April 1990): p. 5.*

the cost of building and maintaining a power plant to increase the supply of electricity. [175]

Several government agencies have also benefited from efficiency improvements in fluorescent lighting. In May 1991, the Office of Technology Assessment reported that "a lighting retrofit by the U.S. Postal Service achieved an astounding 368-percent annual return on investment - - a payback period of a mere three months." [176] By retrofitting one of its buildings the Environmental Protection Agency (EPA) reported a reduction of 57 percent in "electricity use, costs, and power plant emissions". [177]

Space Heating

Good building design can greatly reduce the cost and amount of energy needed for heating. Superinsulated homes like those located in central Canada have heating bills as low as $59 per year. [178] In one 14 house tract in the city of Saskatoon, the heating costs ranged from $59 to $143 per year. [179] In Saskatoon, winter temperatures can drop to lower than 60 degrees below zero (Fahrenheit). To protect their occupants from the cold and high utility bills, these houses feature 12-inch thick exterior walls filled with cellulose (made from recycled newspapers) or fiberglass insulation. Twenty-four inches of insulation is installed in their attics. Additionally, a thin piece of polyethylene plastic, installed in their walls and attics, provides a vapor barrier and blocks drafts. Windows in the houses are triple and in some cases quadruple glazed.

With their tight construction, other heat sources, not normally considered heating devices, provide most of the heat needed to keep the houses comfortable. These sources include heat from lights, cooking, from the refrigerator's motor and compressor, and body heat from the people and pets in the house. With these sources contributing the bulk of the heating needed, forced air heating units came on only during extremely cold periods and for a short amount of time.

Even though the efficiency improvements incorporated into these houses added some to their construction costs, the houses were still built for a competitive $40 to $45 per square foot. [180] Any extra costs, related to improving efficiency, were quickly paid back through energy savings.

Notwithstanding their low heating costs, the Saskatoon houses are by no means the "be all and end all" of efficient building design. In some cases the attic insulation used in the houses was not as effective as expected. Some "builders used crushed blown fiberglass insulation. Tests showed it to be only half as effective as rated". [181] Houses incorporating extra (heat storage) mass and large south facing windows with automatic insulating shutters did not perform as well as other less complicated designs with more normally sized windows. And while most of the windows were triple glazed, new windows now commercially available are 4 to 5 times better at keeping heat in than those used in the Saskatoon houses. [182]

---

[175] *Ibid.*

[176] Romm, Joseph J.. *The Once and Future Superpower*. William Morrow and Company, (1992): p. 124.

[177] *Ibid.*

[178] Meyer, Jane and Craig Sieban. "Super Saskatoon." *Solar Age.*, Vol 7 No. 1, (June 1982): p. 26.

[179] *Ibid. pp. 27-28.*

[180] *Ibid. p. 27.*

[181] *Ibid. p. 31.*

[182] Arasteh, Dariush and Stephen Selkowitz. "A Superwindow Field Demonstration Program in Northwest Montana", Paper presented at the ASHRA/DOE/BTECC/CIBSE Conference on Thermal Performance of the Exterior Envelopes of Buildings IV, December 4-7, (1989), Paper Dated September (1989): p. 1, Lawrence Livermore Laboratory - 26069, TA - 265. See index -

Straw Bale construction, an old idea making a comeback, promises to be even more efficient than the super-insulated houses just cited. With this type of construction, straw bales 18 inches thick, 23 inches wide and 4 feet long are used like large bricks to build walls. Walls made of these "bricks" can have an R value of 35 to 50. [183] The insulating value for exterior walls in the Saskatoon houses is R-30. R value refers to a material's or structure's resistance to heat loss. If the floor, walls, windows, and ceiling of a house have a high R value, it will be able to retain heat very effectively.

In the modern version, straw bales are reinforced with steel and/or structural columns and protected from the elements by plaster and roof overhangs. Well-built straw bale houses can last 100 years or more. Even without modern techniques, some straw bale homes built as early as 1903 are still in good condition. [184]

Protecting Air Quality In Tightly Built Buildings

To preserve indoor air quality, an air-to-air heat exchanger is also included in Saskatoon house designs. In tightly constructed buildings, indoor air pollution can be a problem. An air-to-air heat exchanger turns this problem into an asset. To maintain good air quality, the stale air in a house should be completely replaced every two hours. In a normal drafty house this happens more or less naturally along with an expensive heating or cooling bill. With the heat exchanger stale warm air is drawn out of the building through small tubes that run next to tubes bringing in fresh air from the outside. As the two air flows pass each other, up to 86 percent of the heat in the outgoing air is conducted to the incoming air through the tube walls.

Air quality tests conducted on the Saskatoon houses by R. W. Besant of the Department of Mechanical Engineering, University of Saskatchewan "showed that well-sealed, mechanically ventilated houses in that area do not pose radon-related health problems. Indeed, they may have lower levels of some indoor pollutants than conventional houses." [185]

In the summer, heat exchangers can reduce cooling costs by using the relatively cool inside air to cool the warmer air being drawn in from the outside. If the incoming air is cooled by the earth before it is drawn into a building through its heat exchanger, cooling costs in a well designed building can be close to zero.

The earth can be used for cooling in a number of ways. Building structures partially underground allows a building to use the earth as a heat sink. At a depth of 5 or more feet, the earth maintains a relatively constant temperature of 55 degrees Fahrenheit. If a building is completely or even partially in contact with the earth, such as with a sunken living room with a concrete slab, heat in the room will be absorbed by the earth through the slab.

Outside air can also be cooled if it is drawn through underground pipes before it enters the building to be cooled. When cooling is needed a thermostatically controlled fan pulls air through the underground pipes and into the building. In its passive mode, the system can be activated by letting the warmest air in a building escape out its roof. If the doors and windows of the building are closed, this will create a partial vacuum that will draw air through the underground pipes and into the building.

energy - avoiding heat gain for more details.

[183] Malin, Nadav. "Building With Straw Bales". *Environmental Building News*. Vol. 2, No. 3, (May/June 1993): p. 10.

[184] *Ibid.* p. 10.

[185] Meyer, Jane and Craig Sieban. "Super Saskatoon." *Solar Age*, Vol 7 No. 1, (June 1982): p. 31.

Reducing heating and cooling costs in office buildings is even easier than it is in houses. Office buildings, on average, are larger than houses, thus they contain more enclosed space per square foot of exterior wall. This means that there is less wall area per unit of building volume for heat to escape through in the winter or be gained through in the summer. Ontario Hydro's 20 story office building in Toronto, Canada has no heating system at all. Heating requirements for the building are met by recirculating the heat given off by office equipment, lighting, and employees. [186]

Keeping Cool

In some locations, keeping buildings cool as opposed to warm, is more the issue. In addition to using the earth as a heat sink, there are a number of design and operational strategies that can be used to help a building keep its cool.

Lighting and office equipment produce heat when they operate. If lighting and office equipment are energy efficient, less cooling is needed. Furniture can be designed to radiate warmth toward its occupant or away from them. If cooling is the issue, the wrong kind of furniture can make a person occupying it feel warm even if the air temperature is relatively cool.

Solar heat gain from improperly placed or unprotected windows can cause even a well-designed building to be an air conditioning nightmare. Most designers are aware of passive solar designs as they relate to southern exposures, but much less attention has been focused on the more troublesome east and west exposures.

During the summer the sun rises in the northeast and sets in the northwest (in the northern hemisphere). This means that for several hours in the morning and afternoon, the sun is low enough in the sky to send its rays, even if there is an overhang, directly into windows facing these directions. Thus, a well insulated building can become a heat trap by nine a.m. and stay hot longer in the evening than would be the case if the windows were shaded.

Although heat gain problems can be easily remedied in the design phase of a building and even as a retrofit of an existing building, it is amazing how little is done to avoid them. Some protection from heat gain can be achieved by various window treatments. One gray tinted glass coating is able to reduce heat gain "by 44% while the daylight is only cut by 5%." [187] Some new window designs incorporate dual glazing with a very thin transparent reflective film sandwiched in between the layers of glass. These films reflect some of the unwanted sunlight that hits them back to the exterior environment so it does not enter the building. [188] Interior shades and drapes offer some protection, especially if they are lined with a reflective material on the side facing the glass. If shades are reflective on the window side, some of the light passing through a window is reflected back out the window as light instead of being converted into heat.

One of the easiest ways to avoid solar heat gain is to protect east and west facing windows from direct sunlight altogether. Shading can be as simple as installing roll-down bamboo shades that are lowered manually, the evening before, for windows facing east. Once the sun is high enough and far enough to the south not to cause a heat gain problem, the shade can be raised to let in indirect light and provide a view. For western exposures shades would be lowered in the afternoon

---

[186] *Stobaugh, Robert and Daniel Yergin. Energy Future. Random House, New York, (1979): p. 167.*

[187] *David, Bradley J. "Taking The Heat Out of Sunlight - New Advances In Glazing Technology For Commercial Buildings", Paper Presented at the ACEEE 1990 Summer Study on Energy Efficiency in Buildings, August 26 - September 1, 1990, Asilomar Conference Center, Pacific Grove, California, p. 6.*

[188] *Arasteh, Dariush and Stephen Selkowitz. "A Superwindow Field Demonstration Program in Northwest Montana", Paper presented at the ASHRA/DOE/BTECC/CIBSE Conference on Thermal Performance of the Exterior Envelopes of Buildings IV, December 4-7, (1989), Paper Dated September (1989): p. 1, Lawrence Livermore Laboratory - 26069, TA - 265.*

and raised for optimal benefit just after sunset.

A more sophisticated approach would be to incorporate exterior shades controlled by photo cells which would open and close automatically as needed. In general, exterior shading is more effective than interior shading at blocking solar heat gain. Once sunlight has passed through a glass window and hits objects in a room, most of it is converted into heat which becomes trapped in the room. This is the same phenomenon that makes solar waterheaters and greenhouses work. It is also why we get hot in a car with closed windows when the sun is shining. Light passes readily through glass but once it strikes a drape or other object in a room it is converted into heat. Once in a room, heat can only escape through the glass by heating it and conducting through it. While light passes through glass very easily, glass is a poor conductor of heat.

Even when an interior drape is closed, much of the light that hits it is converted into heat which in turn raises the temperature of the air between the glass and the drape. A reflective drape does this less because it reflects some of the light entering the window back out as light. If the drape is dark, most of the light passing through the window will be converted into heat. A loose woven light colored fabric will also convert light energy into heat energy effectively.

As the air between a window and a drape is heated, the air expands and rises, escaping into the room at the valance above the drape. As the heated air rises, the space between the window and the drape it vacated is filled by cooler air in the room. This new air is heated in turn and so on as long as sunlight is coming through the window. By blocking direct sunlight from entering the window in the first place, this problem is avoided altogether.

Minimizing the use of east and west facing windows is another way to avoid heat gain. While this is the easiest way to solve the problem, it is not always a viable solution. Some rooms require east or west facing rooms due to safety concerns like access to a fire escape route. Daylighting or featuring an attractive view are other reasons for having east or west facing windows.

Solar heat gain can also be reduced by planting trees in appropriate locations. According to a study titled, "The Impact of Summer Heat Islands on Cooling Energy Consumption and CO_2 Emissions, U.C. Lawrence Berkeley Laboratory, July 1988, "three well-placed trees around a house can cut home air conditioning needs by 10 to 50 percent." [189] Additionally, the resulting reduction in air conditioning demand reduces CO_2 emissions 15 times more than the tree could absorb as it grows and it does this at a cost far below almost any other efficiency investment. [190]

If all the ways to use energy more efficiently in buildings were incorporated, adjusted for climate, little if any of the energy now consumed for heating and cooling buildings would be needed. If efficiency was aggressively pursued, the amount of energy used for heating and cooling buildings in the United States could be reduced by 90% or more. [191]

More Efficient Appliances

Big efficiency improvements are possible for appliances. Unless a house is heated or heats water with electricity, refrigeration can account for 25 to 50 percent or more of the typical electric bill. Yet new refrigerator designs are as much as 5 to 10 times more efficient than the refrigerator found in the typical home. [192]

---

[189] *Pearlman, Nancy - Editor. "Costa Rica" The Compendium Newsletter. Vol. 20, No. 4, (July/Aug.): p. 14.*

[190] *Ibid.*

[191] *Author's calculations.*

[192] *Carlock, Marty. "Super-Fridge Can Run On Sunshine." Popular Science. Vol. 227, No. 5, (1985): p. 64.*

The 16 cubic foot Sun Frost refrigerator uses only 17 kwhrs of electricity per month compared to the 75 to 150 kwhrs consumed by comparably sized refrigerators in common use today. In addition to being better insulated and having better seals on its doors, the Sun Frost gains much of its efficiency by mounting the heat producing motor, compressor, and condenser on top of the refrigerator. The motor and compressor are mounted underneath most refrigerators in service today and condensers are attached to or imbedded in the refrigerator's back.

This latter arrangement is like having a fire underneath the refrigerator and a heating pad on its back. To overcome this design contradiction, the motor and compressor have to work much harder and for longer periods of time to achieve the desired temperature inside the refrigerator. In the process they produce much more heat than they otherwise would, if they were arranged more intelligently. Even after such a refrigerator reaches the desired temperature and the motor and compressor shut off, they continue to heat the refrigerator for some time.

Even after the motor and compressor finally turn off, it takes time for them to cool. As they cool they continue to heat the refrigerator. This continued heating causes the refrigerator to rapidly "lose its cool" which causes the motor and compressor to start working and heating again. This built-in contradiction in design is very wasteful.

Commercial refrigeration is generally more efficient than residential. This is because the motors, compressors, and condensers used in commercial refrigeration are usually mounted on the roofs of the supermarkets and restaurants they serve. This avoids the design contradictions inherent in most residential refrigerators. Nevertheless, the efficiency of most commercial refrigeration systems can be improved "by more than 25%." [193]

Although the savings potential is not as dramatic as it is in residential refrigeration, the efficiency of other appliances can be improved if they are equipped with more efficient electric motors. New appliance sized motors can be up to 17 percent more efficient than those in common use today. [194] If care is taken to insure that motors are correctly sized for their task and equipped with non-slip drive systems, efficiencies can be increased further. [195]

A study in the Federal Republic of Germany (FRG) came to a similar conclusion. "At least two-thirds of the electricity used in household appliances (assuming that each household has every appliance) can be saved by good design, with a present FRG payback time under five years." [196]

Beyond using electricity more efficiently, appliances can save energy in other ways. An add-on rotary heat exchanger, designed to recover heat from clothing dryers, is one example. This device, which can be designed into new dryers or retrofitted into existing ones, can cut energy use in clothes dryers in half. Heat being discharged through the heat-exchanger is used to pre-heat the fresh air replacing it. Because it is pre-heated, it takes less energy to get the fresh air up to the desired drying temperature. [197]

---

193 *Cohen, Jon. "Putting the Freeze On Refrigeration Costs". EPRI Journal. (Electrical Power Research Institute), Vol. 13, No. 8, (December 1988): p. 16.*

194 *Rocky Mountain Institute Staff. "New Electric Motor Designs Improves Efficiency." Soft Energy Notes. Vol. 1, No. 2, (1978): p. 22., also see Steve Meyers, "Efficient Motors: Winding Up and Slowing Down." Soft Energy Notes. Vol. 3, No. 2, (1980): pp. 27-29.*

195 *Flanigan, Ted, et al. "Competitek's Drivepower Report Completed." RMI Newsletter. Vol. 5, No. 2, (1989): p. 6.*

196 *Lovins, Amory B. and L. Hunter Lovins. Least-Cost Energy. 2nd Edition, Brickhouse Publishers, New York, (1981): p. XXII.*

197 *Yeaple, Frank. "Laundry Dryer Recuperator Recovers Valuable Heat". Design News. (May 26,1989): p. 122.*

In addition to being more energy efficient, water efficient appliances can also save additional energy. New washing machines and dishwashers use less water. In some cases, this can reduce the amount of energy needed for heating water by 50 percent when compared with their less water efficient counterparts. Though they are not commonly thought of as appliances, new low-flow showerheads and faucet flow-restrictors can reduce the energy requirements for heating household water by 60% or more. [198]

If the efficiency measures discussed here are combined with solar water heating and an instantaneous water heater for backup, non-solar energy use for heating water can be just about eliminated in most climates. This assessment is based on the performance of a Sola Hart thermosyphon water heater equipped with a selective surface collector and a non-freeze heat exchange fluid. If properly sized and used in conjunction with low flow showerheads, faucet aerators and energy efficient hot water appliances, this collector will provide 80 to 100 percent of a family's hot water needs in many areas, even during cold weather and overcast skies.

More sophisticated collector systems can achieve similar results in even very cold and cloudy climates. The output of evacuated (vacuum) heat pipe solar collectors, for example, are "largely unaffected by temperature." [199] The performance of such collectors "drops less than 10 percent when the ambient (out door) temperature drops from 60 degrees Fahrenheit to -20 degrees Fahrenheit (16 degrees C to -29 degrees C)." [200]

Efficiency Improvements In Industry

Efficiency improvements in industry can net energy saving rewards on a number of levels. Attention to details in maintenance and facility upgrades, like fixing broken windows, caulking, adding insulation and installing efficient lighting, can save large quantities of energy and make important contributions to a company's bottom line.

With an investment of $73,000 American Can of New Jersey reduced its energy use by 55% and netted an annual savings of $700,000, nearly a 10 fold or 1,000% return on the investment. [201] The Parker Company, a large manufacturer of auto parts, did even better. The company's investment of $50,000 resulted in a yearly energy cost savings of 1.2 million dollars, a 24 fold return on the investment in just one year. [202]

After their initial payback, investments in efficiency continue to pay dividends in the form of reduced overhead long into the future. In 1982, Dow Chemical ran a contest to find energy saving "projects that cost under $200,000 with a payback time under one year." [203] During the contest 27 qualifying projects were identified in which Dow invested $1.7 million. The average payback to Dow was seven months or a 173 percent return on Dow's investment. [204] Just six years later Dow did even better. In 1988 Dow invested $21.9 million into ninety-five energy saving projects and

---

[198] *Author's calculations based on the use of low flow showerheads and faucet restrictors that can reduce the energy required to heat water by 70%.*

[199] *Mahjouri, Fariborz. "DMS With Solar Hot Water at Baltimore Gas & Electric." Solar Today. Vol. 8, No. 1, (Jan./Feb. 1994): p. 23.*

[200] *Ibid.*

[201] *Stobaugh, Robert and Daniel Yergin Editors. Energy Future. Ballantine Books, (1979): p. 154.*

[202] *Ibid.*

[203] *Romm, Joseph J.. The Once and Future Superpower. William Morrow and Company, (1992): p. 122.*

[204] *Ibid.*

garnered a return on investment of 190 percent. [205]

Although the returns on investment would not always be as spectacular as those just cited, the efficiency of most factory buildings can be improved cost effectively. If all factories in the U.S. were upgraded to the standards demonstrated by buildings in Canada, the energy needed to heat and cool them could be reduced by 90% or more. [206]

Switching to more efficient electric motors is another way that industry can save energy. Industrial motors use around 35% of all the electricity consumed in the U.S. [207] If the use of electric motors in appliances and in industry are included, "electric motors use more than half of all the electricity (in the U.S.) . . . but 28-60 percent of that energy, and tens of billions of dollars per year could be saved if motors and their drive systems became more efficient." [208]

The technologies needed to garner these savings are already well developed and the payback for the cost of their implementation is attractive. Companies that install this equipment, like the Highland Energy Group of Golden, Colorado, are often able to provide their customers with a positive cash flow while the costs of the improvements in efficiency are still being paid. [209] In other words, the savings captured by increased efficiency are often greater that the payments on the new equipment. Once the motor and drive system improvements are paid for, the customer gets all the savings, which can amount to a 60% savings on the purchase of electricity to run their new motors over what they had previously paid. [210]

"A comprehensive 1989 study by Amory Lovins and his colleagues at the Rocky Mountain Institute concludes that the technical potential exists to save an estimated 44 percent of all the energy used by electric motor drivepower systems in the United States . . . at an average cost that is less than the cost of operating, let alone constructing, fossil-fuel or nuclear-power plants to generate an equivalent amount of electricity." [211]

Efficient electric motors even make economic sense when compared with the cost of developing hydro power. "In the case of a proposed dam in Maine, investments in more-efficient industrial motors that could free up equivalent power (what the hydro project would have produced if built) were shown to be one-fifth as costly." [212]

---

[205] *Ibid. p. 123.*

[206] *Author's calculations.*

[207] *Author's calculations based on figures taken from Lovins, Amory. Soft Energy Paths. Friends of the Earth International, Ballinger publishing Company, Cambridge, Mass. (1977): p. 75. Total use of electricity by electric drives (motors) in industry - 2.96 quads, divided by 6.67 quads, both figures relate to the amount of electricity used in the U.S. in 1973.*

[208] *Flanigan, Ted, et al. "Competitek's Drivepower Report Completed." RMI Newsletter. Vol. 5, No. 2, (1989): p. 6. Also see Totten, Michael, et al. The Road to Trillion Dollar Energy Savings. Public Citizen, Washington D.C., (1984): p. 51.*

[209] *Telephone conversation with David Singer, President of the Highland Energy Group of Golden Colorado.*

[210] *Flaningan et. al. "Competiteck's Drivepower Report Completed." RMI Newsletter. Vd. 5, No. 2, (1989): p. 6.*

[211] *Flavin, Christopher, Rick Piltz, and Chris Nichols. Sustainable Energy. Renew America, Washington D.C., (1989): p. 19.*

[212] *Flavin, Christopher. "Yankee Utilities Learn to Love Efficiency". World Watch. Vol. 3, No. 2, (March/April 1990): p. 5.*

Cogeneration: the Art of Using Waste Heat Productively

Beyond the savings potential previously discussed, industry can save even more energy through the use of cogeneration. Typically, industries purchase energy in two forms: electricity to power motors and lights, and oil, natural gas, or coal which is used to make steam or for other processes that require heat.

With cogeneration, industry only purchases a primary fuel like natural gas, oil, or coal and uses it to produce its own electricity. Natural gas, which is more versatile than oil or coal, can be used to make steam to power a turbine or as fuel to power a gas turbine or an internal combustion engine. The turbine or engine, depending on which system is used, turns a generator which produces electricity. The efficiency of converting a primary energy source into electricity ranges from 25% to 40%. Normally, the remaining 60% to 75% of the primary energy involved in the process is lost as "waste heat". But with cogeneration much of this "waste heat" is used to do work like making steam for processes that require it. It can also be used to supply heat for drying, heating water, and for space heating.

Cogeneration means getting more work out of the same energy. First, when it is used to make electricity and second, when the waste exhaust heat is used to do useful work.

Using waste heat can also improve a company's bottom line. The 3M Company is a case in point. "With a one-time capital investment of $690,000, for example, hot exhaust air that had been wastefully pumped into the atmosphere was rerouted to product dryers and reused. The move helped slash annual energy costs by $460,000." [213] From a return on investment perspective, 3M netted a 66 percent return.

The energy savings potential of cogeneration is substantial since "almost half of all the energy used by industry is consumed just to produce steam." [214] If other industrial heating needs are included, close to 60% of the energy consumed by industry could be theoretically supplied by waste heat. [215]

With good design, energy used in cogeneration can be used several times. For example, a primary energy source heats steam under pressure to 1,000 degrees. The steam is released through jets which propel the blades of a turbine which powers a generator. At the end of the turbine's power producing cycle, exhaust steam at 400 degrees can be used in various industrial processes. Exhausted heat from condensing this steam can be used to heat water to 140 degrees, and exhausted heat from heating water can be used for space heating at 80 degrees.

"A number of studies suggest substantial energy -- over 20 percent of total industrial energy use -- could be saved in the United States through cogeneration investments that are economically sound." [216] If the ecological costs of not saving energy through cogeneration are included in the economic equation, the amount of "eco-nomically sound" cogeneration could be markedly increased.

In addition to saving energy in industry, cogeneration can also be used to reduce energy

---

[213] Cook, William J. et al. "Standing Up to Oil Shock". U.S. News & World Report. Vol. 109, No. 9, (Aug. 27/Sept. 3, 1990), p. 37.

[214] Stobaugh, Robert and Daniel Yergin. Energy Future. Random House, New York, (1979): p. 158.

[215] Author's calculations, based on data extracted from: Lovins, Amory B. Soft Energy Paths. Ballinger Publishing Company, Cambridge, Mass. (1977): p. 75.

[216] Stobaugh, Robert and Daniel Yergin. Energy Future. Random House, New York, (1979): p. 160.

consumption in shopping centers, hospitals, office buildings, and apartment complexes. [217] If these facilities produce their own power on-site, the waste heat generated can be used to heat water, space heat, distill water, heat saunas, etc.

More Efficient Industrial Processes

Beyond cogeneration, industry can save additional energy by improving the efficiency of industrial processes. A number of industrialized countries are more efficient than the U.S. in this respect. [218] "Japan and West Germany use less than half the energy per unit of industrial output," as does the United States. [219]

Efficient energy use or lack of it also affects U.S. competitiveness in the world market. "The United States now spends about 10 percent of its gross national product on energy; Japan spends 5 percent. This means that American products cost about 5 percent more on the world market than comparable Japanese products do -- and the gap is expected to widen over the next 10 years as Japan continues to improve its energy efficiency more rapidly than the United States does." [220] Japan's competitiveness in production is also reflected in many of its more energy efficient products - - an attractive selling point for efficiency conscious consumers.

Considering what is possible, however, even Japan has a long way to go before it reaches the limits of cost-effective efficiency improvements in industry. In a study titled "A Soft Path Plan for Japan", Dr. Haruki Tsuchiya, a physicist with the Research Institute for Systems Technology, projected that even if electronics, Japan's fastest growing industry, increased its output by 50%, new silicon chip designs and miniaturization would make it possible for energy consumption in this sector to be halved. [221]

Japan is also improving energy efficiency on other fronts. Some iron forging plants in Japan have reduced their energy consumption by "as much as 50 percent". [222] These savings came primarily from "waste heat recovery, preheating, air screens, and ceramic insulation" which were able to reduce the start up time for furnaces to 1/6th of what it had been. [223] In another related sector, Mutsui Alumina Co. has developed "a new aluminum smelting process" that can reduce the energy consumption per unit of output to as little as 1/10th of previous levels. [224]

---

[217] *Ibid. p. 159.*

[218] *Cook, William J. et al. "Standing Up to Oil Shock". U.S. News & World Report. Vol. 109, No. 9, (Aug. 27/Sept. 3, 1990), p. 37.*

[219] *Flavin, Christopher, Rick Piltz and Chris Nichols. Sustainable Energy. Renew America, Washington D.C., (1989): p. 18. Also See Stobaugh, Robert et al. Energy Future. Random House, New York, (1979): p. 158 and Yukio Suzuki's "Regeneration of the Earth is not an Impossible Dream", The Japan Times Weekly International Edition. Vol 30, No. 39, (October 1-7, 1090), p. 9.*

[220] *Canine, Craig. "The Second Coming of Energy Conservation". Utne Reader. LENS Publishing Company, No. 37, (Jan./Feb. 1990): p. 117, Excerpted from Harrowsmith. (March/April 1989).*

[221] *Harding, Jim. "Soft Paths for Difficult Nations", Soft Energy Notes. Vol. 3, No. 3, (June/July, 1980): p. 21.*

[222] *Totten, Michael, et al. The Road to Trillion Dollar Energy Savings. Public Citizen, Washington D.C., (1984): p. 51.*

[223] *Ibid.*

[224] *Ibid.*

Reduce, Reuse, Recycle: Saving Energy In Industry

As in other sectors, reducing consumption by using resources more efficiently saves energy and reduces negative ecological impacts. Second to cutting consumption, the direct reuse of industrially produced objects is the next best way for industry to save energy and reduce negative environmental impacts related to the procurement of raw materials. For example, "A 12-ounce refillable glass bottle reused 10 times requires 24 percent as much energy per use as a recycled aluminum or glass container, and only 9 to 16 percent as much as a throwaway made of those materials." [225]

If a bottle is used more than ten times, the average energy consumed per use continues to go down. This is because the original energy that went into making the bottle is divided by the number of times it is used, "which can be 50 or more times in areas where refillables dominate the market." [226] This means that reusing glass "saves almost all of the energy needed to make new glass." [227] And after its 50th use a glass bottle can still be recycled into a new bottle.

Today, only 11 percent of the beverage bottles used in the U.S. are refillable. In contrast, 95 percent of the bottles used in Finland are refillable. [228] According to the Environmental Protection Agency (EPA), a return to the national reuse of glass beverage containers "would save 46 million barrels of oil each year--roughly 10 days of imported oil at 1984 levels." [229]

Additionally, "a nationwide return to deposit-and-return beverage bottles would reduce highway beverage container litter by two-thirds; produce estimated annual savings of at least 530,000 tons of aluminum, 1.5 million tons of steel and 5.2 million tons of glass; it would also save 115,000 barrels of oil a day." [230]

Along with these benefits, even the public seems to favor a deposit and return system for bottles. Polls in seven states that have passed some kind of bottle-deposit law "show overwhelming popular approval." [231] Presently, Americans (U.S.) throw away 1.5 million polyethylene terephthalate (PET) bottles per hour and 75 percent of the glass made in the U.S. "goes into single-use bottles and jars." [232] In addition to containers, many other items could be designed to be reusable. True-cost-pricing would encourage the design of products for reuse because it is the most cost effective thing to do if all costs are included in the assessment.

After reuse, recycling is the next best way for industry to save energy related to the use of materials. It takes 50 to 95 percent less energy to make new products out of recycled materials than

---

[225] Young. John E.. *Worldwatch Paper 101 - Discarding the Throwaway Society*. Worldwatch Institute, Washington D.C., (January 1991): p. 23.

[226] *Ibid.*

[227] Gaines, L. L. *Energy and Materials Used in the Production and Recycling of Consumer-Goods Packaging*. Argonne National Laboratory, Argonne, Illinois, (February 1981): p. 5.

[228] Pearlman, Nancy - Editor. " *Use of Refillables Instead of Recycled Bottles"*. *The Compendium Newsletter*. Vol. 20, No. 4. (July/August 1992): p. 10.

[229] Brown, Lester and Edward C. Wolf. "Global Prospects" *Not Man Apart*. (April/March 1885): p. 15.

[230] Horton, Paul B. et al. *The Sociology of Social Problems*, Eighth Edition. Prentice Hall Inc., Englewood Cliffs, New Jersey, (1985): p. 414.

[231] *Ibid.*

[232] During, Alan B. "Junk Food, Food Junk". *World Watch*. Vol. 4, No. 5, (Sept./Oct. 1991): p. 8.

it does to make them from virgin resources. [233]   According to the National Association of Recycling Industries Inc., recycling aluminum uses only 4 percent of the energy that goes into extracting aluminum from virgin ore. The energy required to recycle copper is only 13 percent, paper 30 percent, and lead and zinc 37 percent of the energy needed to extract the same materials from virgin sources. [234]   Likewise, the energy used to produce a ton of steel from scrap, is "only 14 percent of that needed to produce a ton of steel from raw ore". [235]   Distances and modes of transport being equal, it also takes less energy to deliver recycled metals to smelters than it takes to deliver ore. This is because the percentage of metal in recycled scrap is high, in ore it is low.

Saving energy is only one of the benefits that come with recycling. "Recycling steel can result in an 86 percent reduction in air pollution, a 76 percent reduction in water pollution, and a 40 percent reduction in water use." [236]   Recycling steel also eliminates the mining wastes created when steel is made from virgin ore. [237]   Mining wastes are also eliminated when other metals are recycled. Air and water pollution are greatly reduced as well.

The efficiency advantage of recycling over mining and processing virgin materials will undoubtedly increase. As ores with a relatively high concentration of metal are exhausted, more energy will be required to produce a given quantity of metal from ores with a lower metal content. In all, "the extraction and processing of raw materials accounts for about two-thirds of all industrial energy use in the United States, or about 25 percent of all energy consumption." [238]   With extensive recycling this energy expenditure could be cut by two-thirds or more. [239]

Recycling in the packaging sector yields comparable energy savings. Approximately 4% of the primary energy consumed in the United States is used to make packaging materials. [240] Seventy-five percent of this energy is used to make packaging from five materials; paper, glass, steel, aluminum, and plastics (polyethylene, polystyrene, polyvinyl chloride, and polyester). [241] If these five packaging materials were completely recycled, 62% of the primary energy used to make them could be recovered. [242]

---

[233]   Stauffer-Forsell, Roberta. "Energy Savings from Recycling." *Resource Recycling*. (January/February 1989): pp. 24-25, 56, 58-60.

[234]   *Recycling Responds - An Industry at Work for America's Future*. National Association of Recycling Industries, New York, New York, (1978): p. 4.

[235]   Totten, Michael, et al. *The Road to Trillion Dollar Energy Savings*. Public Citizen, Washington D.C., (1984): p. 15.

[236]   Ibid.

[237]   Brown, Lester, et al. "Earth Day 2030". *World Watch*. Vol.3, No. 2, (March/April 1990): p. 17.

[238]   Totten, Michael, et al. *The Road to Trillion Dollar Energy Savings*. Public Citizen, Washington D.C., (1984): p. 15.

[239]   Author's calculations.

[240]   During, Alan B. "Junk Food, Food Junk". *World Watch*. Vol. 4, No. 5, (Sept./Oct. 1991): p. 7, and verified by Author's Calculations based on figures taken from: Gaines, L. L.. *Energy and Materials Used in the Production and Recycling of Consumer-Goods Packaging*. Argonne National Laboratory, Argonne, Illinois, (February 1981): p. 3.

[241]   Author's calculations based on figures taken from: Gaines, L. L.. *Energy and Materials Used in the Production and Recycling of Consumer-Goods Packaging*.Argonne National Laboratory, Argonne, Illinois, (February 1981): p. 3.

[242]   Ibid. pp. 3,4,6,7.

Trash To Energy: Is It A Good Idea?

Fueled by the vision of converting trash into energy, many communities have gotten on the trash to energy bandwagon. While on the surface, turning trash into energy looks attractive, in practice, it is fraught with problems.

Even from an energy perspective, burning trash does not make sense. According to a study by the Argonne National Laboratory for the U.S. Department of Energy, 2.5 times more energy could be saved if the five principal packaging materials were recycled than could be recovered if these materials were burned. [243]

Much more energy goes into making a piece of paper than the piece of paper will give off if burned. Additionally, because of conversion losses, only around 20% of the energy given off if the paper is burned can be converted to electricity. It takes approximately 14,000 Btu's of energy to make one pound of paper. If burned, one pound of paper will release approximately 7,500 Btu's of energy which would, at best, convert to around 2,400 Btu's equivalent of electrical energy or around 17 percent of the original 14,000 Btu's of energy that were consumed in making the paper in the first place. [244]

Jeffrey Morris, a waste management analyst at Sound Resource Management Group, a Seattle consulting firm, comes up with a similar figure. Morris estimates that "recycling paper saves up to five times as much energy as can be recovered through incineration." [245]

If the energy required to mitigate environmental damage associated with mining and processing virgin raw materials and landfilling throwaway objects is included, the energy equation favors recycling even more.

Note: In total, "food packaging accounts for about 20 percent of the nation's tonnage of Municipal solid waste," or "290 pounds per person" per year. [246] "Paper constitutes some 40 percent of the waste going into dumps in the United States. Worldwide, the amount of new paper produced each year -- about 240 million tons -- is four times the weight of the world's total production of new automobiles." [247]

Even if recycling paper and plastic did not save several times more energy than could be produced by burning it, burning such materials instead of recycling them still would not make economic or ecological sense. "A recent study by Barry Commoner's Center for Biology of Natural Systems (CBNS) conducted in East Hampton N.Y., (estimated that) the cost of disposing a ton of garbage under an aggressive recycling program is $127 per ton." The cost of incinerating a ton of garbage is $195-209. [248]

---

[243] *Ibid. p. 3.*

[244] *Author's calculations based on figures taken from - "Recycling Saves Resources", Berkeley Ecology Center Newsletter. (April 1985): p. 1., Also see Holdren, John. Ecoscience.*

[245] *Young, John E.. "Burn Out". World Watch. World Watch Institute, Vol. 4, No. 4, (July/Aug. 1991): p. 8.*

[246] *During, Alan B. "Junk Food, Food Junk". World Watch. Vol. 4, No. 5, (Sept./Oct. 1991): p. 7-8.*

[247] *Ayres, Ed. "Whitewash: Pursuing the Truth About Paper". World Watch. Vol. 5, No. 5, (Sept./Oct. 1992): p. 17.*

[248] *Remba, Zev. interviewing Robert Collins, Director of Clean Water Action's Solid Waste Program. "Recycle First: Countering the Rush to Burn", Clean Water Action News. Vol. 14, No. 1, (Winter 1989): p. 6.*

Recycling is also much less expensive to start up. "Building an incinerator costs $100-300 million. The start up cost of a recycling program may cost $5-10 million, depending on the size of the community." [249] In addition, to being more expensive to establish and energy wasteful, incineration has a number of less obvious costs. Off-site costs include the cost, both economic and ecological, of mining, harvesting, and processing virgin materials to replace those that are burned.

Trash burning plants also carry a number of operational costs. These include toxic air pollution and toxic ash. Pollutants found in air and ash include acid, lead, mercury, cadmium, chlorine, and dioxin. All of these materials can cause serious health problems, even in low concentrations. Dioxins are actually formed during the incineration process. [250] Dioxin is reputed to be the "most toxic substance ever made". [251] Faced with this reality, Ontario, Canada recently declared "a province-wide ban on all future municipal solid waste incinerators." [252] According to Ontario's Environmental Minister, Ruth Grier, "Incineration is an environmental sleight-of-hand which gives the illusion of making waste disappear. . . The people of Ontario need solutions not illusions". [253]

Recognizing its advantages over burning, some countries are aggressively pursuing recycling. "Germany now requires that retailers and manufacturers collect and recycle packaging for a variety of products. By 1995, firms will be required to recycle 80 percent of what they collect - - creating a powerful incentive to reduce packaging and use recycled materials." [254] Additionally, "German auto manufacturers have agreed, under pressure from the federal government, to redesign cars so they are easier to dismantle and recycle." [255]

Great Britain is also an aggressive recycler. "More than half of all the paper and cardboard manufactured in Great Britain is made from recycled paper." [256]

Efficiency Improvements In Transportation

By far, the lion's share of energy used in the United States for transportation is consumed by the automobile. U.S. energy efficiency can be substantially improved by switching to more efficient cars. A study by the Solar Energy Research Institute (SERI) in 1979 estimated that just by using existing technologies a fleet of automobiles could be developed for the U.S. market that would average 103 MPG. In this projected fleet, two passenger sports cars would average 140 MPG, four passenger cars would get 93 MPG, and five and six passenger sedans and small trucks would

---

[249] *Ibid.*

[250] *Karasek, F. W. and L.C. Dickson. "Model Studies of Polychlorinated Dibenzo-p-Dioxin Formation During Municipal Refuse Incineration". Science. Vol. 237, (August 14, 1987): p. 754.*

[251] *Remba, Zev. interviewing Robert Collins, Director of Clean Water Action's Solid Waste Program. "Recycle First: Countering the Rush to Burn", Clean Water Action News. Vol. 14, No. 1, (Winter 1989): p. 8.*

[252] *Young, John E. "Burn Out". World Watch. World Watch Institute, Vol. 4, No. 4, (July/Aug. 1991): p. 8.*

[253] *Ibid.*

[254] *Flavin, Christopher and John E. Young. "Will Clinton Give Industry A Green Edge", World Watch. Vol. 6, No. 1, (Jan./Feb. 1993): p. 30.*

[255] *Ibid.*

[256] *"Vital Signs". World Watch. Vol. 4, No. 5, (Sept./Oct. 1991): p. 6.*

average 70 MPG. [257]

Technological developments since the 1979 SERI study have pushed the auto efficiency potential even further. In their book Changing America: Blueprints for a New Democracy, Hunter and Amory Lovins and co-author Richard Heede state that, "Advances in aerodynamics, new materials, ultra-lightweight construction, new engine and energy-storage technologies, micro-electronics, and computer-aided design and manufacturing can yield a 150-mpg safe, peppy, comfortable, and affordable station wagon." [258] This projected station wagon design is based on the technology used to develop the Voyager, an airplane that circumnavigated the earth on one tank of gasoline.

On the prototype front the four passenger Renault Vesta 2, has an efficiency rating of 78 MPG for city driving and 107 MPG on the highway. [259] In other tests, the Vesta 2 has achieved efficiencies of 124 MPG. [260]

A little closer to production, "is the Volvo LCP 2000, a fully developed prototype with a fuel economy of 63 MPG in the city and 81 MPG on the highway." [261] The LCP 2000 will "comfortably seat four or five people, can accelerate from 0 to 60 miles per hour two seconds faster than the average American car, exceeds U.S. safety requirements, and has an engine that can accommodate alternative fuels." [262]

Volvo is planning to increase the LCP's fuel efficiency by another 20 m.p.g. by adding a flywheel energy storage system and a continuously variable transmission. [263] A flywheel energy storage system would consist of a flywheel looking something like a gyroscope that would spin in a vacuum chamber and ride on magnetic bearings to avoid friction losses. Energy is added to the flywheel by speeding it up. The flywheel slows down as electricity is extracted from it. A continuously variable transmission always keep a car's engine running at its most efficient and least polluting RPM (revolutions per minute) range. "It is estimated that this car could be mass-produced at a cost competitive with today's subcompacts." [264] Volkswagen also has an entry in the efficiency derby. In U.S. tests, an advanced prototype V.W. Golf (Rabbit), averaged 80 to 100 MPG "on the EPA city/highway circuit." [265]

In all, "10 manufacturers have built and tested attractive, low-pollution, prototype cars that

---

[257] *Meyers, Steve and Kathy Slicter. "The Reluctant Revolution."* Soft Energy Notes. *Rocky Mountain Institute, Vol. 3, No. 4, Snowmass, Colorado, (1980): pp. 3-5.*

[258] *Lovins, Hunter et al.* Changing America: Blueprints for a New Democracy. *2nd. Edition, (Reprint) Brickhouse Publishers, New York, (1981): p. 11.*

[259] *Marinelli, Janet.* Garbage Magazine. *Vol. 1, No. 2, (November/December 1989), pp. 31 & 34.*

[260] *Flavin, Christopher, Rick Piltz and Chris Nichols.* Sustainable Energy. *Renew America, Washington D.C., (1989): p. 8.*

[261] *Ibid. - This was also reported in: Romm, Joseph J..* The Once and Future Superpower. *William Morrow and Company, (1992): p. 129. Also see Brown, Lester, et al. "Earth Day 2030".* World Watch. *Vol.3, No. 2, (March/April 1990): p. 16.*

[262] *Ibid.*

[263] *Ibid.*

[264] *Ibid.*

[265] *Lovins, Amory B. and L. Hunter Lovins.* Least-Cost Energy. *p. XXII.*

get 67 to 138 miles per gallon." [266] Additionally, "better designs and stronger materials make some of these (cars) safer than today's cars, as well as more nimble and peppy." [267]

While most people equate efficient cars with small cars, this is not necessarily the case. "Only four percent of past car-efficiency gains came from downsizing." [268] This fact is reflected in some of the prototype cars developed thus far. Some prototypes are large enough to accommodate 4 or 5 passengers comfortably. [269]

Available in today's market, the Japanese-designed 1992 Chevrolet Geo Metro is the fuel efficiency leader. The GEO has an EPA rating of 53 MPG in the city and 58 MPG on the highway. [270] The '92 Honda Civic Hatchback is a close second at 48 MPG for city driving and 55 MPG on the highway. [271] In spite of their reputation for efficiency, fuel efficient cars have a lot of pep. In fact, the Honda CRX, another 50 mpg car, has been criticized for having so much power that it is dangerous to drive. [272] By trading some of its power for efficiency, the CRX could likely exceed the 65 MPG efficiency barrier.

Because automobiles consume the lion's share of the "nearly two-thirds of the oil" used in the U.S. for transportation, even small efficiency improvements can have a big impact. If the current average 19 mpg for U.S. automobiles was improved to just 22 mpg, the oil saved would be equal to all the oil that was imported to the U.S. from Iraq and Kuwait prior to the war in 1990. If average vehicle efficiencies were increased another 10 mpg, it "would displace all oil we import from the Persian Gulf." [273]

Although 86 percent of auto efficiency improvements have resulted from technological improvements rather than weight loss or a shift to smaller cars, many people have erroneously assumed that more efficient cars would be less safe. [274] Even though the average new car efficiency rose from 14 to 27 miles per gallon from 1974 to 1991, "traffic fatalities per 100 millon miles traveled have fallen from 3.5 to 2.1." [275] Even in smaller cars, technology improvements have increased safety. The 81/82 Honda Civic improved fuel efficiency by 10 percent compared to the 79/80 model, "yet had a 40-percent lower death rate (measured over the same time period)." [276] "Volkswagen replaced the Beetle with the Rabbit, a vehicle with a similar weight and wheel base, and yet had a 25-percent improvement in gas mileage and a 44-percent lower death rate." [277] Researchers at the Lawrence Berkeley Laboratory "found no correlation between fuel

---

[266] Lovins, Amory and Hunter Lovins. *"Winning The Peace"*. RMI Newsletter. *Vol. VII, No. 1, (Spring 1991): p. 3.*

[267] *Ibid.*

[268] *Ibid.*

[269] *Ibid.*

[270] Rosewicz, Barbara. *"Japanese Firms Again Dominate Top-Mileage List"*. The Wall Street Journal. *(September 30, 1991): p. C-15.*

[271] *Ibid.*

[272] *"Car Talk", National Public Radio.*

[273] Lovins, Hunter et al. Changing America: Blueprints for a New Democracy.

[274] Romm, Joseph J.. The Once and Future Superpower. *William Morrow and Company, (1992): p. 127.*

[275] *Ibid. p. 127-28.*

[276] *Ibid. p. 128.*

[277] *Ibid.*

efficiency and automobile safety." [278] A United States General Accounting Office (GAO) study concurred. In its study the GAO stated that its "statistical analyses support the view that automobile weight reductions since the mid-1970s have had virtually no effect on total highway fatalities." [279] Presumably, as reinforced passenger compartments, impact absorbing front and rear ends, and air bags become more widely available in smaller cars, this trend toward safer car designs will improve accordingly.

Mass Transit

Expanding the use of mass transit is another way to reduce energy consumption in transportation. An intercity bus, fully loaded with passengers, uses energy around 2.4 times more efficiently, per passenger mile, than a typical car with 4 passengers. Given the same conditions, an intercity rail car is 2.7 times more energy efficient, per passenger mile, than a car carrying four passengers. [280]

Mass transit also saves energy by reducing the amount of energy consumed in making and maintaining roads and building parking lots and parking structures. One study estimated that we would have to add $4 to $5 to the price of each gallon of gasoline sold to cover the cost of building and maintaining roads and the other infrastructural elements that support the auto way of life. [281] According to the World Resources Institute, "U.S. auto subsidies amount to more than $300 billion Annually". [282] This is "more than $1,000 per person, (per year and including children) above and beyond the direct cost to car users." [283]

Two thirds of these costs can be attributed to infrastructural costs, i.e., road building and maintenance, parking facilities, and transportation related police activity. The remaining one-third is caused by congestion. Traffic congestion literally slows the wheels of commerce, increasing the cost of doing business. According to the U.S. General Accounting Office, traffic congestion costs the U.S. economy $100 billion each year. [284] If we continue in the same auto oriented direction these costs will undoubtedly increase. "In Los Angeles, average freeway speed is projected to fall to 11 miles per hour in the next 20 years." [285]

Congestion-related costs also extend to the global economy. In 1989, the London Times reported "that congestion was costing the country $24 billion per year." [286] Traffic congestion reduces economic productivity in Bangkok by 10 percent. [287]

---

[278] *Ibid.*

[279] *Ibid.*

[280] Lowe, Marcia D., *Alternatives to the Automobile: Transport for Livable Cities.* Worldwatch Paper 98, Worldwatch Institute, Washington D.C., (October 1990), p. 13.

[281] Morris, David, "Getting From Here To There: Building a Rational Transportation System. *Paving Moratorium Update*, Issue No. 2, (Fall/Winter 1991-92), Alliance for a Paving Moratorium, p. 6.

[282] Bayless, Lynne. "Car Wars", *Earthword*. No. 4, Eos Institute, Laguna Beach, California, p. 3. For additional details on the true-cost of transportation contact the Campaign for New Transportation Priorities, (202) 408-8362.

[283] Ayres, Ed. "Breaking Away", *World Watch*. Vol. 6, No. 1, (Jan./Feb. 1993): p. 13.

[284] *Ibid.*

[285] *Ibid.*

[286] *Ibid.*

[287] *Ibid.*

Currently, vehicle fees and gas taxes only cover a fraction of true cost of our auto oriented transportation system. The shortfall comes out of property taxes and general tax revenues. In his report <u>Making the Car Pay Its Way</u>, John Bailey "show that more than half (the majority from property taxes) the money spent on Minneapolis roads comes from non-transportation revenue sources." [288] According to his data, shifting the cost of road maintenance and repair to gasoline taxes "could lead to a 40 percent decrease in residential property taxes levied by the city of Minneapolis." [289]

Given that 75% of all auto trips in the U.S. transport a solitary driver, considerable energy could be saved if convenient systems of mass transit were available. If half the single occupant auto trips were substituted for mass transit, an overall transportation related energy savings close to 25% would result, even if the current average auto fuel efficiency average of 20 mpg, did not improve. [290]

Like auto efficiency, the efficiency of air passenger transport is improving rapidly. Between 1973 and 1979 the efficiency of air passenger transport improved by 30 percent from 17.5 passenger miles per gallon (PM/gal.) of fuel to 25 PM/gal. With the "introduction of the new generation of aircraft (Boeing 757 and 767, DC9-80, advanced L-101), this is expected to reach 45 PM/gal" for an improvement in efficiency of 250 percent over the 1973 level. [291] "Boeing's new 777 jet will use about half the fuel per seat of a 727." [292]

Transporting Freight

Efficient energy use can also be increased by expanding and modernizing our national rail freight system. Even with our present somewhat archaic system, "railroads are up to four times more efficient than trucks in intercity freight hauls". [293] The longer the distance that freight is moved, the more efficient it is to send it by rail as opposed to by truck. [294] Notwithstanding its efficiency edge, "more than 3,000 mile of railroad track are abandoned each year". [295]

While the movement of freight by truck and trailer is less efficient than by rail, trucks can go more places. Therefore, more efficient truck and trailer designs can also make a contribution toward increasing efficiency. Large freight trucks are now approaching the 10 MPG barrier. [296] The Fruehauf Corporation has developed a truck/trailer combination that exhibited a 40% increase in fuel efficiency in a standardized road test conducted by the Society of American Engineers. [297]

[288] Lundberg, Jan, Ed. "Get Roads Off Welfare: High Property Taxes Pay for Roads". *Paving Moratorium Update and Auto Free Times*. Issue No. 5, (Summer 1993): p. 25.

[289] Ibid.

[290] Author's calculations.

[291] *Least-Cost Energy*. p. 49. Also see Lovins, Hunter et al. *Changing America: Blueprints for a New Democracy*, and Totten, Michael, et al. *The Road to Trillion Dollar Energy Savings*. Public Citizen, Washington D.C., (1984): p. 50.

[292] Lovins, Amory and Hunter Lovins. "Winning The Peace". *Rocky Mountain Institute Newsletter*. Vol. VII, No. 1, (Spring 1991): p. 3.

[293] Drucker, Charles. "Transportation 2000: The Policy Role." *Soft Energy Notes*. Vol. 4, No. 3, (1981): p. 77.

[294] Drucker, Charles. "Transportation and Energy." *Soft Energy Notes*. Vol. 4, No. 2, (1981): p. 34.

[295] Pearlman, Nancy - Editor. "United States Transportation Mismanagement". *The Compendium Newsletter*. Vol. 20, No. 4, (July/August 1992): p. 9.

[296] Dunne, Jim. "Truckin' Into The Future." *Popular Mechanics*. (June 1986): pp. 65-8.

[297] Krause, Florentine. "Fruehauf Finds 40% Fuel Savings." *Soft Energy Notes*. Vol. 5, No. 2, (1982): p. 43.

Recognizing the efficiency benefits of moving freight by rail, freight hauling trailers have been transported on rail flatcars for many years. Now new trailer designs are improving the efficiency of flat car-freight trailer combination by eliminating the flatcar altogether. This is made possible by equipping trailers with two sets of wheels: one set for the road and a second set for running on rails. At the rail yard, trailers are positioned over the appropriate track and its rail wheels are installed to engage the track. The trailers are then linked together and pulled like box cars. This saves energy by allowing freight to be delivered while avoiding the need to waste energy transporting heavy flat cars. [298]

According to one source, "Trucks hauled only one-fifth of the roughly 2.5 trillion ton-miles (of freight) moved that year (1977) -- but burned four-fifths of the freight fuel budget to perform that much smaller fraction of the work." [299] If this figure is accurate, the movement of freight by rail is around 16 times more efficient than moving the same tonnage of freight by truck. Given this efficiency advantage, if only half the freight ton miles now transported by trucks were switched to rail, the overall energy used to move freight in the U.S. would be reduced by 47 percent, since the additional energy needed for rail transport would almost be negligible. [300] If the remaining freight was hauled by trucks as efficient as the trucks already developed by the Fruehauf corporation, energy used to haul freight would be reduced by another 40 percent. [301]

The efficiency of moving freight by ship can also be improved. A 50 percent improvement in efficiency has been demonstrated by a Japanese ship equipped with a "heat recovery, variable-pitch propeller, and computer operated sails" that allow the ship to substitute wind power for fuel. [302]

Balanced Community Designs

Balanced community designs can greatly assist in reducing energy consumption. When communities are designed to balance the number of living spaces with employment, educational, and recreational opportunities, the need for cars can be substantially reduced. In balanced communities, it is more convenient for most people to walk or bicycle to work, places of recreation, or school, on car-free bicycle and pedestrian pathways. Such pathways are much less costly to build and maintain than roads and match the global trend of increased bicycle use. "Between 1970 and 1990, annual car production increased by 14 million, while bike production grew by 60 million." [303] Worldwide, bicycles already outnumber cars two to one. If current trends hold, bicycles will outnumber cars ten to one by 2030. [304] Bicycles are also safer than cars. "Though they outnumber cars 2 to 1 in the world, only 2 percent of traffic fatalities involve bicycles -- and of those, 90 percent result from collisions with cars. Thus, when bikes and cars are given their own space, the risk of death is 500 times greater in cars," than on bikes. [305]

Balanced community designs are the rule for most European communities and for "just about

---

[298] Swan, Christopher. "Back On The Track-Revitalizing The Railroads." *Soft Energy Notes*. Vol. 4, No. 22, (1981): p. 37.

[299] Drucker, Charles. "Transportation and Energy." *Soft Energy Notes*. Vol. 4, No. 2, (1981): p. 34.

[300] Author's Calculations based on Ibid.

[301] Author's calculations, based on figures taken from Krause, Florentine. "Fruehauf Finds 40% Fuel Savings." *Soft Energy Notes*. Vol. 5, No. 2, (1982): p. 43.

[302] *Least-Cost Energy*. pp. 48-49.

[303] Ayres, Ed. "Breaking Away", *World Watch*. Vol. 6, No. 1, (Jan./Feb. 1993): p. 11.

[304] Brown, Lester, et al. "Earth Day 2030". *World Watch*. Vol.3, No. 2, (March/April 1990): p. 17.

[305] Ayres, Ed. "Breaking Away", *World Watch*. Vol. 6, No. 1, (Jan./Feb. 1993): p. 14.

any town of less than 50,000 people built before the turn of the century." [306] These communities evolved before the advent of automobiles and therefore have amenities in close proximity, "'generally within a 5 minute walk of a person's home.'" [307] In balanced communities, many shop-keeping families live above their businesses. This promotes community stability, identity, and neighborhood security. It also provides employment for community residents. People may still own cars in such communities but use them much less often.

Balanced designs lend themselves to the concept of community-owned vehicle fleets. Instead of individuals owning their own car, truck, or bicycle, these would be owned in common by the community and maintained professionally. Funding for maintaining such a fleet would be generated through fees based on how many miles a user logged during a particular period of time. When a community member needed a vehicle, a simple phone call would make one available. In some European communities, community owned bicycles are available at commuter train stations. When a person arrives at their stop, they hop on a community owned bicycle and ride home. In the morning they return the bicycle by riding it back to the train station on their way to work.

Balanced communities also improve the efficiency of mass transit. With automobile oriented urban sprawl, amenities and communities are more or less homogeneously distributed along major roadways. This dictates that rapid transit vehicles must make frequent stops all along their route. With a balanced design, the role of mass transits is to get people to and from community hubs. Transit vehicles would make only a few stops in a particular community before moving rapidly to the next community nodule. In larger communities small shuttles and bicycles would be available to transport people from transit centers to their homes or other destinations in the community. Balanced community designs could reduce the energy consumed for local transportation by 50% or more. [308]

Telecommuting

Expanding the use of telecommuting is another aspect of balanced community design. Telecommuting, which is working at home or in satellite offices and communicating with colleagues electronically, can reduce transportation related energy consumption even further. In a 1969 study by the U.S. National Academy of Engineering, it was estimated that telecommunications could "theoretically substitute for 80 percent or more of all U.S. transportation." [309]

While replacing such a high percentage of face-to-face contact with electronic communication may not be desirable, the study does illustrate the power of telecommunication technologies to increase efficient energy use. Since telecommunication could eliminate much of the time we spend in our cars, usually alone, it could give us more time to do pleasant things like visiting with friends.

Balanced community designs coupled with telecommuting can save energy in other ways.

---

[306] *Hagerman, Eric. "Small Town Thinking". World Watch. Vol. 4, No. 4, (July/August 1991): p. 7.*

[307] *Ibid.*

[308] *Author's Calculation -- 50% is probably conservative considering that so much of auto travel is related to getting to and from work, school, and for shopping. In a balanced community, served by mass transit, 90 to 100 percent of these travel needs could be met without the use of an automobile.*

[309] *Meyers, Steve. "Microprocessors Vs. Oil." Soft Energy Notes. Vol. 3, No. 4, (1980): p. 17.*

Currently, "two billion hours a year are wasted in urban traffic congestion". [310]   In addition to wasting time, billions of gallons of fuel are also consumed while traffic jammed vehicles creep along at low speeds or sit idling during stops.

"Federal highway officials estimate that over the next 20 years, traffic congestion will increase more than 400 percent on the nation's highway system and 200 percent on other roads." [311] If balanced community designs and telecommuting became the norm, much if not all of this predicted highway congestion could be avoided. Currently, close to "5.5 million workers in the U.S. participate in telecommuting programs and that number is expected to double by the year 2000." [312]

If we combine the elements of community balance, pedestrian and bicycle friendly transport, mass transit and telecommunications into infrastructural designs, many of the reasons for owning a car along with the expense of maintaining, housing, and parking it would be eliminated. Cars and the roads and parking spaces they require use up about half the land in most urban areas. To the degree that cars can be eliminated through good planning, more land can be made available for human use.

Contrary to the popular conception, it may be that the United States' love affair with the car is starting to sour. "In 1991, the U.S. passenger car fleet shrank by half a million cars (from 143.5 million to 143 million) -- the first decrease in 60 years." [313]

While greater population density might evoke images of crowding, with good design this is not the case. "Copenhagen and Vienna -- two cities associated with urban charm and livability -- are of moderate density (measured by the number of residences and jobs in the city, including its central business district and outer areas), with 19 people per acre and 29 people per acre respectively. By contrast, low density cities such as Phoenix (5 people per acre) often are dominated by unwelcoming, car oriented commercial strips and vast expanses of concrete and asphalt." [314]

People commonly associate high-density land use with poverty, squalor, and crime. But so far there is no scientific evidence to support this view. "Data in a recent report on the world's 100 largest cities by Washington, D.C.- based Population Crisis Committee indicated that Hong Kong -- the most densely populated city at 163 people per acre -- has fewer murders per capita than all but 11 other cities (cited in the report). Additionally, its infant mortality rate, seven deaths per 1,000 live births, is lower than that of all but five other cities." [315]

If We Put All The Ways To Save Energy Together, How Energy Efficient Can We Get?

Technically, the only limit on how energy efficient we can become is our ingenuity. And research to date is bearing this out. According to studies by the Rocky Mountain Institute and Friends of the Earth, we "can sustain our present affluent lifestyle with one-fifth the energy we use

---

[310]   Pearlman, Nancy - Editor. "Telecommuting As A Transportation Alternative". *The Compendium Newsletter*. Vol. 20, No. 5, (Sept./Oct.): p. 10.

[311]   Ibid.

[312]   Ibid.

[313]   Ayres, Ed. Editor. "Vital Signs". *World Watch*. Vol. 6, No. 6, (November/December 1993): p. 37.

[314]   Lowe, Marcia D. "City Limits". *World Watch*. Vol. 5, No. 1, (Feb. 1992): p. 20.

[315]   Ibid, p. 21.

now", and in ways that "are cost-effective investments on narrowly economic grounds alone." [316] Similarly, efficiency can cost-effectively reduce oil consumption to one-fifth of 1993 consumption levels "and the cost of saving each barrel would be less than $5." [317] Even with out true-cost-pricing, oil currently costs around $16 a barrel.

A study conducted by the Umweltbundesamt, the (West) German EPA, concurs. "With present state-of-the-art technology we can increase the efficiency of our buildings ten to hundred fold, increase the miles-per-gallon of our cars five-fold, raise the efficiency of lighting and appliances four-fold, triple the fuel efficiency of industrial processes and freight transport, and double the service per unit of energy from planes and industrial drives." [318]

A detailed study by Amory and Hunter Lovins on the potential to use energy more efficiently in the German economy came to a similar conclusion. Their analysis shows that "technical measures that stop well short of what is technically feasible or economically worthwhile" can increase the efficiency of the Federal Republic of Germany (FRG) economy 3.3 to 5 times beyond what it was in 1973. [319] This conclusion is all the more remarkable, considering that the Western German economy was already roughly twice as energy efficient as the U.S. economy in 1973. If the same measures were applied to the U.S. economy it would end up being 6 to 10 times more efficient than it was in 1973. [320] Even though the U.S. and Germany have both improved in efficiency since 1973, Germany is still about twice as energy efficient.

Dr. Haruki Tsuchiya, a physicist with the Research Institute for Systems Technology in Japan, has a similar view. In his study titled "A Soft Path Plan for Japan", Dr. Tsuchiya "shows that Japan's energy use could be cut 38 percent over a 33 year period without reducing standards of living." [321] Dr. Tsuchiya's study comes to this conclusion, even though it assumes that healthy economic growth will continue along with Japan's current population growth rate of .5 percent per year. [322]

The potential for efficiency improvements indicated by Dr. Tsuchiya's study is even more impressive when compared to current U.S. energy consumption. Currently, Japan's per capita energy consumption is only 40% of the per capita use in the U.S.. "We in the United States use about 11.5 kilowatts (kW) per person (all energy for all uses by all sectors of the economy, divided by all people), compared with Germany's 6, Japan's 5 and the average Third World country's 1." [323] For reference, if a constant primary energy out-put of one kW is converted to electricity at 30 percent efficiency, it would power three 100 watt light bulbs continuously. [324]

If Japan's population grew only .5 percent per year (the present rate of growth) over the 33 years covered by Dr. Tsuchiya's study, a 38% drop in national energy consumption would reduce

[316] Krause, Florentine. "Carbon Dioxide: Fate or Folly?", *Not Man Apart*. (December 1983): p. 14.

[317] Lovins, Amory and Hunter Lovins. "Winning The Peace". *Rocky Mountain Institute Newsletter*. Vol. VII, No. 1, (Spring 1991): p. 3.

[318] Krause, Florentine. "Carbon Dioxide: Fate or Folly?", *Not Man Apart*. (December 1983): p. 14.

[319] *Least-Cost Energy*. p. 68.

[320] Author's calculations.

[321] Harding, Jim. "Soft Paths for Difficult Nations", *Soft Energy Notes*. Vol. 3, No. 3, (June/July, 1980): p. 21.

[322] Ibid.

[323] Hayes, Dennis. "A Wake-up Call". *Solar Today*. Vol. 6, No. 6, (Nov./Dec.): p. 38.

[324] Author's calculations.

Japan's per capita energy use to 21% of the current U.S. per capita consumption. [325]

In other words, if all the efficiency improvements suggested by Dr. Tsuchiya's study were in place in the United States today, U.S. per capita energy consumption would be 21% of what it is now. At this level our energy consumption nationally would be just under 18 quads instead of the 85 quads now used. [326]

Even this may be underestimating the potential for efficiency to save energy. In their book, Least-Cost Energy, Amory and Hunter Lovins conclude that even the studies just cited understate the potential for efficiency improvements. Their approach was to analyze the strengths and weaknesses of the numerous studies on the potential to use energy more efficiently. They then combined the more comprehensive aspects of these studies with new information and projected their findings to a global scale.

They concluded that by the year 2030 a world population of 8 billion people with a robust industrially-based economy could run quite effectively on 40 percent less energy than is used today. Included in their assumptions are the use of efficiency measures that are cost-effective in today's market place (even without true-cost-pricing), that poor countries would be 10 times richer than they are now, and that rich countries would still be ten times richer than poor countries. [327] In other words, if the efficiency measures projected in Least-Cost Energy were in place in the U.S. today, the U.S. economy would be running quite nicely on less than 1/8th (10.6 quads) the energy it uses today. [328]

If true-cost-pricing was the economic measure, many more efficiency measures would become cost effective and even less energy would be required to provide the services we desire. This is because many ecological and social costs, connected to our present energy choices, are not included in the studies cited, just as they are not included in the business as usual energy use balance sheet. [329]

---

[325] *Author's calculations. - A .5 percent increase in population per year would increase Japan's population by 17% in 33 years. Even if national energy consumption remained the same a 17% population increase would reduce the per capita energy use in Japan to 83% of what it is today or only 33% of present per capita energy consumption in the U.S. A 38% reduction in Japan's national energy use on top of this would reduce Japan's per capita energy use to around 21% of the per capita energy use prevalent in the U.S. today.*

[326] *Author's calculations.*

[327] *Lovins, Amory and L. Hunter Lovins. Least-Cost Energy. p. XXVII, XXVIII.*

[328] *Author's calculations.*

[329] *Lovins, Amory and L. Hunter Lovins. Least-Cost Energy. p. 119.] (See section on the true cost of energy.*

Chapter VIII

ECO-NOMIC SECURITY AND RENEWABLE ENERGY

Synopsis

From an economic perspective, investing in efficiency improvements provides a better return than investing in even the most cost-effective energy supply system. But renewable energy is the next best investment if the social and environmental costs associated with conventional energy sources are included in the economic analysis.

Investing in efficiency and in renewable energy resources is also the best way to eliminate our dependence on non-renewable energy resources altogether. The more efficient we become, the easier and less costly it will be to replace non-renewable energy sources with renewables. From a purely security perspective, this strategy would eliminate dependency on imported energy supplies and, if executed properly, make energy supply and distribution systems much less vulnerable to natural phenomena or intentional human acts.

The Potential

Given the studies cited in the last chapter, it seems reasonable to assume that the present U.S. economy could run quite nicely on one-fifth or less of the energy it currently consumes, if all the cost-effective efficiency measures available were in place today. Indeed, with true-cost-pricing, energy consumption could be cost effectively reduced even further.

In addition to saving energy, becoming more energy efficient also makes it easier to replace non-renewable energy sources with various forms of solar energy. Although combining energy efficiency with solar energy makes the most sense from an eco-nomic security perspective, even without efficiency, we have plenty of solar energy.

On a global scale, "if solar cells with only 10-percent conversion efficiency were placed over one quarter of the Sahara, they could supply 3.5 x 10 (to the 14 power) kilowatt-hours or 40,000 gigawatt-years of energy each year -- the projected world energy demand in 2050" (without efficiency improvements). [330] Forty thousand gigawatt-years is just under 1195 quads or 40 terawatts (TW) of energy. This is 8 times as much energy as would be required globally each year in 2050, if state-of-the-art efficiency measures (best available in 1982) were in place. [331]

Dennis Hayes, the founder of Earth Day, comes up with a similar solar availability scenario. According to Hayes, "if we convert the insolation (sunlight) striking 1/2 percent of the land area (on our planet) at 20 percent efficiency, we can harness 26 TW" or around three times what we inefficiently consume today globally or would need in the year 2050 with efficiency. [332]

---

[330] Rowe, William D. *"Renewable energy: Target for 2050". IEEE Spectrum. (February 1982): p. 58.*

[331] Lovins, Amory and L. Hunter Lovins. *Least-Cost Energy. pp. XXXIII, 126. Also see Totten, Michael, et al. The Road to Trillion Dollar Energy Savings. Public Citizen, Washington D.C., (1984): pp. 42-43.*

[332] Hayes, Dennis. "A Wake-up Call". *Solar Today. Vol. 6, No. 6, (Nov./Dec.): p. 38. 26 terawatts is Hayes' figure. My statement -- three times what we inefficiently consume today or would need in the year 2050 with efficiency -- is based on figures developed by Amory and Hunter Lovins in their book Least Cost Energy.*

"Sunlight falling on the U.S. landmass (yearly) carries about 500 times the 85 quads of energy the United States (currently) consumes in a year." [333]   Obviously, not all of this energy can be captured. But, according to the book Cool Energy, published by the Union of Concerned Scientists, "if just 1 percent of U.S. land were adapted to collecting solar energy at 25 percent conversion efficiency, over 100 EJ (96 quads) would be made available each year." [334]

Although possible with today's technology, producing 96 quads of energy per year on 1 percent of U.S. land area is probably a bit optimistic. One of the best collectors yet developed and field tested, that would be suitable for such a task, is the McDonnell Douglas Parabolic Dish/ Stirling Engine Solar Electric Generating System. During clear sunny periods, this system achieves overall efficiencies of 23 percent with efficiencies as high as 30 percent during midday periods. In other words, 23 percent of the sunlight intercepted by a McDonnell Douglas collector, on a clear day, is converted into electricity.

If the overall efficiency of the McDonnell System could be boosted to 25 percent, the collector surface needed to produce 96 quads of electricity would be approximately .5 percent of the land area of the United States. This equals half the 1 percent U.S. land area projected in the Union of Concerned Scientist's book Cool Energy.

But, in addition to collector surfaces, solar collectors also need to have space between them. This is especially true for dual axis tracking collectors like the McDonnell Douglas system. Given today's technology, two axis tracking is necessary to achieve an overall efficiency of 25 percent. Since the collector surface needed to produce 96 quads of electrical energy each year is .5 percent of U.S. land area, the Ground Cover Ratio (GCR) of the Cool Energy 1 percent projection, would be 50 percent. The percentage of land at a collector site that is actually covered by collectors is called the Ground Cover Ratio or GCR. Unfortunately, a GCR of 50 percent means that about 14 percent of the sunlight that could have been collected and converted into electricity each year, would be lost. This is because collectors packed in so tightly would partially shade each other in the morning and afternoon when the sun is low in the sky.

For perspective, one percent of U.S. land area equals one-tenth the land area currently devoted to agriculture in the United States. [335]

Ultimately, the most eco-nomically secure energy system for a region or country would include as many forms of renewable energy as are available. Additionally, this system would be configured to be as decentralized as is practical. This approach would make it difficult for natural phenomena or intentional human acts to interrupt large parts of a region's or country's energy supply.

But, for purpose of getting a better idea about how much renewable energy is out there, let us assume that if the efficiency measures discussed in Chapter VII were in place today, national energy consumption would only drop to 25 percent of its current level. In other words, instead of using 85 quads of energy per year as we do now, we would only be using 21 quads. Since the sun does not shine or the wind blow 24 hours a day, we will add another 9 quads extra capacity for

---

[333]   Brower, Michael. Cool Energy. A Report by the Union of Concerned Scientists, Cambridge, Mass. (1990): p. 18.

[334]   Ibid.

[335]   Ibid. p. 19.

storage for a total of 30 quad energy supply for each year. [336] (It will be shown later that this is probably much more storage than is actually needed. See index - Energy storage, for more details.) Further, let's assume that we will supply all of this energy in the form of electricity made from renewable resources.

If we set the goal of producing 30 quads of electrical energy each year, how much land would be required, given the following assumptions:

1.   That the collectors we use will have and overall conversion efficiency of sunlight into electricity of 23 percent, (the McDonnell Douglas system has already achieved this level of efficiency.)

2.   A ground cover ratio of 33 percent.

      A GCR of 33 percent as opposed to 50 percent would make building a system more cost effective by reducing the number of collectors required. A ground cover ratio of 33 percent instead of 50 percent would also reduce the problem of collectors shading each other. With more distance between them, collectors would shade each other less in the morning and afternoon than would be the case if more of them were packed into the same space. On the positive side, this would increase the total output from each collector system -- less shading equals more power. On the negative side, increasing the space between collectors, would reduce the amount of total electricity that could be produced per unit of land. In addition to being affected by numerous factors like available sunlight, collector efficiency, and shading, the optimal GCR for an area would also need to reflect the cost of land in comparison to the cost of collectors.

3.   A daily average of 7 kwhrs of heat energy delivered (reflected) to receivers per square meter of collector per year.

      This is approximately the amount of sunlight available in a number of locations in Southeast California, Arizona, New Mexico, Southern Nevada, and Southern Colorado. [337]

      Note: As collectors follow the sun, the solar energy they intercept is reflected to a receiver where the concentrated solar light is transformed into heat which drives a heat engine that powers an electric generator.

4.   That the systems would be 95 percent reliable.

      In other words, 19 out of every 20 solar electric devices would be fully operational, whenever there was sufficient solar insolation to produce power at a site. Once in operation, system reliability could exceed 95 percent considering that:

      □   System components like heat engines, generators, tracking motors, tracking sensors, and mirrors can be modular, ie. designed so that any component needing repair could be replaced in a few minutes; and

---

[336] *A quad of energy equals a quadrillion (1x10 to the 15th power or 1 followed by 15 zeros) Btus. A Btu is the amount of energy needed to raise the temperature of a pound of water 1 degree Fahrenheit.*

[337] *Based on data extracted from National Renewable Energy Laboratory, NREL. Interim Solar Radiation Data Manual. NREL, Golden, Colorado, (November 1992): pp. 10-72.*

☐   More extensive repairs could be done at night.

Given the assumptions just discussed, it would require approximately 6,000 square miles of collector surface to produce 30 quads of electricity annually. With a ground coverage ratio of 33 percent, the land occupied by these collectors would be 18,000 square miles. If located in one place 18,000 square miles would cover an area of land 140 miles by 140 miles.

Eighteen thousand square miles is approximately .5 percent of the land area (excluding areas covered by water) of the United States. [338]

Eighteen thousand square miles is roughly equivalent, in area, to 60 percent of the land currently occupied by military bases located on U.S. territory. [339] It is also equal in area to about 5 percent of the land area currently used for agriculture in the United States. [340]

In the past, large scale solar plants have been criticized as being more land intensive than conventional energy sources. Research now indicates that this is not the case. Studies conducted by the Office of Conservation and Renewable Resources at the U.S. Department of Energy in 1989 have shown that coal and uranium have comparable land requirements, but at different stages in the electricity production cycle. Solar and wind power require the use of land at the generating site whereas coal and nuclear energy "consume land at fuel-extraction sites." [341]

Further, mining is only one of many steps in the extraction, processing, transportation, use, and disposal cycle through which coal or any other non-renewable resource must pass to derive usable energy from it -- steps which have multiple impacts which consume land and hurt the plants, animals, and people that inhabit it.

Though it requires less land than for coal and uranium, drilling for oil and natural gas also has large impacts. Land is impacted during the process of exploring for oil and gas and when they are extracted after discovery. Additionally, land and water are contaminated by oil spills. Oil contaminates oil fields and oil spills, particularly in coastal areas, can devastate large fishery and wild life habitat areas. After oil and natural gas are located, more land is impacted by the construction and maintenance of pipe lines and burning all fossil fuels causes acid rain.

Another factor is that extracting uranium, or any other non-renewable energy resource, consumes new land on an on-going basis. Once a source of non-renewable energy is consumed, more land has to be impacted to continue the supply. With solar energy this is not the case. Once a solar or wind system is in place it will continue to produce the same amount of energy forever, if maintained. And it will never use another square meter of land unless its capacity is expanded. Even biomass (plants grown as energy crops) can be grown in the same location indefinitely, if the nutrient rich ash from burning them is returned to the growing site. And solar energy in all its forms is not an energy resource we have to worry about using up.

---

[338]   *Author's calculations based on figures taken from: The World Almanac and Book of Facts 1993. World Almanac, Scripps Howard Co., St. Martin's Press, New York:(1992), p. 456.*

[339]   *Author's calculations based on figures taken from: The World Almanac and Book of Facts 1993. World Almanac, Scripps Howard Co., St. Martin's Press, New York:(1992), p. 456.*

[340]   *Author's calculations based on numbers taken from Brower, Michael. Cool Energy. A Report by the Union of Concerned Scientists, (1990): p. 19, and The World Almanac and Book of Facts 1993. World Almanac, Scripps Howard Co., St. Martin's Press, New York:(1992), p. 456.*

[341]   *Hubbard, Harold M. "The Real Cost of Energy". Scientific American. Vol. 264, No. 4, (April 1991): p. 40.*

When all the costs are considered, it is clear that use of conventional energy resources impacts far more land, in numerous interdependent ways, than would be impacted if the same amount of energy was produced using renewable energy resources.

This is not to say that solar technologies are completely benign. In addition to land requirements, they also require metal and other materials to be extracted and processed for their construction. They also need to be maintained. But, once in place, their impact is minimal. This will be especially true if the devices (solar collectors, windmills, etc.) are installed and maintained in ways that are sensitive to the habitat needs of installation areas and designed to be easily recycled when they wear out - which would be standard procedure with true-cost-pricing.

Using Solar Generated Electricity as a Primary Fuel

When electricity is generated by burning fossil fuels or through nuclear fission, about 1/3 or less of the energy embodied in the original fuel (the primary energy source) is converted into electricity. This thermodynamic (heat) loss is an unavoidable aspect of changing a primary form of energy into electricity. If the energy consumed by the whole fuel cycle (locating an energy source, extracting and processing it, getting it to a power plant, and disposing of its combustion wastes) is included, the amount of electricity produced is an even smaller fraction of the total energy involved.

Because of these inefficiencies, electricity is usually reserved for tasks which only it can perform, like powering electric lights and electric motors. It is not normally used for tasks like heating water, unless a primary energy source like natural gas is unavailable. Once it is delivered to a water heater, however, close to 100 percent of the electricity used is converted into hot water. But when the conversion losses discussed earlier are included we see that the actual efficiency is no better than 100 percent of 33 percent (even without discounting fuel cycle losses) of the original primary energy source used to create the electricity. Whereas, if natural gas is used to heat water directly, around 70 percent of the primary gas energy will be converted into hot water.

However, if solar energy is used to make electricity, it makes sense to approach the concept of efficiency from a different perspective. Even though using solar energy to generate electricity is subject to thermodynamic losses similar to those experienced when a non-renewable resource is used for the same purpose, these losses can be largely discounted.

Unlike converting non-renewable energy resources into electricity, converting solar energy into electricity is more related to the land or roof area required to produce the desired amount of electricity, not the energy lost in the conversion process. The availability of non-renewable energy resources is finite while the supply of solar fuel is infinite. Solar conversion efficiencies are important, not because of the waste of fuel, but because higher efficiencies can reduce the amount of land and collector hardware needed to produce the desired amount of power. And as was previously discussed, solar energy already uses less land to produce a given amount of electricity, than do non-renewable energy resource. If photovoltaic cells are installed on roof tops, it could be argued that other than procuring the raw materials to make them, photovoltaics use no land at all.

Conversion Efficiencies: Comparing Complete Fuel Cycles

Actually, the 23 percent conversion efficiency achieved by the McDonnell Douglas system in converting solar energy into electricity probably exceeds the conversion efficiencies of some non-renewable energy resources, if the energy consumed by their complete fuel cycles is included. Delivering a form of non-renewable energy to the power plant where it can be used to generate power requires the expenditure of energy on a number of levels. Considerable energy is used in finding a resource, mining or drilling for it, processing it, and transporting it, before it ever gets to a power plant. It also requires energy to control, store, and dispose radioactive waste and coal ash sludge after the electricity is produced. Added to this is the energy consumed in mitigating the numerous environmental and social costs that are caused by using of non-renewable energy resources.

If these energy expenditures are included in the efficiency equation, generating electricity using devices like the McDonnell Douglas system may prove to be more efficient over all than producing electricity from either fossil fuels or nuclear power. Indeed, using solar generated electricity produced at an overall efficiency of 23 percent may even be more efficient for direct heating than using non-renewables like natural gas and oil if a true-cost analysis of all the energy used up in their fuel cycles are included. Even without true-cost accounting, one source projects that "'it will be pointless to continue exploring for oil and gas'" after 2005 in the United States because "after that more energy would be used to look for these fuels than the oil and gas we found would contain." [342]

Note: With the exception of solar energy in its various forms, the real efficiency of any energy source is the amount of energy that actually ends up providing a service divided by the amount of energy consumed during that energy source's fuel cycle. This includes the energy required to mitigate any social and environmental damage that the fuel cycle precipitated. Solar energy does not fall under this definition because, over time, the amount of solar energy available on our planet is infinite, and solar energy has no fuel cycle liabilities with the possible exception of biomass--growing plants as energy crops.

Unlike non-renewable energy resources, solar fueled systems do not even have fuel cycles. The possible exception to this is biomass (energy crops) which have to be grown, harvested, and delivered to a power plant or a processing facility. For systems that use a form of solar energy directly, the energy is delivered directly to the collector field or wind farm ready for use and its use produces no wastes. Constructing and maintaining collector fields or wind farms does require energy for mining and processing metal and mineral ores and to assemble and maintain collectors. But, as preceding chapters have shown, the energy consumed in creating a collector field and the environmental damage sustained during the process of creating it is decidedly less damaging than those that occur when any non-renewable energy resource is used.

Using Solar Generated Electricity
As a Primary Energy Resource

It is therefore practical to use solar generated electricity as a primary energy source except where direct solar heating can do the job. For example, it makes more sense to heat water with a solar water heater than to use solar energy to generate electricity for this purpose. However, using solar generated electricity as the backup energy source for a solar water heating system is probably more efficient than using natural gas, when all the fuel cycle and environmental costs associated with using natural gas are included.

Another argument for using solar generated electricity as a primary energy source is that electricity is more efficient at its point of use than other energy sources. Once it is produced, electricity is more efficient at getting a task accomplished than any other energy source except direct solar for heating things like water and space. When water is heated with natural gas, 20 to 30 percent of the energy released by burning the gas is lost out the exhaust stack. If electricity is used, the water is heated by a heating rod inside the tank from the inside out. Therefore, almost 100 percent of the energy applied is converted to hot water. [343]

---

[342]   Gever, John, et al. *Beyond Oil*. A Project of Carrying Capacity Inc. Ballinger Publishing Company, Cambridge, Massachusetts, (1986): p. 20.

[343]   Author's calculations.

If direct solar collectors for heating water or making steam are backed up with solar generated electricity instead of natural gas, 20 to 30 percent less energy is required to perform the same backup function. In other words, if 100 units of gas energy are needed to provide backup energy for a solar water heating system per year, only 70 to 80 units of electrical energy would be required to do the same work. Instead of needing a collector area large enough to produce 100 units of electrical energy to replace 100 units of gas energy, the 100 units of gas energy can be replaced by 70 to 80 units of electrical energy. Because less energy is needed, the amount of collector area needed to get the job done can be reduced accordingly.

This is even more true for transportation than for heating water if vehicles are powered by solar generated electricity instead of by internal combustion engines. If 100 units of energy in the form of a fuel like gasoline are consumed in a vehicle powered by an internal combustion engine, only about 20 units of the energy in that fuel will be converted into vehicular motion. [344] Because of internal combustion engine inefficiencies, 80 percent of the energy in the gasoline is lost as waste heat. If we include the energy used up in finding, extracting, delivering, and processing the oil to make the gasolines, the overall efficiency of the vehicle will be considerably less than 20 percent.

If the same vehicle is fueled by 100 units of energy in the form of electricity, 65 units of energy in the electricity will be converted into vehicular motion. Well designed electric motors are 90 to 95 percent efficient at converting electricity into work. [345]

Even if we include energy losses associated with battery charging and the small amount of energy that is used up when batteries are charged and discharged, we still end up with efficiencies of around 65 percent. [346] In other words, if we start with 100 units of energy in the form of electricity and use it to charge the batteries of an electric vehicle, around 65 units of the electricity we started with will be converted into motion. This efficiency advantage means that powering the same number of vehicles over the same distance with electricity would require less than one-third the energy needed to move them the same distance with fossil fuels. [347] And again, if we start our energy calculations from when the oil to make the gasoline was still in the ground, the advantage of powering vehicles with solar generated electricity becomes even more attractive.

If the fleet average for all U.S. automobiles is 100 miles per 120,000 Btu's of gasoline (approximately 1 gallon), it would only require 40,000 Btu's of electrical energy to move the car the same distance. In other words, we do not need to produce as much solar generated electricity to do the same work as if we used gasoline or natural gas to do it.

This efficiency advantage has a positive implication related to how many solar collectors or windmills we would actually need to meet our energy needs. If 5 quads of gasoline energy are required to power the U.S. auto fleet, it would only require 1.6 quads of electricity to power the same number of electric cars the same distance. In terms of collector area, this efficiency advantage means that the 18,000 square mile collector area projected in our thirty quad scenario could be

---

[344] *Busch, Lawrence and William B. Lacy Editors, Food Security in the United States. Westview Press, Boulder, (Colorado) - London, (1984): p. 107.*

[345] *Meyers, Steve. "Efficient Electric Motors: Winding Up and Slowing Down". Soft Energy Notes. Vol. 3, No. 2, (April 1980): p. 28.*

[346] *Telephone conversation with Mark Delucchi at the University of California at Davis Institute of Transportation Studies.*

[347] *Author's calculations.*

reduced by approximately 2,000 square miles if all cars were powered by solar generated electricity.[348]

By substituting electric powered auto transport wherever practical with electric powered light rail, even more energy can be saved. Electric powered light rail is powered directly and does not suffer from efficiency losses related to charging and using batteries. The more that electric powered cars are replaced by electric powered mass transit, the less collector area needed to provide enough energy for the same service.

Collector Distribution

Although it would be possible to locate a concentrating collector system in one place, it would actually be more efficient as well as more secure from a national defense or natural disaster perspective if it was distributed along the sun belt from Florida to the deserts of California. This would reduce storage requirements because the energy being produced would better match peak energy use across the country.

Peak energy use occurs during the day when most people work and when both work-places and homes are being heated in the winter or air conditioned in the summer. This period of peak use continues to a lesser extent into the early evening when people are cooking, taking showers, and watching television. Many stores and other commercial enterprises also remain active in the early evening.

If collectors are distributed across the southern states, their output in the southeast would closely match the energy needs of the east coast in the morning and throughout the day. As the earth rotated, collectors further west would come on line to supply energy directly to the eastern and central states into the evening and supply the far western states during the daylight hours.

Additional generating capacity would go into storage to supply the west coast with energy in the evening and for cloudy periods. With this type of distribution, it is less likely that more than a small portion of the overall system would be under clouds at any one time. Although the yearly average amount of sunlight available in the eastern portion of the sunbelt is less than that in the western portion, the difference would be made up by minimizing the amount of energy needed for storage.[349]

The Advantages Of A Diversified System

As has been shown, it would be relatively straightforward to fill all our energy needs using solar concentrating systems located in the southern part of the United States--especially if efficient

---

[348] *Author's Calculations based on a projected U.S. fleet of vehicles equivalent to the number of cars on the road today, driving the same number of miles, but with cars that are four times more efficient, on average, than today's average car and still fueled by a gasoline powered internal combustion engines. If a fleet of cars built to the same specification were powered by a battery or flywheel storage system, the same number of units of energy, in the form of electricity, would allow the fleet to go three times as far as the same fleet fueled by gasoline powered internal combustion engines.*

[349] *The average solar insolation in the south west desert states is around 7 kwhrs of solar energy, in the form of heat, per square meter per day. In the best areas of Florida, the per square meter daily average is just under 5 kwhrs. Taken from the National Renewable Energy Laboratory (NREL). Interim Solar Radiation Data Manual. NREL, Midwest Research Institute Operated for the U.S. Department of Energy, (November 1992): pp. 13-72.*

energy use was aggressively pursued. Nevertheless, it would be even more efficient, require less land and energy storage capacity, and be better for national security if a more diversely based renewable energy system was developed.

Ideally, this system would be a mix of the various forms of renewable solar energy available in a particular region or country.

Wind Energy

Of the various forms of solar energy available, wind energy can be a big contributor to this energy mix. Even if we only consider land areas with suitable average wind speeds (12 mph and higher) that are not being used for non-compatible purposes, the potential energy production from wind power in the U.S is between one and four trillion kwhrs of electricity per year or 3.4 to 13.6 quads. [350]

According to the U.S. Department of Energy, thirty-seven states have sufficient wind power resources "to support development of utility scale power plants, and there are ample winds for small, residential-size wind turbines in all 50 states." [351]

Since 1981 the performance of wind power systems has improved steadily. [352] In response to these improvements, "Wind generated electricity has risen from 6,000 kWh in 1981 to almost 2.8 billion kWh in 1991." [353]

Biomass

Biomass could also be a substantial contributor to the U.S. energy mix. Unlike direct solar or wind, which are intermittent, biomass stores energy that can be used to supply energy when wind and solar are inadequate.

Forestry and agricultural wastes alone can supply 3 to 5 quads of primary energy per year. These sources alone come close to meeting U.S. fuel needs for transportation if transportation efficiencies approached what is currently technologically feasible. [354]

If provisions to grow energy crops are included, biomass could supply 9.6 to 23 quads of primary energy per year. [355] John I. Zerbe, the manager of the Energy Research, Development, and Application Program for the U.S. Forest Service's Forest Products Laboratory (maintained in cooperation with the University of Wisconsin) holds a similar view. He believes that a strong Federal Department of Energy "commitment (to biomass) could lead to the production of 6.2 quads by (1995)

[350] Brower, Michael. *Cool Energy*. Union of Concerned Scientists, Cambridge, Mass. (1990): p. 46.

[351] Swisher, Randy, et. al. "Wind Energy -- A Resource for the 1990s And Beyond". American Wind Energy Association, (Feb. 15, 1991), p. 2.

[352] Swisher, Randall and Paul Gipe. "U.S. Wind Farms: An Expanding Market." *Solar Today*. Vol. 6, No. 6, (Nov./Dec. 1992): p. 17.

[353] Ibid.

[354] Lovins, Amory B. and Hunter L. Lovins. *Least-Cost Energy*. Rocky Mountain Institute, Second Edition, Brickhouse Press, New York p. 112.

[355] Brower, Michael. *Cool Energy*. Union of Concerned Scientists, Cambridge, Mass. (1990): p. 57.

-- and 10 quads by 2000." [356]

A study by the Stanford Research Institute called the <u>Effective Utilization of Solar Energy To Produce Clean Fuel</u> reported yields of eucalyptus as high as 312 cubic meters per hectare "on rich land in Brazil". [357] At .7 tons per cubic meter (air dried), this represents a yield of 88 tons per acre per year. [358] Eucalyptus wood, air-dried to 6 to 12 percent moisture content, contains 25% more energy pound for pound than lignite coal. Air dried eucalyptus contains 8,500 btu's per pound verses 6,330 btu's per pound for lignite coal. [359] Additionally, if growing areas are treated properly the yield will continue indefinitely whereas coal can only be extracted from a particular area once.

One way biomass could be utilized would be to link freeway landscaping and urban forestry. Irrigation and fertilizer for such operations could be supplied by recycled sewage water and composted sewage sludge. Once this system was established, trees would be harvested and replanted as part of an ongoing cycle. Once harvested, wood would be converted into liquid fuels to power vehicles and clean burning charcoal which could be used like coal to produce electricity.

Using current technologies, around 50 percent of the energy contained in a biomass material is lost in the process of converting it into a liquid fuel. But if solar generated electricity supplied the necessary conversion energy, all the energy embodied in the biomass could be converted into liquid fuels and charcoal. Additionally, the amount of electrical energy required to do the conversion work would be less than if biomass was used to supply it. This is because electricity could provide the needed heat internally, which would avoid the 30 percent stack loss that providing the conversion energy with biomass would incur. Using solar generated electricity for biomass conversion would also maximize the amount of biomass that could be stored as a back-up energy source. Taking this approach, biomass becomes a storage battery that can be burned like coal in power plants to supply electricity during periods when direct solar, wind, or hydro power was producing less electricity than required.

In some parts of the country natural brush lands could be harvested as energy crops. Chaparral, which has a higher energy content than eucalyptus, periodically burns off on average every thirty five years but reaches a semi-climax or dormant stage at about 20 years. [360] By harvesting every 20 years, the semi-dormant stage of the chaparral cycle can be shortened. Shortening the dormant period would increase the amount of plant material produced in an area over a given time. This is because vigorous growth will be taking place during what otherwise would have been a dormant period of almost no growth. Reducing the period of dormancy could also improve conditions for animal life. Like fires, harvesting would remove low production, hard to penetrate (by people and wildlife) growth which would be replaced by accessible productive growth.

---

[356] Zerbe, John I. *"Biofuels: Production and Potential".* Forum for Applied Research and Public Policy. *(Winter 1988): p. 38.*

[357] Alich, John, A. Jr. and Robert E. Inman. Effective Utilization of Solar Energy To Produce Clean Fuel. *Stanford Research Institute, Menlo Park, California 94025, (1974): pp. 34 & 35.*

[358] Author's calculations based of figures taken from: Alich, John, A. Jr. and Robert E. Inman. Effective Utilization of Solar Energy To Produce Clean Fuel. *Stanford Research Institute, Menlo Park, California 94025, (1974): pp. 34 & 35.*

[359] Ibid. pp. 34 & 98.

[360] Telephone conversation with Walter Graves, Farm Advisor with the University of California Extension Service, San Diego, California.

To keep the harvest cycle viable, nutrients would have to be applied to the harvest area to replace the nutrients embodied in the woody materials removed from the site. When harvesting virgin sites, imported nutrients would be applied as an area is being harvested. During subsequent harvests, nutrient balances would be maintained by returning the ash residues from previous harvests to the growing area.

To protect wildlife, harvesting would be suspended during animal breeding seasons. In addition to the moral issues of protecting wildlife, a viable wildlife population is vital to healthy watershed maintenance. (See index for more entries.)

The economics of using chaparral as an energy crop looks promising. One study conducted at San Diego State University in California projected that chaparral, harvested and processed for burning, could be delivered for $28 per dry ton to a steam-electricity generating facility. [361] At that price, the energy value of a ton of chaparral would make it equivalent to purchasing oil at ten dollars a barrel. [362]

Chaparral economics is even more attractive when fire control benefits and reduced insurance costs are included in the economic package. Tens and, in bad years, even hundreds of millions of dollars worth of property are lost when chaparral dominated brush areas erupt into wildfires. If an attentive harvest regimen was followed, much of this loss could be avoided. Including some of these savings in the economics of harvesting chaparral makes this energy option all the more attractive.

Hydropower

Though its contribution is not likely to increase substantially (most of the good dam sites have already been used), hydroelectric power already contributes 3.1 quads of electricity. [363] There appears to be a considerable amount of small scale hydropower (small dams and small turbines) potential around our planet. But installing such systems will not be practical unless the watersheds that deliver water to them are protected.

Renewable Energy: Putting An Integrated Package Together

Considering only the conservative estimates for the amount of energy available from wind, biomass, and hydropower, the total is over 16.1 quads. [364] This would mean that 13.9 quads of energy would still have to be powered by solar thermal systems to meet our 30 quad energy budget. The area of land required, using the previously discussed assumptions, to produce 13.9 quads of electrical energy would be approximately 8,340 square miles or an area 90 miles by 90 miles if located in one place.

---

[361] LaRue, Steve. *"Scientist Says Chaparral Is Energy Source."* San Diego Union, *(November 14, 1982): p. b-1.*

[362] *Author's calculation.*

[363] Brower, Michael. Cool Energy. *Union of Concerned Scientists, Cambridge, Mass. (1990): pp. 19 & 68.*

[364] *Ibid. pp. 19, 46, 55, - Based on existing hydro power (3.1 quads) low end wind power potential (3.4 quads) and the average of the estimates for biomass potential using the low numbers from the estimates given on page 55 where the estimates are given as a range. (9.6 quads).*

If we assume that the potential for wind and biomass is half-way between the low and high estimates in each category, the total energy available is almost 27.9 quads. [365]   In this scenario, the need for the solar thermal production of electricity is almost eliminated. If we deduct the 3.3 quad savings in transportation energy gained through electric powered cars, we would have a 1.2 quad surplus even without using solar thermal systems. (See index - Solar electricity as a primary energy source.)

Indeed if we include the 30 quads of electrical energy from concentrating solar collectors, we get a total of 57.9 quads or almost twice what we actually would need in our 30 quad scenario. [366]

Photovoltaic (Solar) Cells

Additionally, there are still other renewable energy options available. For example, if the typical house in the U.S. was up-graded to the efficiency level, adjusted for climate, of the super-insulated houses in Canada and equipped with efficient lighting, appliances, and a solar water heater, it could be kept comfortable and perform all of its functions on 5 kwhrs of electricity per day or less. [367]   A one hundred square foot photovoltaic panel could supply this amount of electricity quite easily in areas of the country that are reasonably sunny. Even if the need was 10 kwhrs per day, it could be produced by a roof-top solar cell panel 10 feet wide and 20 feet long. [368]

At least half of all the buildings in the U.S. are in climate zones that would allow them to be partially or completely energized by installing solar cells on their rooftops. Roof mounted solar cells on buildings and parking structures could be used to charge-up batteries in electric cars -- directly during daylight hours while they are parked at work. In the evening, vehicles could extract energy from batteries or a flywheel that had been charged up by solar cells mounted on the roof of one's home during the sunny part of the day. **(See index for more details.)**

At their current cost, without true-cost-pricing, it is difficult to justify the use of photovoltaic (PV) cells for some applications. Nevertheless, in 1988, approximately $150 million worth of solar cells were sold. [369]   This represents a generating capacity of over 30,000 kilowatts, enough power "to supply 10,000 homes." [370]   Although still more expensive than other solar electric options, the cost of solar cells continues to fall. Currently, photovoltaic cells can be purchased for $4.50 per peak watt of production. [371]   At this price PV cells are cost effective for many applications such as for homes and equipment located in places where grid connection would be more costly.

The Rocky Mountain Institute estimates "that PVs and efficiency can often beat a 400-meter (power) line extension." [372]   A case has been made that even where power grids are close at hand, it may be cost effective to equip new homes with a photovoltaic system for producing

[365]   *Brower, Michael. Cool Energy. Union of Concerned Scientists, Cambridge Mass., (1990): p. 46, (For Wind Energy), p. 55, (For Biomass), pp. 19, 68 (For Hydropower).*

[366]   *Author's calculations.*

[367]   *Author's calculations.*

[368]   *Author's calculations.*

[369]   *Flavin, Christopher. "Selling Solar Cells". World Watch. Vol. 1, No. 5, (Sept./Oct. 1988): p. 42.*

[370]   *Ibid.*

[371]   *Lovins, Amory and Hunter Lovins. "Winning The Peace". Rocky Mountain Institute Newsletter. Vol. VII, No. 1, (Spring 1991): p. 7.*

[372]   *Ibid.*

electricity and a bank of batteries for storage. This is called a stand-alone system. Typically, utilities charge $7 to $15 per foot to extend a local utility grid. Even if the grid only has to be extended 200 feet, the cost of the extension would be $1,400 to $3,000. If this money is applied to the purchase of photovoltaic cells and storage batteries instead, it can sometimes tip the economics in favor of solar cells. Especially if the house in question is equipped with the most efficient appliances and lighting system.

New breakthroughs in photovoltaic technologies promise to bring the price of solar cells down even further. A partnership between Southern California Edison and Texas Instruments has resulted in the development of a new less costly solar cell. This cell, which is expected to sell at around $2 per peak watt, is scheduled to be introduced into the marketplace late in 1994. [373] At this price, solar cells would be competitive in almost any application with most other energy production systems even without true-cost-pricing.

Wave And Tidal Power

Other potential renewable energy sources include wave and tidal power. Wave power can be used to drive hydraulic pumps which pressurize hydraulic fluid to drive generators. Where tidal differences are extreme, tidal flows can be used to turn generators to produce electricity. Tidal systems should be used cautiously since they can cause serious ecological problems to marine ecosystems.

Aquatic Biomass

Aquatic plants like kelp can be grown as energy crops along the continental shelves or in deep ocean areas. Dr. Howard Wilcox, the principal researcher for the Deep Ocean Kelp Project, envisions floating deep ocean kelp rafts that could supply all of the world's energy needs in the foreseeable future.

In Wilcox's system, free drifting juvenile kelp plants would attach themselves to a polypropylene grid suspended at a depth of 100 feet from buoys in the deep ocean. Since surface waters in the deep ocean have very few nutrients, these would be supplied by pumping nutrient rich water from a depth of a 1,000 feet to the surface. This takes very little energy because the pumping action involves lifting water through water. Lifting water through water 1,000 feet requires the same amount of energy as lifting the same water 1 foot above the surface. To harvest the energy, the tops of the kelp plants would be periodically harvested using standard kelp cutting technology. After valuable materials like algin were extracted, the kelp residues would be loaded into digesters where anaerobic bacteria would convert it into methane gas. (Methane gas is the same as natural gas.) Once produced, the gas would be piped or transported by tankers to land based natural gas pipe line grids. Digester residues would be used for animal feed and fertilizers. [374]

Although a Wilcox-like system would have the same vulnerability to natural phenomena and to terrorism as does our present energy production and delivery system, these problems can be largely avoided if aquatic plants like kelp are grown and used locally. Kelp forests grow along the coast lines of many countries. They grow by attaching themselves to rocky reefs where there is sufficient sunlight and nutrients to promote growth and where wave action is not too severe. If reefs with established kelp forest communities were expanded, the production of kelp could be increased

[373] Parrish, Michael. "Solar Power Cells May Cut Bill by One-Third." *Los Angeles Times*, Times Mirror, (April 3, 1991): p. A-1.

[374] Wilcox, Howard. *Ocean Food and Energy Farm Project.* Integrated Science Corporation, 1532 Third Street, Suite 201, Santa Monica, California, (March 1, 1980): pp. 4-21.

substantially. These reefs could be expanded by depositing clean, landfill bound, materials like concrete rubble and the porcelain portion of old toilets, sinks, and bathtubs as add-ons to appropriate reefs along a coast. A similar technique has been used in China to expand its Seaweed growing Industry. Floating rafts are also being used successfully to expand China's kelp growing potential even further. [375]

Once they were in place, these materials would be stabilized through the electro-deposition of minerals. In this process, which was developed by Wolf Hilertz, a wire mesh is draped over and attached to the previously placed rubble. Next, low voltage electricity would flow through the wire mesh which would cause calcium carbonate, extracted from the water column to be deposited on to it. Over time this depositing action would stabilize the reef by fusing or cementing it together with calcium carbonate. [376] As these reef extensions stabilized, they would gradually be colonized by the neighboring kelp forest community. In addition to increasing the amount of energy available, expanding kelp systems would create many permanent jobs involved in expanding and managing kelp forests. Other jobs would involve extracting and processing kelp directly or the other life forms for which the kelp forest is the food chain base.

Energy Storage

Solar energy in the form of biomass can be stored indefinitely. Other forms of solar energy like direct solar and wind power are intermittent and therefore require storage, though not as much as might be imagined. This is especially true with a diversified system where numerous forms of solar energy are integrated, i.e., the wind may be blowing even if the weather is cloudy. Considering just wind alone, however, "an interconnected network of wind farms could supply electricity with 95 percent reliability if 24 to 48 hours of storage capacity were built into the system." [377] For reference, nuclear power plants have a reliability of around 60 percent. [378]

For openers, some solar systems inherently have less need for storage than others. Passive solar for space heating and direct solar water heating require little storage because they work quite well even in cloudy weather. [379]

The availability of wind energy and direct solar is also particularly well matched to peak energy demand. The best periods of direct solar and wind availability coincide with peak periods of industrial, commercial, and residential energy demand. The energy collected by solar thermal plants "at temperatures ranging from 350 to 1,000 degrees plus centigrade (660 - 1830+ F) "can be economically stored in commercial quantities with less than 1 percent loss per day." [380] One storage medium is molten salt which has a large heat storage capacity per volume. "Hot salt can

[375] Bird, Carolyn J. and Mark A. Ragan Editors. *Eleventh International Seaweed Symposium*. Paper by C.K. Tseng. "Phycological Research in the Development of the Chinese Seaweed Industry." Dr. W. Junk Publishers, Dordrecht, Boston, Lancaster, (1984): p. 9.

[376] Telephone conversation with Bill Wilson, an Environmental Planning and Engineering consultant based in Maui, Hawaii.

[377] Brower, Michael. *Cool Energy*. Union of Concerned Scientists, (1990): p. 51.

[378] Ibid.

[379] Mahjouri, Fariborz. "DMS With Solar Hot Water at Baltimore Gas & Electric," *Solar Today*. Vol. 8, No. 1, (Jan./Feb. 1994): p. 23.

[380] Vant-Hull, Lorin L. "Solar Thermal Central Receivers". *Solar Today*. Vol. 6, No 6, (Nov./Dec. 1992): p. 13.

be stored for several weeks with negligible loss." [381]

Biomass, stored as wood chunks or converted to liquid fuels and charcoal, can be brought on-line to provide energy during periods when wind or direct solar are inadequate. Biomass reserves can be stretched by using solar generated electricity instead of biomass energy to convert biomass materials into alternative fuels. Biomass can be converted into gas, liquid fuels, and charcoal by heating it up in an oxygen free chamber. Solar generated electricity and direct solar energy where practical can be used as the heat source. Using solar energy to power biomass conversion processes, like pyrolysis, would save biomass energy which would have been used up in providing conversion energy. The pyrolysis of biomass consists of heating biomass in an oxygen free chamber. As the biomass is heated, volatile gases are driven off and converted into liquid and gaseous fuels. The residue from the process is charcoal which can be burned like coal to make electricity or provide direct heat. Because it is almost pure carbon, charcoal is a relatively pollution free fuel.

One of the most efficient and straightforward ways to store energy is to pump water that has already been used to generate hydro-electric power back into storage so it can flow through the hydro-turbines again. To protect downstream ecologies, the amount of water that could be used for pump storage would have to be limited. But even with such limitations, the potential for pump storage is substantial. [382]

Another way to store energy is by compressing air into tanks or underground caverns. Exhausted natural gas reservoirs would be possible locations for compressed air storage. When energy is needed the compressed air would be released to drive air turbines to produce electricity.

Battery or chemical storage is another option. Under ideal conditions batteries can deliver as much as 86% of the energy charged into them. New battery technologies on the horizon hold the promise of being even more efficient, lighter, and storing more energy in a smaller package.

Energy can also be stored in flywheels. Energy storing flywheels are gyroscope type devices mounted on magnetic bearings in vacuum chambers. Mounting flywheels on magnetic bearings and in vacuum chambers avoids friction losses from roller bearings and air. Energy is added to flywheels by speeding them up. Energy is extracted by making the flywheel into a generator by creating an electric field around it. As electricity is produced the flywheel is slowed. Pound for pound flywheels can store close to four times as much energy as can be stored in lead-acid batteries. [383] Additionally, "flywheels should last 10 years or more, while lead-acid batteries must be replaced every two to three years." [384]

If It's So Easy, Why Hasn't It Happened?

The question naturally arises, if it's so easy, why haven't we taken advantage of efficiency technologies and renewable energy resources a long time ago? The answer goes back to earlier discussions about true-cost-pricing.

---

[381] *Ibid. p. 15.*

[382] *Brower, Michael.* Cool Energy. *Union of Concerned Scientists, Cambridge, Mass. (1990): p. 68.*

[383] *Author's calculations based on information published in Dart, Guy. "Alternative Fuels",* The Energy Report. *(November 15, 1993): p. 678.*

[384] *Dart, Guy. "Alternative Fuels",* The Energy Report. *(November 15, 1993): p. 678.*

Currently, there are a number of direct as well as indirect or hidden subsidies that support our non-renewable energy dependency. Direct subsidies include resource depletion allowances which allow resource extractors to reduce the taxes on their profits in relationship to the rate at which they deplete the resource they are extracting. In other words, the faster the extractor depletes the resource, the less they are taxed on the profits they make in the process.

Other direct subsidies in the conventional energy sector include publicly funded nuclear power research and research directed toward developing safe storage areas for spent fuel rods and other radioactive refuse.

The public is also on the hook for part of the cost of decommissioning nuclear plants at the end of their life span and for tax supported accident insurance to cover clean up and repair costs in the event of a serious nuclear power accident. According to the book Energy Future, published by the Harvard Business School, direct subsidies for conventional non-renewable energy systems could be as high as "$50 billion per year or more." [385] Other sources put direct subsidies even higher. [386]

In addition to direct supports, there are a host of indirect subsidies that make conventional energy resources appear less costly than efficiency and renewables. These costs, which are incurred when oil, coal, natural gas, and uranium are drilled for or mined, when the raw materials extracted in these operations are processed, and when these materials are used, - are paid for through tax funded environmental clean ups and repairs and increased health costs.

These costs include; crop, forestry, and fishery losses related to acid deposition (acid rain, fog. etc.), and the buildup of greenhouse gases like CO_2 in the atmosphere. Health costs, like lung cancer, related to coal and uranium mining and health costs resulting from breathing polluted air or drinking polluted water also come out of the public's coffers. These costs do not show up when we purchase electricity for lighting, fuel oil or natural gas to heat our homes, or at the gas pump. Instead, they are hidden in general tax revenues, out-of-pocket health costs, and in higher prices for food and forestry products.

Pollution from conventional energy sources even causes our personal possessions to deteriorate more rapidly. Acid deposition, particulates, and other conventional energy related pollutants attack the paint and roofing on our homes, cause our clothing to wear out faster, and corrode the paint and metal on our cars. Though the connection between these pollutants and their economic effects is not often made, the money that the public pays, either out-of-pocket or through taxes, to deal with them is a direct subsidy toward maintaining the energy status quo.

True-Cost-Pricing And Solar Energy

From a true-cost-pricing perspective renewable energy systems have numerous advantages over systems dependent on non-renewable energy sources. U.S. manufactured solar systems do not cause trade balance problems like imported oil or produce pollution when they operate. With the exception of biomass, the social and environmental cost associated with renewable energy is primarily sustained during the procurement of the resources needed to create solar collectors and windmills and to maintain them after they are installed. Though it is not a point by point comparison, the replacement of the energy (in the form of electricity) that goes into the production and installation of the equipment, unique to a solar thermal plant (reflectors or heliostats, receivers, storage, etc.),

---

[385]   *Stobaugh, Robert and Daniel Yergin. Energy Future. Random House, New York, (1979): p. 226.*

[386]   *Hubbard, Harold M. "The Real Cost of Energy". Scientific American. Vol. 264, No. 4, (April 1991): p. 37.*

is 18 months. [387]

Similarly, a solar thermal plant will recoup the energy used to create it, with the exception of "particulates (mostly dust from mining and steel making)" in the form of electricity "in about 14 months, or 5 months on a process heat basis or in terms of displaced fossil fuel." [388] In other words, a solar thermal plant operating for 30 years would produce pollution free electricity for 96 percent of the time it is in operation.

With true-cost-pricing, all the subsidies associated with the use of non-renewable energy resources would be eliminated. If this happened, market forces would quickly develop an energy system grounded in efficient energy use and renewable energy resources. It's not that efficiency and renewable energy do not have ecological and social costs, but their costs are far less than the costs associated with our present non-sustainable energy direction.

---

[387] Vant-Hull, Lorin L. "Solar Thermal Central Receivers". _Solar Today_. Vol. 6, No 6, (Nov./Dec. 1992): p. 16.

[388] Ibid.

Chapter IX

ECO-NOMIC SECURITY AND WATER

Synopsis

Our water security, the availability of clean water in sufficient quantities to meet our needs, is decreasing. This decrease in our water security is caused by human activities which are contaminating our surface and groundwater. Human activities are also damaging the ability of our watersheds to recharge our groundwater systems.

All these problems can be corrected. And though it is not widely recognized, all the technological know-how needed to make these corrections already exists and is in use in various locations on our planet.

Water Problems

Until our sun burns out some 5 billion years from now, water on our planet is infinitely recyclable. Unlike oxygen which depends on plant life for renewal, the hydrological cycle needs only the evaporative energy of the sun to set it in motion. Changed into a gas through the absorption of solar energy, water vapor is transported by the wind throughout the atmosphere. Here it condenses as rain, fog, snow, or dew and returns to replenish the earth's land, waterways, and groundwater storage basins.

Even though the amount of water on our planet has not diminished, our water security (the availability of clean water in sufficient quantities to meet our needs) is certainly decreasing. This decrease in water security is primarily caused by human activities which are:

❑ causing the water on our planet to become increasingly polluted,

❑ reducing the effectiveness of our watersheds to store water and recharge groundwater storage areas; and

❑ extracting groundwater at rates that far exceed the rate of recharge. The United States, "as a whole uses 21 billion gallons a day (BGD) of groundwater in excess of local recharge rates." [389]

Although the present situation is becoming increasingly serious, there are a number of things we can do to reverse this trend.

Increasing Water Security

One way to increase water security is to use water more efficiently. By using water efficiently we reduce the drain on surface and groundwater supplies and the need to build or expand costly and ecologically damaging water storage and delivery systems. Efficient water use will also reduce the per capita cost of wastewater treatment. With more water efficient toilets and showerheads less sewage is generated per person.

Efficient water use does not mean doing without the productivity, usefulness, and enjoyment that the use of water can bring. It does not mean taking fewer or shorter showers or flushing toilets less often. It does mean using better technologies like low-flow showerheads and water efficient

---

[389] Gever, John, et al. *Beyond Oil*. Carrying Capacity Inc., Ballinger Publishing Company, Cambridge, Mass. (1986): p. 168.

toilets.

Efficient water use also means that we can have luxuriant landscapes and productive agriculture by growing plants that are adaptable to local climates and by using water efficient irrigation technologies and strategies where irrigation is required.

Investing in water efficiency also makes good economic sense. The payback, or time needed to save enough money on reduced water purchases to pay for the cost of water saving equipment, is almost always less than 5 years and often less than two years. [390] These paybacks would be considerably shorter if government subsidies which keep water prices artificially low were removed. If the true eco-nomic costs associated with damming rivers, building and maintaining aqueducts, depleting aquifers, using energy for pumping, and wastewater treatment were included in the accounting, the payback on saving water through efficiency would be close to instantaneous. [391] Just in the arena of energy, "California's vast State Water Project uses almost as much electricity to pump water around the state as all the people of Los Angeles use". [392]

California farmers that benefit from the federally subsidized Central Valley Project (CVP) "have repaid only 5 percent of the project's cost over the last 40 years, with the total subsidy exceeding $930 million." [393] Additional subsidies came in the form of "at least $200 million in water subsidies" that were given to farmers by the Bureau of Reclamation "in 1986 to grow crops that the Department of Agriculture was paying other farmers not to grow because of surpluses." [394]

Such subsidy-loaded policies have been resistant to change, and even when changes occur they tend to be incremental. Recently, the government raised one of its irrigation district water costs from $3.50 to $14.95 per acre foot when the district's contract came up for renewal. While this represents a 400 percent price increase, it is "still only 28 percent of the water's true cost." [395] Even this 28 percent figure is misleading since it only includes costs like building and maintaining dams and aqueducts and the cost of moving the water around. It does not include the ecological and social costs associated with our present water policies. If these costs were included in the analysis, the subsidies taxpayers are paying to keep the present systems going would loom even larger.

In all, "the government (taxpayers) is spending more than $534 million a year to provide cheap irrigation water to western farms, many of which in turn are producing surplus crops that reap additional federal farm subsidy payments, according to a new Interior Department report." [396]

---

[390] *La Ganga, Maria L. "Maverick Farmer's Drought Solution", Los Angeles Times. (June 2, 1991): pp. D - 1, 7, also see "The West's Water Future: A Continuing Sunset SPECIAL REPORT", Sunset Magazine. March 1987, p. 93 and September 1987, p. 157.*

[391] *Author's calculations.*

[392] *Adler, Jerry, and William J. Cook, et al. "The Browning of America". Newsweek. Vol. XCVII, No. 8, (Feb. 23, 1981): p. 27.*

[393] *Postel, Sandra. "Trouble On Tap", World-Watch. Worldwatch Inst., Vol. 2, No. 5, (Sept/Oct. 1989): p. 19.*

[394] *Ibid. pp. 19-20.*

[395] *Ibid. p. 20.*

[396] *Peterson, Cass. "Cut-Rate Water, Surplus Crops". Washington Post, (August 8, 1988): p. A-17.*

Efficient Water Use In Agriculture

To maximize water security, it is important to use water efficiently in every way we can. But more efficient water use in agriculture could save more water than all other efficiency measures combined. Worldwide the amount of water used in agriculture "accounts for some 70% of global water use", greatly exceeding the quantity of water used for domestic and commercial purposes. [397] In countries like the U.S. that have well-developed irrigation infrastructures, up to eighty-five percent of all water used is consumed by agriculture. [398]

One of the most troubling aspects of this water use in agriculture is how rapidly it is depleting groundwater supplies. In 1986 the U.S. Department of Agriculture reported "that one-fourth of the 21 million hectares (52 million acres) of U.S. irrigated cropland was being watered by pulling down water tables anywhere from six inches to four feet per year." [399] The depletion of water tables because of crop irrigation is also a problem in countries like China and India. [400]

Strategies for Increasing Water Security

Whether in the United States or abroad, much of the water used by agriculture can be saved through the use of efficient irrigation practices and by growing climate appropriate crops.

The most prevalent form of irrigation in the world today is to periodically flood fields with water. This form of irrigation is inexpensive to establish where land is flat but it is not particularly efficient. [401] This is because a large percentage of water often runs off a field before it has time to soak into the soil. In porous soils substantial quantities of water can be lost because it percolates to underground levels beyond the reach of plant roots. [402] If this water returns to the aquifer from which it was extracted, this can be positive but not if the water becomes contaminated with pesticides and chemical fertilizers along the way.

Sprinkler systems are generally more water efficient than flooding because the amount of water applied and the evenness of its distribution is more easily regulated. [403] On the negative side, sprinkler systems are expensive to install and maintain. Sprinkler systems also increase the amount of water lost to evaporation. Water evaporation is increased as it is dispersed in small droplets through the air and as water sits on plant foliage. Such losses can be avoided to a large

---

[397] *Postel, Sandra. World Watch Paper 93. Worldwatch Institute, Washington D.C. (Dec. 1989): p. 6.*

[398] *Wiles, Richard, Project Director, Committee on the Role of Alternative Farming Methods in Modern Production Agriculture. Alternative Agriculture. National Academy Press, Washington D.C. (1989): p. 50.*

[399] *Brown, Lester R. "The Growing Grain Gap". World Watch. Vol. 1, No. 5, (Sept./Oct. 1988): p. 14.*

[400] *Ibid.*

[401] *Postel, Sandra. World Watch Paper 93. Worldwatch Institute, Washington D.C., (Dec. 1989): p. 6. Also see Postel, Sandra. World Watch Paper 62. Worldwatch Institute, Washington D.C., (Dec. 1984): p. 39.*

[402] *Postel, Sandra. World Watch Paper 62. Worldwatch Institute, Washington D.C., (Dec. 1984): p. 39.*

[403] *Postel, Sandra. World Watch Paper 93. Worldwatch Institute, Washington D.C., (Dec. 1989): p. 38.*

extent if sprinklers are used at night when the humidity is usually higher than it is during the day.

The efficiency of large sprinkler systems can also be enhanced by attaching "drop tubes" to sprinkler arms. "Called low-energy precision application (LEPA), these systems deliver water closer to the ground and in large droplets, cutting evaporation losses." [404]   The efficiency of flooding and sprinkler systems can be improved if fields are precisely leveled. Laser technology can be used to guide farm equipment to insure accurate leveling. [405]

Drip irrigation, a technology developed in the 1960s in Israel, is a further advancement in the efficient use of water for growing plants. This method delivers water directly to each plant by means of small tubes that supply just enough water to saturate plant root zones. [406]   Other drip technologies include soaker hoses and various specialized emitters suitable for different crops. Soaker hoses, for example, are good for many row crops because they weep water along their whole length. Drip irrigation devices can be used on the surface, on the surface below mulch, or below the surface depending on plant requirements. Losses to evaporation can be almost completely eliminated when emitters are installed below mulch or beneath the soil surface.

While drip equipment is relatively costly, increased crop yields coupled with money saved by reducing water consumption can result in a quick payback on the investment. In Israel, where drip systems are used to "supply water and fertilizer directly onto or below the soil...experiments in the Negev Desert have shown . . . yield increases of 80 percent over sprinkler systems." [407]

Computer technologies are also being mobilized to increase water use efficiency in agriculture. One devise called a tensiometer, measures the moisture content of the soil and the amount of moisture in the soil that is actually available to plants. [408] This second feature is important because some soils, like those with a high clay content, are so absorptive that they do not give up the water they hold easily to plants. Sandy soils, on they other hand, do not hold water like clay soils. They may have a relatively low moisture content but almost all the moisture in a sandy soil is available to plants. When tensiometers sense that the moisture content of a particular soil is too low to meet plant needs, they activate an automated irrigation system. Tensiometers can also be read manually for more low tech applications.

Automated irrigation systems can be programmed so that irrigation water is only applied at night to minimize the loss of irrigation water to evaporation. Automated systems can also be designed to detect leaks, compensate for wind speed, control the application of fertilizer, and optimize the effect of the fertilizer used. Though they are costly to install, such "systems typically pay for themselves within 3 to 5 years through water and energy savings (using less water means that less energy is needed for pumping) and higher crop yields." [409]

---

[404]   *Ibid.*

[405]   *Ibid.*

[406]   Postel, Sandra. <u>World Watch Paper 62</u>. *Worldwatch Institute, Washington D.C., (Dec. 1984): pp. 39-40.*

[407]   *Ibid.*

[408]   *The Hydrovisor is a tensiometer devise which performs this function. It is available through Water Conservation Systems Inc., 141 So. Spring Street, Claremont CA 91711, (741) 621-5806.*

[409]   Postel, Sandra. <u>World Watch Paper 62</u>. *Worldwatch Institute, Washington D.C., (Dec. 1984): p. 41.*

A new development in the efficient water use arsenal is to combine water efficient technologies with weather monitoring programs. The University of Nebraska's Institute of Agriculture and Natural Resources has developed a computer program called "IRRIGATE" that compiles information gathered across the state of Nebraska from small weather stations. By calling a telephone hot line, farmers can "find out the amount of water used by their crops the preceding week, and then adjust their scheduled irrigation dates accordingly." [410]

The California Department of Water Resources is involved in a similar program. The California Irrigation Management System (CIMIS) that is aiming to save 740 million cubic meters of water annually by the year 2010. [411] (740 million cubic meters equals a little more than 600,000 acre feet or about the same amount of water used in 1990 by the 2.4 million people living in San Diego County, California, USA.)

Like Nebraska and California, Wisconsin has developed its own system of weather monitoring to assist farmers. This system, which is called the Wisconsin Irrigation Scheduling Program (WISP), is managed by irrigation specialists through the University of Wisconsin. [412]

Appropriate Crops

Efficient water use in agriculture can also be improved by minimizing the practice of growing water intensive crops in climate zones that have little rainfall and high rates of evaporation. With water efficient cropping, the water requirements of a particular crop should be reasonably close to the natural precipitation that could be expected in the climate zone where it is grown. Irrigation for such crops would be relegated to evening out yearly rainfall totals and as a way to supply water during periods when rainfall is below normal.

To date, research in the development and use of low water use crops has been poorly funded. "Perhaps 15% of the $82-millon University of California budget for agricultural research is spent on water conservation, but mostly to improve existing crops." [413]

Nevertheless, there are a number of promising plants now being grown, some commercially and others experimentally. Sweet sorghum, for example, is already widely grown. It requires a third less water and half the fertilizer required by corn to produce a crop and sweet sorghum is an excellent animal food. Currently, most of the corn grown in the U.S. is used for animal feed. [414]

According to Steve Staffer, an alternative crop expert with the California Department of Agriculture, sweet sorghum can also outperform corn as an energy crop. An acre of corn can be processed into 360 gallons of ethanol. Processing an acre of sorghum can produce 600 gallons. Staffer estimates that by growing low water use plants like sorghum, "California could produce 25%

---

[410] *Ibid. p. 40.*

[411] *Ibid. pp. 40-41, Additionally there are publications available on CIMIS from the State of California Dept. of Water Resources Office of Water Conservation, 1416 Ninth St., P.O. Box 942836, Sacramento, CA. 94236-0001, (916) 653-5791.*

[412] *Arthur, Tom. "Computer Helps Reduce Irrigation Costs". American Vegetable Grower. Vol. 38, (Feb. 1990): pp. 14, 17.*

[413] *Daniel Akst. "New Crops May Hold Promise on Drought", Los Angeles Times: Business Section. p. D-1.*

[414] *Ibid.*

to 30% of its energy needs, without affecting our price of food". [415] Given Staffer's projections, producing ethanol from sorghum alone could more than supply all the energy needed in California today if the efficiency measures described earlier were in place.

Other promising low water use crops include:

☐   canola, a seed bearing plant, which is used to produce "one of the healthiest cooking oils around and takes just a fraction of the water required by many other crops grown in the (Sacramento, California) region";

☐   buffalo gourd, a perennial that is native to the Mojave Desert, has seeds that can be processed into lubrication oil and a starchy root that can be used to make alcohol;

☐   guayule, a plant that yields rubber, kanaf, an African plant which can be used as food, clothing fiber, packing material, carpet backing, and as high quality newsprint that is so absorbent that the hands of newspaper readers stay clean; and

☐   tepary bean, a drought-tolerant high yield food crop that contains "as much or more protein than most edible legume crops." [416]

While the strategy discussed above may seem obvious, farmers who benefit from federal subsidies, which allow them to purchase water at rates as low as 1/10 the price that urban dwellers pay, have little incentive to grow things that make more sense in the desert. [417]

Alice In Waterland Economics

In his book Cadillac Desert, Marc Reisner points out such subsidies lead us into absurd situations. In 1986, four low value crops grown in California [pasture (grass and hay), alfalfa, cotton, and rice] consumed 5.3, 3.9, 3.0, and 2.0 million acre feet of water respectively. Added up, this is almost three times as much water as was consumed by the 27 million people living in California, including all the water they used to irrigate landscapes and keep their swimming pools full. [418]

Even if all these low value crops were totally discontinued and no more water efficient crops were grown in their place, the economic loss to the state would be $1.7 billion or less than one third of one percent of the $550 billion California economy. [419] "That $1.7 billion loss of revenue, by the way, is exactly the cost of the proposed Auburn Dam (in northern California) that farmers want taxpayers to build for them. By simply retiring the land we'd get 75 times more water for our money." [420]

Additionally, if we converted a little over half the land now used just to grow grass and hay to grapes or other speciality crops with a similar or greater dollar value, the $1.7 billion loss would

---

[415]   *Ibid.*

[416]   *Ibid.*

[417]   *Rogers, Peter. "Water: Not as Cheap as You Think",* Technology Review. *Nov. - Dec., (1986), p. 33.*

[418]   *Reisner, Marc. "The Next Water War: Cities Versus Agriculture."* Issues in Science and Technology *(Winter 1988-89): p. 99.*

[419]   *Ibid. pp. 98 & 99.*

[420]   *Ibid. p. 99.*

be erased. [421] Grapes require roughly the same amount of water per acre as grass and hay pasture.

This is a perfect example of how the lack of true-cost-pricing promotes practices that are not in anyone's long term interest. This even includes the farmer whose over-irrigated soil is becoming increasingly unproductive as salt and other minerals, are concentrated.

Another example of Alice in Waterland economics is the proposed Peripheral Canal (also in California). In his book Water and Power, Harry Dennis presents a well documented case that increasing water use efficiency will easily meet the water needs of California, into the foreseeable future, at a considerably lower cost both economically and to the environment. [422] If constructed, the 42 mile long Peripheral Canal and its associated projects would ultimately cost the public $23 billion or in excess of $100,000 per foot to build. [423] An essay by John Burnham, the Metropolitan Water District's only accountant until he retired, argues that even if water was delivered to Southern California by a completed Peripheral Canal, its $1,267 per acre foot cost would be over three times what people would actually pay for most uses. [424]

Water Beefalow

A parallel aspect of growing low water use crops is related to the production of meat. Currently, "Over half the total amount of water consumed in the United States goes to irrigate land growing feed for livestock." [425] To put this fact into perspective, a 50% reduction in the production of livestock nationally would free up almost twice as much water as is currently used in the U.S. domestically, commercially, and by industry combined. [426] Though the production of meat in all its forms is water intensive, growing beef requires the most water. It takes approximately 2,500 gallons of water to produce a pound of beef. [427]

Given this 2,500 gallon figure it takes up to 100 times more water to produce a pound of beef as it does to produce a pound of wheat. "Rice takes more water than any other grain, but even rice requires only a tenth as much water per pound of production as meat." [428]

Efficient Water Use In The Residential Sector

Although residential water use accounts for only about 8% of the water used in the United States, from an ecological security perspective it is important to use water more efficiently on every front. Using residential water more efficiently also makes good economic sense.

---

[421] *Ibid. p. 100. - Growing grapes in California is a $1.5 billion industry yet it uses only a little over half the land area that is now used to grow pasture.]*

[422] *Dennis, Harry. Water and Power. Friends of the Earth, San Francisco, (1981): p. 11-12.*

[423] *Author's calculations based on Ibid.*

[424] *Ibid. p. 101-103.*

[425] *Robbins, John. Diet for a New America. Stillpoint Publishing, Walpole, New Hampshire, (1987): p. 367.*

[426] *Author's calculation. Also see Lazear, Edward p., "Water for the People, Los Angeles Times. (February 5, 1991): p. B-7.*

[427] *Robbins, John. Diet For a New America. Stillpoint Publishing, Walpole, New Hampshire, (1987): p. 367.*

[428] *Ibid.*

Even from the business as usual economic perspective a number of municipalities and agencies are getting on the efficiency bandwagon. For example, the city of Glendale Arizona passed an ordinance that gives residents up to a $100 cash rebate for installing low flow toilets (1.6 gallons or less). [429] This is because city leaders realized that rebating the toilets was much less expensive than increasing water supplies and sewer capacity. The California Department of Water Conservation estimates "that installing a low flow toilet can save a family of four $25 to $50 a year on water bills." [430] The producers of Consumer Reports magazine reported an even larger savings potential. "By our own calculations, an average family that uses municipal water can save as much as $50 to $75 per year on water and sewer bills by switching to low-flow showerheads and low-flush toilets." [431].

In addition to saving money on water, low flow shower heads and water efficient appliances also save on energy costs. Just changing from a 6 gallon per minute to a 2 gallon per minute showerhead can save over half the energy used in a home to heat water. [432] This can amount to an energy savings of $50 per year. [433]

Faucet restrictors, automatic shut off faucets, and water-efficient appliances can also save water and energy. Faucet flow restrictors and automatic shut-off faucets can cut the use of sink water in half while reducing energy consumption for water heating. State-of-the-art washers and dishwashers use only 70 to 75 percent of the water and energy consumed by less efficient models. [434] If all the efficiency measures just described were in general use, household water consumption in the U.S. could be reduced by 60% or more. [435]

The use of water in toilets can be eliminated entirely through the use of dry or composting toilets. Composting toilets come in a variety of designs ranging from the old-fashioned outhouse to the modern chambered versions where the composted residues are periodically removed and used as fertilizer. These modern systems usually include a port for adding kitchen scraps which are composted along with toilet wastes. Sawdust or other similar material is added after each use to control odors. [436] Some composting toilets work better than others. Check the following footnote reference for details. [437]

[429] Marken, William Editor. "Water Efficiency in the Home," *Sunset Magazine*. September 1987, p. 158.

[430] *Ibid.* p. 156.

[431] *Consumer Report Staff.* "How To Save Water". *Consumer Reports*. Vol. 55, No. 7, (July 1990): p. 465.

[432] *Author's calculations.*

[433] *Consumer Reports Staff.* "How To Save Water". *Consumer Reports*. Vol. 55, No. 7, (July 1990): p. 465.

[434] Postel, Sandra. *World Watch Institute Paper 62*. Worldwatch Institute, Washington D.C., (1984): p. 45.

[435] *Author's calculations.*

[436] Kourik, Robert. " Toilets: Low Flush/No Flush." *Garbage*. Vol. II, No. 1, (Jan./Feb. 1990): p. 22 & 23.

[437] *Ibid.*

Water Recycling

Water recycling is another way to improve residential water use efficiency. Water recycling can occur on several levels. Home gray water systems (bath and sink water) may be as simple as draining bath and wash water into one's yard. Depending on the particular situation, more sophisticated systems may involve filtering, pumps, and disinfection. [438]

Graywater includes bath, sink, and water from washing clothing. It excludes toilet wastes. Food scraps and many soaps and shampoos present in graywater are not usually a problem since they can be broken down by soil organisms into nutrients that are used by plants.

In some states, home gray water recycling is illegal. [**Check with local health officials**] The reason for this prohibition is that graywater may be contaminated by harmful bacteria, viruses and parasites. Contamination can occur in a number of ways, such as washing diapers at temperatures too low to kill harmful organisms, or from the small amounts of fecal material that is washed off our bodies when we bathe. For this reason, gray water that has not been disinfected should not be used to directly water vegetable parts that are to be eaten or on lawn areas where direct human contact is likely. Although the use of graywater could be potentially harmful, "it's worth noting that health officials we consulted knew of no documented case of illness caused by gray-water use." [439]

Since there is a small possibility that diseases could be transmitted by graywater contact, graywater should be used carefully. [440] Graywater can be used safely to water fruit and other trees, or in landscaping. It can also be used for vegetables if it is applied sub-surface with a soaker hose or by some other sub-surface system. Sub-surface application is the most preferred way to use graywater because direct exposure to graywater is eliminated and soil organisms kill pathogens. [441]

Soaker hoses can also be used with relative safety on the surface in gardens since water applied by them does not splash onto the edible parts of plants. Although the uptake of pathogens by root crops does not take place, root crops watered with graywater should be carefully washed and/or well cooked before they are consumed.

To maximize safety, graywater can be disinfected before it is applied. Historically, water has been disinfected by adding chlorine. Chlorine does disinfect but its use can also result in the creation of compounds like chloramine. Chloramine, which is toxic to soil and aquatic organisms, results when chlorine reacts with the carbon in water borne organic materials. If the level of organic materials is low, the amount of chloramine created is small. But if the organic load is high, the amount of chloramine produced becomes a problem. Chlorine is also toxic to soil and aquatic organisms but it dissipates faster than chloramine.

If water is disinfected with ozone, this problem is avoided. Ozone, a form of oxygen that links three atoms of oxygen together, is even more effective at killing pathogens than chlorine and does not cause harmful side affects. It can also break down many organic pollutants and can be used to remove heavy metals through a process of precipitation.

---

[438] *Ibid. p. 3.*

[439] *Marken, William Editor. "Collecting and Reusing Gray Water". Sunset. (May 1981): p. 116.*

[440] *Ibid.*

[441] *Kourik, Robert. Graywater Use In The Landscape. Metamorphic Press, Santa Rosa, California, (1991): p. 7.*

used to remove heavy metals through a process of precipitation. [442] Though the adoption of ozone water treatment systems in the U.S. has been slow, ozonization has replaced chlorine in 99% of the swimming pools in Western Europe. [443]

Soaps containing phosphates can also be used without negative consequences in most graywater recycling situations. Phosphate is a much maligned nutrient because it stimulates aquatic plant growth in lakes and waterways. These plant "blooms" can cause fish to die from suffocation. At night aquatic plants need oxygen which they extract from the water. If the number of aquatic plants in a volume of water is excessive, oxygen levels can drop below levels that can support fish. [444]

Excessive plant growth also threatens fish with suffocation when plants die in the autumn. With large quantities of dead plant material available, decay bacteria multiply rapidly. These bacteria require oxygen and can quickly reduce the oxygen content in a body of water to levels below which fish can survive. [445] In soil, however, phosphate is a nutrient readily useable by plants and need only be avoided if there is a possibility that the phosphate will enter a waterway instead of becoming part of a terrestrial plant.

Though they are usually thought of as waste elimination processes, septic tank leach field systems can be excellent water and nutrient recyclers. A leach field is made up of lines of perforated pipe buried 4 to 5 feet deep on level contours so that the wastewater is evenly distributed throughout the whole leach field. Additionally, leach pipes are surrounded by coarse sand and an 18" layer of one inch rocks to keep the perforated pipes from getting clogged by soil or plant roots. When wastewater leaves a house it passes through a septic tank where some of the solids are biologically broken down. From the tank the partially processed wastewater flows into the leach field where it seeps through the perforations in the pipe into the surrounding rock and then into the soil.

Once in the earth, soil organisms complete the process of killing pathogens and converting the wastewater borne nutrients into inorganic compounds which plants can use. The water that carries these waste materials provides irrigation. The recycling process is completed when plants watered and fertilized in this way lose their leaves, or die and decay to become part of the surface soil. These plant materials can also be recycled by collecting and composting them so the nutrients they extracted from the leach field can be used as fertilizer in other locations. Since leach fields pipes are typically laid at a depth of five feet it is essential that the plants grown in conjunction with them have roots that go deep enough (6 feet or deeper) to take advantage of the water and nutrients available. If leach field pipes are installed closer to the surface, plants with shallower root systems can also be used.

On whatever level it occurs, it is important to keep toxic and caustic materials, like some drain openers, out of recycling systems. These materials can damage or kill the various organisms that help in the recycling process. With the exception of lead from pipe solder or silver, which is a waste from photo processing, heavy metals and other industrial toxins are not usually found in graywater. But where industry is hooked into municipal treatment systems such materials are often

[442] Stopka, Karel. " Meeting Federal Drinking Water Standards with Ozone" *Pollution Engineering*. September 1990, p. 101.

[444] Harper, David. *Eutrophication of Freshwaters, Principles Problems, and Restoration*. Chapman and Hall, New York, New York, (1992): p. 139.

[445] Clark, Mary E. *Contemporary Biology*. Second Edition, W. B. Saunders Company, Philadelphia, London, Toronto, (1979): pp. 180-81.

present.

Heavy metals and other toxins can concentrate in the food chain when water or composted sludge contaminated with them is used to irrigate and fertilize plants. [446]

Community Scale Water Recycling

In dense urban areas, where many residences do not have yards, community sized wastewater recycling systems are a more practical choice for recycling wastewater. As with individual residence systems it is important to keep toxic and caustic materials out of all wastewater collection and recycling processes. If this is done there are a number of processes that can be used to clean up wastewater so it can be used for irrigation. In general such recycling systems use both biological and mechanical methods to clean wastewater.

Biological systems can be used exclusively where land availability is not an issue. In Arcata California a marsh system is used to treat the community's sewage. As the sewage flows through the marsh, aquatic organisms consume and convert the waste into nutrients that marsh plants then convert into plant growth. While the water in this system is not reclaimed for irrigation it does enhance the marsh's aquatic environment. [447]

Where land area is limited or expensive, the land area required for biological treatment can be reduced by additional human manipulation. The new Alchemist Institute under the direction of John Todd has developed a treatment process which uses greenhouses and translucent tanks to maximize decomposition and photosynthesis. As the wastewater flows through a series of semi-transparent tanks a complex community of aquatic plants and animals purify the water by consuming and converting the organic waste into animals and plants (biomass). At the end of the process, the clean water can be used for irrigation or it can be safely discharged into streams. In addition to water, the process also produces a crop of fish and other aquatic organisms and aquatic plants that can be composted and used as a soil amendment. [448]

A third approach has been developed in Tijuana, Mexico. The treatment plant in Tijuana is called Eco-Parque. The Mexican system combines biological and mechanical methods to process wastewater to minimize the amount of land needed for treatment. The treatment process involves mechanical screens, biological filters, clarification (slowing the flow of water so solids can settle out) and disinfection. The goal of this project is to recycle all the water and nutrients that pass through it. The recycled water is being used for irrigation and the nutrient rich solids are composted and used as soil amendments. [449]

---

[446] Lefferts, Lisa Y. "Something Fishy: How Safe is Your Seafood." *New Age Journal*. Vol. 6, No. 4, (July/Aug. 1989): p. 113.

[447] Hammer, Donald A. *Constructed Wetlands For Wastewater Treatment*. Lewis Publishers, Chelsea, Michigan, (1989): p. 116.

[448] Todd, John. "Adventures of an Applied Ecologist". *Whole Earth.*, No. 62. (Spring 1989): pp. 36-39.

[449] The author was the Co-project director of this project during its design and construction. Also see Protillo Jr., Ernesto. "Thousands of Trees Envisioned", *San Diego Union*. March 25. 1991, pp. B-3, B-5 and LaRue, Steve. "Low-tech Facility in Tijuana Hailed as One Sewage Solution." *San Diego Union-Tribune* (Wednesday, Oct. 20, 1993).

Climate Appropriate Landscaping

As in other areas, water use for landscaping and gardening can be significantly reduced. In low rainfall areas, the amount of water used for residential landscape irrigation can average 50 or more gallons per day per capita. [450] The use of water efficient irrigation equipment and selecting landscaping schemes and plants that are suitable for the climate where they are located can greatly reduce this requirement. Efficient water use in landscaping does not mean that landscaping themes have to be sparse. Even in arid areas there are numerous beautiful plants from which to select. [451] Nor does such a strategy preclude having a vegetable garden, fruit trees, or grass. Reducing water use in other parts of a landscape frees up water for these purposes.

If climate appropriate landscaping is combined with water efficient irrigation equipment, even more water can be saved. Water efficient irrigation equipment ranges from various drip irrigation systems and low flow drip emitters and sprinklers to sophisticated irrigation control tools called tensiometers. Tensiometers are electronic devices that are installed in the soil where they measure soil moisture content. They can be read and water applied accordingly or they can be used to activate automated irrigation systems when water is needed.

On the plant side, there are literally hundreds of attractive drought tolerant trees, shrubs, vines, and ground covers that can be included as part of a low water use landscape palette. [452] Additionally, there are numerous drought tolerant plants that produce food and other useful materials. These plants include the California Black Walnut tree, the fig family, the Oriental Persimmon, the Quince tree, members of the grape family, the Guava family, loquat trees, Aloe, Bamboo, and many more. [453]

Even modest efforts toward coupling water efficient irrigation systems with climate appropriate plants in landscaping could cut irrigation requirements in low rainfall areas in half. [454] If climate appropriate plants are used exclusively, irrigation requirements can be reduced to zero after plants become established. If graywater recycling systems are incorporated, even relatively water intensive landscapes can be successful without using potable water for irrigation.

Efficient Water Use In Industry

Just as in the residential sector, commercial and industrial users can cut water consumption through water recycling and use of water efficient fixtures and appliances. Changes in operational strategies and manufacturing processes can increase efficient water use even more. In 1978, U.S. manufacturing industries used each unit of water 3.4 times before it was discharged. By the year 2,000, experts predict that the water reuse rate for industry will have increased to over 17 times before discharge. [455]

---

[450] *California Department of Water Resources. <u>Water Conservation In California</u>. Bulletin 198-84, State of California, Sacramento, California, (July 1984): p. 11.*

[451] *The Editors of Sunset Books and Sunset Magazine. <u>Sunset New Western Garden Book</u>. Lane Publishing Co., Menlo Park, CA, (1981), See Appropriate Climate Zones.*

[452] *Ibid.*

[453] *Ibid.*

[454] *Author's calculations.*

[455] *Brown, Lester R. <u>State of The World 1986</u>. Worldwatch Institute, Washington D.C., W. W. Norton and Company, New York, London, (1986): p. 49.*

Some innovative firms have already achieved or exceeded this level of efficiency. "Armco steel mill in Kansas City, Missouri, which manufactures steel bars from recycled ferrous scrap, (scrap iron and steel) draws into the mill only 9 cubic meters of water per ton of steel produced, compared with as much as 100-200 cubic meters per ton in many other steel mills -- the Armco plant uses each liter of water 16 times before releasing it after final treatment, to the river." [456] "One paper mill in Hadera, Israel, requires only 12 cubic meters of water per ton of paper (produced), whereas many of the world's paper mills use 7-10 times this amount." [457]

Pioneer Metal Finishing, a plating firm in New Jersey, has developed a water recycling process that totally eliminates sewer discharge. In the Pioneer process, all water is recycled and most of the chemicals and metals extracted from it are reused. Pioneer is now looking for a use for the small quantity of dry residue left over from their recycling operation. [458]

Water use in industry can also be cut by using non-chemical water treatment processes to prevent biological fouling and water scale buildup in boilers, water lines, and cooling systems. Non-chemical water treatment consists of exposing water to magnetic and electrostatic fields to prevent mineral scale from attaching itself to pipes and other metal surfaces and to remove such deposits where they already exist. Non-chemical treatment also creates an environment hostile to the growth of water borne bacteria, fungus, and algae.

The buildup of scale and bacterial slime reduces the efficiency of heating and cooling systems by restricting water flow rates and by insulating heat exchange elements. A 1/16 inch scale buildup requires 15% more fuel to achieve the same heating results. A 1/4 inch buildup increases fuel consumption by 39%. [459]

In the U.S., chemicals have been the predominant method used for treating such problems. But chemical treatments are relatively labor and material intensive because they need regular chemical mixture adjustments. Maintenance is also high because chemical treatments reduce the rate of scale build up but do not prevent it. This means that heating and cooling systems have to be drained and manually cleaned on a regular basis. Additionally, all the water in chemically treated systems must be periodically purged because evaporation losses increase the concentrations of chemicals and minerals beyond acceptable levels. This purging wastes water and releases treatment chemicals like algaecides, fungicides, bactericides, and phosphates into the environment. [460]

Non-chemical treatment minimizes or avoids most of these problems. Although they have been slow to catch on in the U.S., non-chemical treatment systems have been the preferred treatment choice in Europe and in the Russian Commonwealth for decades. But this is changing as is evidenced by the numerous high profile firms like Kodak, IBM, Hewlett Packard, Ford Motors, Holiday Inn, Pepsi Cola, Coca Cola, Marriott, and Bantam Books that have already switched to non-

---

[456]   Postel, Sandra. *World Watch Paper 67*. Worldwatch Institute, Washington D.C., (1985): pp. 29-30.

[457]   *Ibid.* p. 29.

[458]   *NOVA Broadcast*, "Are You Swimming In A Sewer," Transcript of the Broadcast, WGBH Educational Foundation, Boston Mass. (1986): pp. 16-17.

[459]   Cummings, Gil. "A Clear Look At Water Conditioning", *Restaurant Business*. April 10, 1985, p. 232.

[460]   "IBM Engineer Shuns Chemicals in Favor of Electrostatic Device for Water Treatment", *Air Conditioning & Refrigeration News*. April 27, 1987, p. 6.

chemical treatment processes. [461]

Efficient Water Use, Other Benefits

In addition to saving water, using water more efficiently has other benefits. Efficient irrigation practices and growing water efficient crops help to avoid the build up of salt and other minerals in soils. As rainwater runoff travels over and through the ground, salt and other minerals are dissolved into it. When this mineral laden water is used for irrigation the salts and minerals it contains are left in the soil when the water evaporates or is transpired by plants.

If irrigation water is used efficiently there is less water to evaporate and thus less of a salt and mineral build up. A smaller mineral buildup makes it easier for rainfall or intentional periodic flooding to leach the accumulated minerals and salts out of the soil. Rainwater runoff from efficiently irrigated agricultural soils is also less salty than it would be with less efficient irrigation practices and is thus more useable for other purposes.

Efficient water use saves energy and minimizes energy related pollution by reducing the amount of energy required to pump water out of the ground and to deliver it from distant sources. It also means that fewer rivers will be dammed or otherwise modified, and that smaller less costly conveyance systems can be used to deliver water when local supplies are inadequate. More efficient water use also means that stored water will last longer during periods of drought.

Though the relationship is less direct, efficient water use also minimizes the environmental impact of building wastewater treatment facilities to treat urban sewage. With smaller quantities of water to treat, less energy, concrete, and other resources are needed to build and operate treatment centers. Reducing the amount of energy and materials needed to build and operate treatment systems also reduces the amount of watershed damage related to the procurement of such resources. By reducing pollution it also reduces the amount of pollution entering waterways and groundwater deposits.

Protecting Watershed Function

Another aspect of creating a more water secure future is the vital need to protect watersheds and the waterways and groundwater storage areas which they supply. A watershed is a drainage basin composed of a valley and the surrounding slopes which collect and direct the flow of rainfall and snow melt runoff.

Watersheds are also the home of complex interdependent plant and animal communities which are vital to watershed function and its health. Many watersheds are small. Usually smaller watersheds empty into larger ones. The great rivers of the world are all supplied by runoff from numerous smaller watersheds that result in one large watershed or drainage basin for each river. Actually all land areas above sea level are part of one watershed or another.

In a healthy watershed, rainwater runoff carries very little sediment and nutrients. Even when rainfall is heavy, streams and rivers run clean. This is because plant leaves and the ground carpet they form when they fall protect the soil from pounding rain. [462] Plant root systems, along

---

[461] *Ibid.*

[462] *Callahan, Robert Z. Callahan, Robert Z. California's Shrublands. Report No. 5, Wildlands Resources Center, Division of Agriculture and Natural Resources, University of California, Berkeley, California, (Feb. 1985): p. 4. Also see Postel, Sandra. "A Green Fix To The Global Warm-Up". World Watch. Vol. 1, No. 5, (Sept./Oct. 1988): pp. 33-34.*

with tunneling soil organisms, also help store water by making it easier for water to be absorbed into the soil. Rainwater and snow melt runoff are also slowed by this process.

By slowing runoff and storing water, watershed communities perform three important functions. First is the function of self preservation. By storing water and slowing runoff the watershed's plant and animal community perpetuates itself by insuring that it has an adequate water supply during dry periods. Second, the slow release of watershed stored water through springs evens out the flow of rivers and streams so they continue to flow long after the wet season has past. [463] Finally, this slowing and storage process helps to increase groundwater supplies by allowing more time for water to percolate down into groundwater aquifers for storage. In addition to providing the services just discussed, all the organic material in our planet's soils have been produced by the plant and animal communities that inhabit the world's watersheds.

In a healthy watershed, the processes described above happen naturally. But if we use watersheds inappropriately and extract resources from them incorrectly, the watershed community and the functions it performs will be crippled and can even collapse.

Watershed communities worldwide are under attack. If present practices persist, human activities will be driving "100 species (of plants and animals) to extinction every day," over the next three decades. [464] This "is at least 1,000 times the pace that has prevailed since prehistory." [465] At this rate, not only are we losing species, but whole ecosystems, the "nurseries of new life forms." [466] Harvard biologist E.O. Wilson describes this phenomenon as the "'death of birth.'" [467] "Wilson estimates that people have recently begun to extinguish lesser creatures at a pace 10,000 times the typical natural rate." [468] "British ecologist Norman Myers has called it the 'greatest single setback to life's abundance and diversity since the first flickerings of life almost 4 billion years ago.'" [469]

One might argue that the extinction of one or even thousands of species of life, in a world that is home to millions of species, is of little consequence. But the long-term effect of the loss of even a single species is not easily known. [470]

History has shown that eliminating certain organisms from an ecosystem can have unanticipated effects. Early in the 20th Century people in Kern County California waged a 20 year battle "against annoying predators: skunks, foxes, badgers, weasels, snakes, hawks, owls." [471] In 1924 the war against predators was escalated when Kern County sheep herders "hired a U.S.

---

[463]   Horton, Paul B. et al. *The Sociology of Social Problems*, Eighth Edition. Prentice-Hall, Inc. Englewood Cliffs, New Jersey, (1985): p. 420.

[464]   Linden, Eugene. "The Death of Birth". *Time*. Vol. 133, No. 1, (Jan. 2, 1989): p. 32.

[465]   Ibid.

[466]   Ibid.

[467]   Ibid.

[468]   Easterbrook, Gregg. "Everything You Know About The Environment Is Wrong". *The New Republic*. Vol. 202, No. 18, (April 30, 1990): p. 25.

[469]   Linden, Eugene. "The Death of Birth". *Time*. Vol. 133, No. 1, (Jan. 2, 1989): p. 32.

[470]   Horton, Paul B. et al. *The Sociology of Social Problems*, Eighth Edition. Prentice-Hall, Inc. Englewood Cliffs, New Jersey, (1985): p. 422.

[471]   Ibid.   416.

Biological Survey team to wipe out the coyotes." [472]   By 1926 crop yields were the best ever, but by the following Spring the lack of predators resulted in Kern County being inundated by 100 million starving field mice which even killed and ate sheep in their hunger. [473]

Even when the target of animal control measures is the prey rather than the predator, problems can emerge. This was borne out in an experiment where rodents and rabbits were intensively poisoned and trapped in one area and then had their population levels compared with those of another area where such measures were not applied. The study found that the population levels of rabbits and rodents in the area where poisons and traps were used was soon larger than the comparison area where nature was not interfered with. The reason given for this phenomenon was that as poisoned animals died they were eaten by predators which died as well. With fewer predators available to eat them, the rodent/rabbit population quickly grew beyond previous natural levels. [474]

Even if poison is not used to kill prey animals, a substantial reduction in the prey animal population could cause a similar imbalance. If the population of prey animals is greatly reduced by any means, predator populations will fall as well as the result of starvation or through migration to where food is more plentiful. In the absence of predators, prey population will quickly grow beyond normal levels until the slower reproducing predator population can rebound.

Eco-nomic Watershed Use

We are still quite a ways from fully understanding all the intricacies of watershed mechanics. But in a general sense we know how present practices harm them and how watershed resources can be used in ways that minimize negative ecological impacts.

Agriculture

Agriculture, as it is commonly practiced, is not as effective at slowing runoff and storing water as the plant and animal communities it replaces. With conventional agriculture land is frequently unprotected by vegetation. Even when crops are grown the soil is often only partially protected compared with natural vegetation. When land previously farmed is converted to grassland or woodland "it will store roughly 16 more tons of carbon (embodied in plant material) than when it was cultivated." [475]   Without protection, topsoil is easily eroded by pounding rain. Hard rainfall on bare soil often has the effect of sealing the soil surface so as to block water absorption. This speeds runoff and increases erosion down stream.

The use of chemical fertilizers in lieu of organic fertilizers can also increase soil erosion. Conventional agriculture often relies on chemical fertilizers to supply plant nutrients instead of using organic materials like manure and plant residues. A reduction in the amount of organic material in soils translates into less food for soil organisms. Fewer soil organisms means that there are fewer passageways in the soil through which water can be absorbed. Less absorption translates into more runoff which increases soil erosion. It also reduces the amount of water stored in the soil and as groundwater.

---

[472] *Ibid.*

[473] *Ibid.*

[474] *Ibid. p. 422-23.*

[475] *Postel, Sandra. "A Green Fix To The Global Warm-Up". World Watch. Vol. 1, No. 5, (Sept./Oct. 1988): pp. 35.*

Once set in motion, the loss of fertile topsoil tends to perpetuate itself, making it harder for watershed communities to recover after they have been damaged. A weakened watershed function results in more erosion which further weakens the watershed community which causes more erosion and so forth. This is true whether agriculture is continued or if a natural watershed community tries to re-establish itself after agriculture has been discontinued.

Watershed Friendly Agricultural Practices

Even though many of today's agricultural practices are watershed damaging there are a wide variety of techniques that can be adopted to maximize the watershed function of agricultural systems.

One way to blunt the effects of pounding rain and runoff from rainfall and snow melt is to leave crop residues in the field. Plant residues can either be left standing or used on the soil surface as a mulch or in combination with mulch. Because its root systems are intact, standing vegetation can offer additional protection from water and wind erosion. Leaving plant residues in the field also helps watershed function by providing food for soil organisms. The tunnels they create in the pursuit of food make it easier for water to be absorbed by the soil.

There are a variety of tillage methods that can be used to prepare soils for planting that minimize the impact of agriculture on the watershed fabric. These include chisel plowing, strip tillage, ridge tillage, and no-tillage methods. Chisel plowing, a method of plowing that only opens a narrow furrow of soil, can reduce erosion losses by up to 50% over more commonly used cultivation practices. [476] "The use of no tillage, strip tillage, and ridge tillage ... can decrease erosion by 75% or more." [477]

Growing nitrogen fixing legumes along with crops and as rotation crops can also improve the watershed function of agricultural systems. These crops protect the soil from wind and water erosion and provide food for soil organisms which, in turn, make the soil more permeable by their tunneling activities. Adding organic materials to the soil, like manure, also improves watershed function. Manure-like materials absorb water like a sponge and provide food for tunneling soil organisms. "Increasing soil organic matter by applying livestock manure increased the water infiltration rate by more than 90% (Meek and Donovan, 1982; Sweeten and Mathers, 1985) mainly by decreasing the rate of water runoff (Mueller et al., 1984)." [478]

Planting trees and shrubs to form windbreaks is a good way to protect soils from the erosive effects of the wind. "Soil particles do not ordinarily blow away until wind velocity is about 13 miles per hour 1 foot above the ground." [479] A well established windbreak can provide full protection against wind blown soil losses "10 times the height of the trees measured in the direction the wind is blowing. And they give some protection as far out as 20 times the height of the trees." [480] Windbreaks also "make sprinkler irrigation more effective" by protecting "the spray against shifting

---

[476] *Committee On The Role of Alternative Farming Methods in Modern Production Agriculture. Alternative Agriculture. National Academy Press, Washington D.C., (1989): p. 119.*

[477] *Ibid.*

[478] *Pimentel, David. Food and Natural Resources. Academic Press Inc., Harcourt Brace Jovanovich, San Diego, California, (1989): p. 305.*

[479] *Ferber, Arthur E. Windbreaks for Conservation. U.S. Dept. of Agriculture, Soil Conservation Service, Agricultural Information Bulletin 339, Washington D.C., (October 1969): p. 2.*

[480] *Ibid. p. 3.*

winds." [481]

The use of windbreaks can also increase crop yields. "In a project aided by CARE in the Majjia Valley of Niger, for instance, trees planted to form windbreaks around cropland boosted grain yields more than 20 percent and also produced wood needed for fuel and timber." [482] Windbreaks also "increase both dew fall and the number of birds and small animals by providing cover, food, nesting sites, and storm protection. In summer, farmstead windbreaks raise humidity and produce an air conditioning effect. In winter, they decrease livestock deaths, heat, and feed needs." [483]

Though it is just one aspect of food production, the grazing of livestock on rangeland has a particularly negative effect on watershed function. Livestock grazing on range and forest lands decreases the water holding capacity of watersheds by removing soil protecting vegetation. [484] This translates into soil erosion which, in turn, results in less and weaker vegetation leading to further soil loss and eventually the formation of gullies. Topsoil loss in the U.S. is around 3.1 billion tons per year. [485] Around 85 percent of this loss can be attributed "to the feet of grazing livestock or to the production of livestock feed." [486]

As early as 1974 the Bureau of Land Reclamation reported "that less than one-fifth of the grazing lands in the United States were in '"good to excellent'" condition. [487] Even in forestlands, where one would expect that tree canopies would protect against erosion, livestock grazing has a negative impact. Soil erosion on grazed forestlands is "six times the rate experienced on non-grazed forestlands." [488] Grazing, especially grazing cattle, is particularly damaging to streams and stream related vegetation. Cattle cause damage because they break down stream banks and trample stream vegetation. "A 1990 EPA report stated that '"riparian areas through much of the West (in the late 1980s) were in the worst condition in history.'" [489] Livestock grazing has a similar effect on the rest of the planet. "Livestock grazing and livestock crop production cause accelerated soil loss over more of the globe than any other land use." Even if we do not count the land used to grow grain and other supplemental food for livestock, overgrazing livestock alone is the largest cause of

---

[481] *Ibid. p. 2.*

[482] *Postel, Sandra. "A Green Fix To The Global Warm-Up". World Watch. Vol. 1, No. 5, (Sept./Oct. 1988): p. 36.*

[483] *Grossman, Joel. "Entomological Society of America's 1988 Annual Meeting IPM Highlights - Part Eight" The IPM Practitioner. Vol. XI, No. 11/12, (Nov./Dec. 1989): p. 9.*

[484] *Wuerthner, George. "The Real Cost of a Hamburger". Earthwatch. Vol. XII, No. V, (July/August 1993): p. 25.*

[485] *Committee on the Role of Alternative Farming Methods in Modern Production Agriculture. Alternative Agriculture. National Academy Press, Waqshington D.C., (1989): p. 119.*

[486] *Jacobs, Lynn. Waste or the West: Public Lands Ranching. Arizona Lithographers, Tucson, Arizona, (1991): p. 80.*

[487] *Horton, Paul B. et al. The Sociology of Social Problems, Eighth Edition. Prentice-Hall, Inc. Englewood Cliffs, New Jersey, (1985): p. 421.*

[488] *Sampson, R. Soil Erosion, Farmland or Wasteland - A Time to Choose. Rodale Press, (1981): p. 118.*

[489] *Wuerthner, George. "The Real Cost of a Hamburger". Earthwatch. Vol. XII, No. V, (July/August 1993): p. 25.*

soil degradation on our planet. [490]

If it is done carefully, domestic animals can be grazed on some range land areas without seriously compromising their watershed function. But to avoid serious damage, grazing and its timing need to be carefully regulated. Considering the damage that they cause to watersheds in general and to streams and ponds in particular, it may be advisable to prohibit livestock grazing, particularly cattle, which cause the most damage, in most range and forest land areas. The overall economic impact of such a policy in the U.S. would be relatively minor since only three percent of the beef grown nationally is rangeland fed. [491] It would be important however, to work with ranchers who earn their livings raising range fed cattle to mitigate any negative economic impacts that such a policy would create for them.

Watershed Function And Forestry

Timber harvesting is another way that human activity impacts watershed function. Clear cutting, the most prevalent method of timber harvesting, completely eliminates large stands of vegetation during the process of harvesting trees. This results in the almost total disruption of the plant and animal communities that are essential to the retention of forest soils, the water they store, and the water that percolates through them into groundwater storage basins. Though professional foresters do not agree completely as to the best strategy or strategies for both harvesting timber and protecting watershed communities, some general strategies are emerging.

If more than a few trees are harvested in one area they should be harvested in narrow bands along contours to minimize the problem of erosion. Harvesting vegetation counter to contours opens the soil up to the formation of erosion gullies. Trees close to waterways should only be harvested individually and if they can be harvested in a way that avoids waterway siltation. Stream siltation has been identified as a factor in the decline of salmon, and cut-throat-trout in the Pacific Northwest. [492] Forest floor debris or duff should be spread on soil areas disturbed by felling or from dragging trees or by logging equipment. This practice minimizes the effects of erosive rainfall.

Road building in forested areas should be limited. Often the grading of access roads can be just as destructive to watersheds as the harvesting itself. [493] In one study, a single road slide (caused by erosion) contributed to 40% of the sediment lost from the watershed area being examined during the study year. [494]

To avoid the need for roads, timber harvested in remote areas should be moved to transport centers by helicopters, horses, or balloons. Currently, around 8 percent of the logs harvested in the

---

[490] *World Resources 1992 - 93*. The World Resources Institute, The United Nations Environmental Programme, and The United Nations Development Programme. Oxford Press, New York, (1992): p. 114, 115.

[491] Jacobs, Lynn. *Waste of the West: Public Lands Ranching*. Arizona Lithographers, Tucson, Arizona, (1991): p. 566.

[492] Wilson, Alex. "The Northwestern Timber Debate". *Environmental Building News*. Vol. 2, No. 3, (May/June 1993): p. 16.

[493] School of Forestry and School of Engineering, Oregon State University. *Studies on the Effects of Watershed Practices on Streams*. U.S. Environmental Protection Agency, Washington D.C. (1971): pp. 41-45.

[494] *Ibid.*

Pacific Northwest are moved to loading areas by one of these methods. [495] Only the tree boles, the main wood portion of a tree, should be removed from the forest. This portion of a tree is low in nutrients and its removal represents a relative minor nutrient loss to the forest ecology. Small branches and foliage, rich in nutrients, should be left in the forest. [496]

Some experts argue that forest ecosystem management practices should also permit some form of clearcutting as long as it mimics "nature and the effects of natural disturbances" like fire. [497] While this view certainly deserves study, it should be noted that logging in any form is not "natural" in that harvested trees and the micro-nutrients they embody are removed from the forest environment. Although there are parallels between clearcutting and forest fires, we should be careful not to establish forestry policies based on such parallels until we are sure that such policies are truly sustainable. The negative impacts of clear cutting, like stream heating (**See index for more details**) and siltation and the accelerated loss of nutrients, certainly indicate the need for further study.

Under the general heading of "New Forestry" there are a number of experiments being conducted toward the development of sustainable forestry strategies. The U.S. Forest Service is currently experimenting with "the use of low-impact logging techniques to minimize the worst aspects of conventional forestry: soil erosion, habitat fragmentation, and homogenization of forests." [498] Forest homogenization refers to the condition caused when one species of same age trees are planted over a large area after it is clearcut.

In an experiment in the Shasta Costa Valley in Southwestern Oregon, "foresters will carefully select the trees to be logged and those left behind as biological "legacies" that aid the recovery of the land. Mimicking the fires that occur on a 50-to-90 year cycle in the area, timber cutters will concentrate their work on the valley's dry ridges and avoid the sensitive stream side areas altogether. By concentrating timbering near existing roads on the valley's degraded edges and relying on helicopter logging for the rest, the project will minimize road building and the soil and habitat loss it causes." [499]

The University of Oregon is also getting into the sustainable forestry act. In one experiment "one-half acre patches of trees were harvested, creating a mosaic of small openings and wooded areas; researchers are studying whether young douglas firs can grow in these filtered light patches." [500] Other researchers are creating intentional snags in larger clear cut areas. In these areas, the tops of remnant trees in larger clear cuts "were either cut off or blown off with explosives (they are trying to determine which approach works better) to provide cavity-nesting trees for wildlife." [501] A third experiment leaves a fairly large number of trees standing after harvest. These "leave trees" are

---

[495] Wilson, Alex. "The Northwestern Timber Debate". *Environmental Building News*. Vol. 2, No. 3, (May/June 1993): p. 14.

[496] Perry, David A.. "An Overview of Sustainable Forestry." *Journal of Pesticide Reform*. Vol. 8, No. 3, Fall (1988): pp. 9-10.

[497] Wilson, Alex. "The Northwestern Timber Debate". *Environmental Building News*. Vol. 2, No. 3, (May/June 1993): p. 17.

[498] Ryan, John C. "Oregon's Ancient Laboratory." *World Watch*. Vol. 3, No. 6, (Nov./Dec. 1990): p. 7.

[499] Ibid. p. 8.

[500] Wilson, Alex. "The Northwestern Timber Debate". *Environmental Building News*. Vol. 2, No. 3, (May/June 1993): p. 15.

[501] Ibid.

designed to create a mixed aged forest and a multi-level tree canopy. [502]

The goal of selective timber harvesting is to minimize the ecological trauma that results from clearcutting. Indicative of this trauma is the change in stream temperatures after clearcutting. In one study, stream temperatures went from a maximum of 57 degrees fahrenheit to a maximum of 85 degrees after clearcutting occurred. [503]

Soil erosion is another trauma caused by clearcutting. This is particularly true where rainfall is heavy. "In the Amazon Forest, for example, a hectare (2 1/2 acres) of land may lose no more than 3 pounds of topsoil a year through erosion; when the land is stripped of its forest cover the erosion losses rise to 34 tons per hectare." [504]

A controlled deforestation experiment in the Hubbard Brook Experimental Forest revealed a number of other impacts. In this experiment "six contiguous watersheds, ranging in size from 12 hectors (30 acres) to 43 hectors" (106 acres) were studied as normally functioning forested areas. [505] During this period, forest inputs and outputs (nutrients, water, etc.) were measured to develop a baseline of information to compare with the second half of the experiment. This second phase consisted of completely leveling all the vegetation on one of the study watersheds with an area of 15.6 hectors (38.5 acres). After it was leveled, no material was removed "and great care was taken to prevent disturbances of the surface of the soil that might promote soil erosion." [506]

As the experiment continued, changes in the watershed were measured for several years and compared with the previous information. Even though the soil surface was not damaged and no vegetation was removed from where it was felled, the "deforestation had a pronounced effect on runoff." [507] In the first year after deforestation, runoff "exceeded the expected amount by 40 percent." [508] Runoff rates during one four-month period were over 4 times what would be normally expected. [509] Additionally, loss of key nutrients like potassium, calcium, and nitrate dramatically increased along with the organic soil base. [510] In short, the experiment illustrated how clearcutting, even when vegetation is not removed, sets up a situation where rainwater runoff, soil erosion, and loss of key nutrients substantially increases. [511]

While clearcutting dominates the forestry industry today, not all forests are harvested in this way. The 91,000 acre Collins Almanor Forestry operation in north eastern California is a case in

---

[502] *Ibid.*

[503] *School of Forestry and School of Engineering, Oregon State University.* <u>*Studies on the Effects of Watershed Practices on Streams.*</u> *U.S. Environmental Protection Agency, Washington D.C. (1971): pp. 6, 7.*

[504] *Horton, Paul B. et al.* <u>*The Sociology of Social Problems,*</u> *Eighth Edition. Prentice-Hall, Inc. Englewood Cliffs, New Jersey, (1985): p. 420.*

[505] *Bormann, Herbert F. and Gene E. Likens. "The Nutrient Cycles of an Ecosystem".* <u>*Scientific American.*</u> *Vol. 223, No. 4, (October 1970): p. 95.*

[506] *Ibid.*

[507] *Ibid. p. 97.*

[508] *Ibid.*

[509] *Ibid.*

[510] *Ibid. p. 100.*

[511] *Ibid. p. 101.*

point. Recently, the media has made much out of the apparent conflict between saving the forest from clearcutting and preserving jobs for loggers. Meanwhile, the Collins Almanor foresters have been quietly harvesting timber sustainably and profitably for over 50 years. [512]

When they began harvesting the forest in 1941 it was estimated that it contained 1.5 billion board feet of lumber. A board foot of lumber is 12 inches by 12 inches by one inch thick. Since 1941, 1.7 billion board feet of lumber have been harvested from the forest--more lumber than the forest contained when harvesting first began. Yet, after over 50 years of harvesting, 1.5 billion board feet of unharvested timber still remain in the forest. "Even after decades of cutting, most stands in the Collins Almanor Forest still contain some magnificent 200- and 300-year-old trees with diameters reaching five and six feet." [513]

Over the 51 year harvest period "only a few trees were snaked out of the woods at a time" matching the forest's natural rate of regeneration. [514] Wood debris (leaves, needles, branches, etc.) is "left on the forest floor after logging, so more nutrients return to the soil." [515] Through this method, the forest has been profitably harvested while "wildlife, clear water, and recreational possibilities abound, even on land that has just been cut." [516]

To increase the forest's value as a wildlife habitat, some potentially harvestable trees are left in the forest to die. When the crowns of these trees break off they become snags which provide nesting habitats for "woodpeckers and other animals that require dead or dying trees." [517]

Further, the Collins Almanor forest does not contain tree stands of "even-age, single species management stands that clearcut logging produces; instead the stands have a variety of species and ages, the kind of mix that comes from letting the forest reproduce itself without artificial planting." [518] To protect streams from siltation, "logging roads are set well back from streams. The forest, in short looks and feels like a forest rather than a tree farm that is periodically mowed down and replanted." [519] Greg Apiet, a specialist in forest health for the Wilderness Society, has described the Collins Almanor forestry system as "impeccable." The management direction of the Collins Almanor forestry operation is not accidental. It was the vision of Trueman W. Collins who "envisioned a new kind of forestry operation that would yield a perpetual supply of timber for a mill that would never close". [520] In addition to receiving praise from the environmental community, the Collins Almanor Forestry Operation had been certified as sustainable by Scientific Certification Systems, a national independent environmental certification organization.

---

[512] Kenworthy, Tom. "One Tranquil Story of Timber Cutting". *The Washington Post*. (Wednesday, Oct. 14, 1992): p. A-3.

[513] Ibid.

[514] Zuckerman, Seth. "Old Forestry". *Sierra*. Vol. 77, No. 2, (March/April, 1992): p. 44.

[515] Kenworthy, Tom. "One Tranquil Story of Timber Cutting". *The Washington Post*. (Wednesday, Oct. 14, 1992): p. A-3.

[516] Zuckerman, Seth. "Old Forestry". *Sierra*. Vol. 77, No. 2, (March/April, 1992): p. 44.

[517] Kenworthy, Tom. "One Tranquil Story of Timber Cutting". *The Washington Post*. (Wednesday, Oct. 14, 1992): p. A-3.

[518] Ibid.

[519] Ibid.

[520] Ibid.

Scientific Certification Systems has also certified two other forestry operations as sustainable. The Menominee Tribal Enterprise forestry operation has been harvesting forestry products sustainably since 1854 in Wisconsin. Outside the U.S. the Noh-Bec and the Tres Garantias forest operations, which provide support for the community of Quintana Roo, Mexico, have also been certified as sustainable. [521]

In addition to timber, there are a number of other products that can be harvested sustainably from forests. A study conducted by botanists Robert Mendelsohn of Yale University and Michael Baick of the New York Botanical Gardens concluded more income could be generated in tropical forests by harvesting native medicinal plants instead of logging or using the land for agriculture. [522]

Another study in Peru demonstrated that "your average savvy forest dweller" could make almost $700 per year "by harvesting nine varieties of fruit, wild chocolate, rubber, and an occasional tree" from a plot of land "about the size of a suburban lot." [523] By comparison, if the lot were clearcut it might gross $1,000, but of course a considerable time would have to pass before the plot could be harvested again if at all. [524] Studies of deforestation data "shows as much as 55 percent of the forest that is logged over eventually becomes deforested." [525] Globally, the rate of tropical deforestation has increased by 50 percent since the early 1980s. [526]

On another front related to using forests sustainably, "the pharmaceutical firm Merck and Company has signed a precedent setting agreement with Costa Rica's National Biodiversity Institute." [527] As part of the agreement Merck will "train Costa Rican biologist how to test specimens for medical properties" and provide them with the necessary equipment to do the job. [528] Merck will also pay a million dollars for the right to screen any promising plant or animal for pharmaceutical properties. [529]

The abundance of life forms in tropical forests makes them especially fertile ground for the discovery of pharmaceuticals. "Tropical forests cover only 7% of the earth's surface, but house 50%

---

[521] *Scientific Certification Systems, 1611 Telegraph Ave. Suite 1111, Oakland CA 94612-2113, (510) 832-0359.*

[522] *"Rain Forest Drugs Cure Deforestation". Earth Watch, Vol. XII, No. II, (Jan./Feb. 1993): p. 6.*

[523] *Christensen, Jon. "Letting The Amazon Pay Its Own Way". Whole Earth. No. 66, (Spring 1990): p. 96.*

[524] *Ibid.*

[525] *"The Disappearing Forests". United Nations Environmental Programme -Environment Brief No. 3. Nairobi, Kenya, Second Edition, (1991): p. 3.*

[526] *World Resources 1992 - 93. The World Resources Institute, The United Nations Environmental Programme, and The United Nations Development Programme. Oxford Press, New York, (1992): p. 118. Also see Monastersky, Richard. "The Fall of the Forest". Science News. A Science Service Publication, Washington D.C., Vol. 138, No. 3, (July 21, 1990): p. 40-41.*

[527] *Pearlman, Nancy - Editor. "Costa Rica" The Compendium Newsletter. Vol. 20, No. 4, (July/Aug.): p. 12.*

[528] *Ibid.*

[529] *Ibid.*

to 80% of the planet's species." [530]   To date, "some 25% of the pharmaceuticals in use in the U.S. today contain ingredients originally derived from wild plants." [531]

Forestry And True-Cost-Pricing

As in other economic sectors, forestry practices are affected by economic conditions, not all of which are market driven. For example, U.S. "taxpayers lost $50 million in below-cost timber sales on Montana public lands alone" in 1991. [532]   "Nationally, the Forest Service timber program lost more than $5.6 billion in the last decade." [533]   Such subsidies undoubtedly have an impact on the economic choices the forestry industry makes. With true-cost-pricing such subsidies would be eliminated along with unsustainable forestry practices.

Land development And Watershed Function

Land development is another way that watershed function is compromised. Current development practices often involve grading and rearranging the topography of large tracts of land. This process totally destroys watershed function.

A better approach is to minimize grading and topographical changes and protect native plant and animal habitats as much as is possible. Where grading and land movement are unavoidable, the area should be re-vegetated as soon as possible, after it has been disturbed. These practices will minimize the negative impact that development has on watersheds and will result in community and neighborhood designs that avoid the topographic monotony that characterizes most contemporary urban layouts.

Protecting Watersheds from Pollution

Watershed pollution is another threat to water security. Whether it comes from industrial or urban activities or from forestry and agricultural practices, once released, pollution is fated to be spread by the forces of wind and water throughout the whole watershed where it occurs and beyond.

Ultimately, the only way to control watershed pollution is to control it at its source. Admittedly, this is a very large task since it involves using new methods for doing almost everything we now do. Fortunately, many of the these methods have already been developed and are being put to use, though not even close to the scale that is needed.

Avoiding Pollution In And Around Our Homes

One way to reduce watershed pollution is to use more ecologically benign products and practices around our homes. Many of the products we use in and around our homes contribute to watershed pollution. These products include pesticides, paints, cleaners, and auto maintenance products. Less common pollutants include silver and other chemicals related to home film processing and residues from other home business and hobby activities. Until major changes are made in how some of the products we use are formulated, some watershed pollution is inevitable, but 90% or more of it can be avoided right now if consumers are selective when they purchase

---

[530]   Linden, Eugene. "The Death of Birth". *Time*. Vol. 133, No. 1, (Jan. 2, 1989): p. 32.

[531]   *Ibid.* p. 33.

[532]   "Carrying Capacity Checkup and Connections". *Carrying Capacity Network Clearinghouse Bulletin*. Vol. 3, No. 2, (March 1993): p. 5.

[533]   *Ibid.*

products and use them carefully. [534]

Purchasing products that are ecologically benign also sends a powerful message to manufacturers. It is the most direct way to let them know what we expect from the products we buy. How we spend our money in the present has a great deal to do with the kind of world we will have in the future.

For watershed friendly cleaning, look for biodegradable soaps and detergents. Avoid cleaners with chlorine based bleach in favor of those using oxygen bleach. Phosphorous-free soaps and detergents should be used in areas where wastewater may be discharged into aquatic environments. In aquatic environments phosphorous, a nutrient, causes excessive plant growth. Plants produce oxygen during the day but use it up at night. If too numerous, plants can deplete the dissolved oxygen in water during the night to levels so low that fish suffocate. [535] Excessive plant growth can also cause oxygen depletion in the autumn when aquatic plants die. When aquatic plants die, decay bacteria multiply. With an abundance of dead plant material, these bacteria, which require oxygen, can become so numerous that oxygen levels drop below what is needed to support fish. [536] These two phenomena, which are forms of eutrophication, can be avoided by keeping excessive nutrients out of aquatic environments.

Auto maintenance is another aspect of protecting watersheds from pollution. "According to the EPA, 91 percent of home oil-changers dispose of their used oil improperly, releasing 193 million gallons into the world at large each year." [537] Similarly, antifreeze and to a lesser extent brake, power steering, and transmission fluid frequently become watershed pollutants via the home mechanic route. Plus, used tires, batteries, oil filters, and other auto parts are often discarded improperly.

Because of the nature of the fluids and parts involved, a completely ecologically benign way to deal with them does not exist in most instances. But with proper handling their ecological impacts can be reduced as follows:

1. Oil and antifreeze can be recycled. A new antifreeze called Sierra is being advertised as biodegradable. Call your County Waste Management or recycling agency to find out where oil and antifreeze can be recycled. Oil can be recycled and reused but it is often mixed with fuel oils and used as heating oil.

2. Brake, power steering, and transmission fluid can be recycled in some areas. Call your County Health Department for information on where these fluids can be recycled.

3. Tires that are not too worn can be retreaded and reused. Used tires have also been shredded and used in roofing tiles and rubber mats and added to asphalt and used as a

---

[534] *Author's personal experience.*

[535] *Conversation with biologist Steve Neudecker, Executive Director of the Chula Vista Nature Center and Bay Front Conservancy Trust. Also see Harper, David. Eutrophication of Freshwaters, Principles Problems, and Restoration. Chapman and Hall, New York, New York, (1992): p. 139.*

[536] *Clark, Mary. Contemporary Biology. W.B. Saunders Company, Philadelphia, PA, (1979): p. 35.*

[537] *Lecard, Mark. "Road Worrier". Sierra. Vol. 77, No. 6, (Nov./Dec. 1992): p. 20.*

paving material. [538]   Ultimately, tires should be designed to be easily recycled and biodegradable so that the materials that wear off them will break down in nature.

4.   Watershed pollution can also be reduced if we use fewer paper products. Most paper products are bleached with chlorine or chlorine derivatives. A by-product of using chlorine in the papermaking industry is dioxin, a family of highly toxic compounds which includes Agent Orange, the notorious defoliant used during the Vietnam war. [539] Dioxin and other pollutants enter watersheds when paper mills discharge their wastewater.

In addition to the fear of general dioxin contamination, concerns have "been raised about direct exposure to humans, not only at bleaching plants but in dioxins leaching out of bleached paper products such as milk cartons and tissues. In Sweden, the use of chlorine in the bleaching of such products is now banned." [540]   Actually, dioxin "is only the most notorious and highly publicized of about 1,000 chemicals emitted by pulp mills. Many are carcinogenic, and the effects of others are only now being discovered." [541]

The consumption of paper products can be reduced by using washable dinner napkins and kitchen towels instead of paper napkins or towels. Use the backs of paper printed on one side for notes and memos. Where the use of paper products is necessary, look for paper products that are not bleached or that are processed with oxygen prior to bleaching. Oxygen processing does not eliminate the use of chlorine but it does reduce the amount used. [542]

Use paper products made from post-consumer recycled paper. Post consumer paper is made with paper that someone has already used as opposed to many recycled paper products that are made from factory trimmings. A high percentage of post consumer paper in a product translates into fewer natural forest trees being cut to produce it and less natural habitat disruptions caused by plantation style pulp farms. Where the use of paper is unavoidable, choose unbleached paper products made from post consumer recycled paper. This is the best way to avoid paper related watershed pollution.

Using watershed-safe pest control products in our homes and yards is another way to protect watersheds from pollution. Many watershed-safe pest control products are already commercially available and the number of these products on the market is growing. But before buying pest control products, attention to house and garden keeping details, as the first line of defense against pests, should be explored. To control household pests, caulk cracks around baseboards and plug up holes around plumbing and heating ducts and electrical wiring. Make sure eave and basement vents are covered with screen mesh.

The primary pest control strategy in gardens is to maintain healthy plants. Healthy plants, like healthy people, naturally resist the attacks of pests and diseases. The key to maintaining

---

[538]   *Ibid.*

[539]   *Miller, Fred. "Exposure", The Monthly Journal of the Waste and Toxic Substances Project. Environmental Action Foundation, Washington D.C., July/August, (1983): p. 3. Also see Science News. (2/18/89): p. 104., and (8/5/89): p. 94.*

[540]   *Ayres, Ed. "Whitewash: Pursuing the Truth About Paper". World Watch. Vol. 5, No. 5, (Sept./Oct. 1992): p. 24.*

[541]   *Ibid.*

[542]   *Ryan, John. "Sweden Says No To Polluting Paper".   World Watch. Vol. 3, No. 2, (March/April 1990): p. 39.*

healthy plants is to insure that they get the balance of nutrients they need from a healthy soil. Though nutrients in the form of chemical fertilizers can be added to the soil to make up for deficiencies it is better for soil health if organic materials like composted manures and plant residues, are used instead. As soil organisms consume these materials, nutrients are released at rates more closely matched to plant needs. The tunneling action of soil organisms also makes it easier for water and air, both essential for healthy plants, to enter the soil.

The slow release of nutrients by soil organisms also avoids the problem of nutrients getting into waterways and groundwater aquifers. With chemical fertilizers nutrients are often released faster than plants can use them. Thus water soluble nutrients are carried by runoff into waterways or leached into groundwater supplies. The findings of a national five-year Environmental Protection Agency study show this to be an increasing concern. Based on samplings taken from over 1,300 community water systems and rural wells, "the agency estimated that 57% of rural domestic wells contain nitrate, while 4.2% contain one or more pesticide and 3.2% contain both nitrates and pesticides." [543] This same EPA study showed that, "52% of community water systems contain nitrates, with 10% showing one or more pesticides and 7% containing both nitrates and pesticides." [544]

Beyond house and garden keeping details, the next level of pest control is the use of non-toxic mechanical measures. These include adhesives like flypaper, glue type mouse and roach controls, and sticky ant barriers like Tanglefoot. Flea combs and frequent vacuuming are effective flea control measures. Alternative pest control products are increasingly available in retail outlets that had previously carried mostly toxic pest control products. [545]

Using insects and other animals to control pests is another non-toxic strategy. Ladybugs, lacewings, and praying mantises are just a few examples of insects that eat other insects. Providing nesting boxes for insect-eating birds can also be an effective control strategy. Bats are valuable allies in the control of flying nocturnal insects like mosquitos which carry malaria and other diseases and moths whose larvae attack garden plants. Bat boxes, designed to accommodate sleeping bats, are useful tools in keeping bats around. Lizards, frogs, and toads are valuable insect consumers. Some lizards have been used effectively inside buildings to control roaches, flies, and other household insects.

On the microscopic end of the control spectrum are biocides or pest pathogens like BT (Bacillus Thuringiensis). BT is composed of the spores of a bacterium that are fatal to the larvae or worm stage of insects in the butterfly family. Included in this family are cabbage worms, tomato hornworms, and other leaf-eating insect larvae. Still in the research stage is the celery looper virus. This virus, which is effective at controlling a wide spectrum of pests is naturally occurring and could be commercially available in the next five years. [546]

Using homemade and commercial insecticidal soaps is another non-toxic way to control house and garden pests. Depending on the materials included in the mix, such concoctions can be totally benign or mildly irritating. Commercial products often contain alcohol as an emulsifier.

---

[543] Abramson, Rudy. *"Study Discovers Nitrate in Half of Nation's Wells"*, *Los Angeles Times*. (November 14, 1990): p. A-18.

[544] *Ibid.*

[545] *"Be Eco-logical!"*, *Ecological Buying Guide*. Environmental Health Coalition, San Diego, California, (1991): p. 1, (619) 235-0281.

[546] Wood, Marcia. *"Microbe Blows Those Hornworms Away"*. *Agricultural Research*. Vol. 4, No. 6, (June 1992): p. 4. For more in-depth coverage on the biological control of pests see Biocide Use in Agriculture, page 179.

Insecticidal soap sprays are effective against house pests like fleas and garden pests like aphids. Herbs can also be used for pest control. Some herbs, though not fatal to fleas, are useful in repelling them. [547]

Diatomaceous earth is another useful insect control material. Diatoms are the skeletons of tiny sea organisms. Diatomaceous earth kills insects by dehydrating or desiccating them when it comes in contact with their bodies. Though it is not toxic, it can be irritating to mucus membranes and lungs. Care should be taken to avoid breathing diatomaceous dust during its application. For indoor use diatomaceous earth can be applied directly to rugs to kill fleas and the excess can be vacuumed up after a few hours. In gardens it can be applied like any other pest control products on or around plants. [548]

Boric acid, only moderately toxic to mammals, marks the next level of the pest control regimen. Boric acid is the active ingredient in many commercial roach killers. It comes in both tablet and powder form. In tablet form it is mixed with a bait which is eaten by roaches along with the boric acid. In powdered form, insects walk through it and ingest the boric acid when they lick the dust off their legs. Since boron is toxic to plants in more than trace amounts, care should be taken when using boric acid around plants. If roaches are a problem around plants, boric acid tablets can be placed around them in upturned jar lids. This gives roaches access to the tablets and keeps the tablets out of direct contact with the soil. Where sprinklers or rainfall are an issue the tablet containers will need rain caps to keep them dry. Since boric acid is harmful to mammals if eaten, it should not be applied where children or pets can get to it. [549]

Pyrethrin, an insecticide originally derived from the chrysanthemum flower and now produced synthetically, is another relatively safe control measure. While quite toxic to insects, pyrethrin degrades rapidly into harmless byproducts and it is relatively non-toxic to animals and people. Nevertheless, pyrethrin should be used carefully since it is known to provoke asthma and allergy attacks in children and people with respiratory problems. [550] Pyrethrin is also toxic to fish and should not be used where ponds and streams would be directly affected.

Weed Control

For the urban gardener, pulling and/or hoeing weeds, in combination with mulching is one of the best and least labor intensive non-toxic weed controlling strategies. Where plants are already established, pull weeds or cut them down and cover with a four to six inch layer of leaves, grass clippings, straw, or sawdust. Do not use sawdust that has paint in it unless the paint is non-toxic and biodegradable. If properly covered by mulch, very few weeds will survive and the few that do manage to break through the mulch are easily pulled. Periodically more mulch will have to be added to keep weeds at bay. This is because soil organisms will be constantly turning the mulch into beneficial soil amendments from the bottom up. [551]

---

[547] "Be Eco-logical!", *Ecological Buying Guide*. *Environmental Health Coalition, San Diego, California, (1991): p. 1, (619) 235-0281.*

[548] *Ibid.*

[549] *Ibid.*

[550] *Ibid.*

[551] *Author's personal experience.*

Watershed Pollution And Agriculture

Adopting non-polluting agricultural methods is another way to protect watersheds from contamination. The EPA has identified agriculture as the largest non-point source of surface water pollution. [552] Compared with the 9 percent of stream pollution that comes from industry, non-point pollution from agriculture approaches 65 percent. [553] "Pesticides and nitrate from fertilizers are detected in the groundwater in many agricultural regions." [554]

In the United States, groundwater supplies 95 percent of the drinking water in rural areas and 50 percent of the drinking water for all residents. [555] "Yet, according to a 1987 EPA report, at least twenty pesticides, some of which cause cancer and other harmful effects, have been found in groundwater in at least twenty-four states. In California alone, fifty-seven different pesticides were detected in ground water." [556] Though this problem will be with us for some time, the rapidly expanding use of organic and other alternative farming methods, less dependent on petrochemicals, promises to reduce this kind of watershed pollution.

Using Organic agriculture To Avoid Watershed Pollution

Organic farming is an alternative farming method that totally excludes the use of pesticides, chemically derived fertilizers, and other non-natural inputs. In organic farming nutrients are supplied by adding manures to the soil and by growing crops that convert atmospheric nitrogen into nitrogen compounds beneficial to plants. [557] Healthy soil makes for healthy plants which are naturally resistant to pests and disease. This is borne out by the fact that modern commercial organic agriculture is proving to be just as productive as is its petrochemical counterpart and less costly to practice even without including its true-cost advantages. (See chapter X for details.)

Watershed Pollution From Business And Industry

Watershed pollution from industrial and commercial operations can also be eliminated or reduced. Prior to World War II, U.S. "factories produced very few toxic by-products." [558] By 1985, the United States had "an estimated 50,000 toxic dumps as well as 180,000 toxic pits, ponds, and

---

[552] Committee on the Role of Alternative Farming Methods in Modern Production Agriculture. *Alternative Agriculture*. National Academy Press, Washington D.C., (1989): p. 3.

[553] Easterbrook, Gregg. "Cleaning Up". *Newsweek*. Vol. CXIV, No. 4, (July 24, 1989): p. 36. Also see Easterbrook, Gregg. "Everything You Know About The Environment Is Wrong". *The New Republic*, (April 30, 1990): p. 26.

[554] Committee on the Role of Alternative Farming Methods in Modern Production Agriculture. *Alternative Agriculture*. National Academy Press, Washington D.C. (1989): p. 3.

[555] Mott, Lawrie, and Karen Snyder. "Pesticide Alert". *The Amicus Journal*. Vol. No. (Spring 1988): p. 22.

[556] **Ibid. pp. 22-23.**

[557] Committee on the Role of Alternative Farming Methods in Modern Production Agriculture. *Alternative Agriculture*. National Academy Press, Washington D.C., (1989): pp. 258-59.

[558] Horton, Paul B. et al. *The Sociology of Social Problems*, Eighth Edition. Prentice Hall Inc., Englewood Cliffs, New Jersey, (1985): p. 414.

lagoons." [559]   According to the EPA at least 14,000 of these sites are potentially dangerous. [560]

In 1985, 60 to 70 thousand chemicals were produced by the U.S. chemical industry and "approximately 1,200 new organic chemical products, with potential commercial value, are created in laboratories each year." [561]   Of these new chemical compounds commercially produced each year, the EPA lists less than 50 thousand. Of those listed, "next to nothing is currently known about the toxic effects of almost 38,000 of them. Fewer than 1,000 have been tested for acute effects and only about 500 for their cancer-causing, reproductive, or mutagenic (gene mutating) effects." [562]

Three of the most common toxic contaminants of groundwater, chloroform, trichloroethylene, and trichloroethane, are produced by the organic chemical industry. [563]   In all, "the U.S. Environmental Protection Agency has found that man-made chemicals have contaminated roughly 20 percent of the country's drinking water aquifers." [564]

While they are not the only generators, "a 1984 Environmental Protection Agency report found that organic chemical plants emitted almost 40 percent of air emissions of selected chemicals from industrial sources." [565]   The organic chemical industry also "accounts for 83 percent of industrial discharges of hazardous organic chemicals to rivers." It also manufactures "over 5 billion pounds per year" of 14 organic chemicals, nine of which are hazardous. [566]

In practice, the volume of hazardous waste is much greater than the official numbers would indicate. This is because hazardous materials contaminate other materials like water which then become hazardous as well. In 1988, "manufacturers generated more than 290 million tons of hazardous waste regulated under RCRA (Resource Conservation & Recovery Act). Less than 5% was solid waste, the rest was wastewater." [567]

Besides the chemicals themselves, their production and use creates even greater quantities of toxic waste. "Air emissions of potentially toxic organic chemicals exceed five billion pounds per year." [568]   Responding to federal regulations requiring them to report releases of toxic air

---

[559]   *Ibid.*

[560]   *Ibid. Also see Easterbrook, Gregg. "Everything You Know About The Environment Is Wrong". The New Republic. Vol. 202, No. 18, (April 30, 1990): p. 25.*

[561]   *Sarokin, David J., et al. "Cutting Chemical Wastes". An INFORM Report. INFORM, Inc., (1985): p. 1.*

[562]   *Langone, John. "A Stinking Mess". Time. Vol. 133, No. 1, (Jan. 2, 1989): p. 47.*

[563]   *Sarokin, David J., et al. "Cutting Chemical Wastes". An INFORM Report. INFORM, Inc., (1985): p. 3.*

[564]   *Arrandale, Tom. "Land Use and The Invisible Cesspool". Governing. (May 1993): p. 62.*

[565]   *Sarokin, David J., et al. "Cutting Chemical Wastes". An INFORM Report. INFORM, Inc., New York, New York, (1985): p. 3.*

[566]   *Ibid.*

[567]   *Hanson, David. "Hazardous Waste Management: Planning To Avoid Future Problems". Chemical and Engineering News. Vol. 67, No. 31, (July 31, 1989): p. 9.*

[568]   *Sarokin, David J., et al. "Cutting Chemical Wastes". An INFORM Report. INFORM, Inc., New York, New York, (1985): p. 14.*

pollutants, industry reported the release of up to 2.7 billion pounds per year. [569] (The discrepancy between 5 billion and 2.7 billion pounds probably has more to do with reporting methods than any appreciable reduction of toxic air emissions between 1985 and 1989 when the articles citing these figures were released.)

Another 412 million pounds of toxic waste are dumped into sewage treatment plants and rivers. [570] The "federal EPA estimated that more than 580 billion pounds of hazardous solid wastes are generated annually -- more than one ton for every person in the U.S." [571]

As large as the numbers just cited are, they do not tell the whole story. Specifically exempted from RCRA regulations are a host of other "high volume, low hazard" wastes. These include "cement kiln dust, utility company ash and sludge, phosphate mining wastes, uranium and other mining wastes, and gas and oil drilling muds and oil production brines, and some chemical process wastes." [572]

Of these exempted wastes, the mining industry is the largest contributor. According to former Secretary of the Interior Stewart Udall, "mining generates twice as much hazardous waste each year as all other industries and municipal landfills in the United States combined". [573]

The total "amount of unregulated waste is not known, but it is believed to be a much larger volume than regulated waste. In fact, various estimates inside and outside government put the amount of RCRA-regulated hazardous waste at just 10 to 50% of the total waste volume." [574]

Public Health And Toxic Waste

Obviously, coming into direct contact with toxic materials can be dangerous but direct contact is only part of the problem that toxic waste presents. Through a process called **biological magnification** some toxic materials can affect us by becoming increasingly concentrated as they move to higher levels of the food chain. Many of the chemicals we introduce into the environment are carried by rainwater runoff into streams, lakes, and estuaries. Once there, they are ingested by simple marine organisms which are eaten by small fish, which are eaten by bigger fish and so on. According to Larry Skinner, the principal fish-and-wildlife ecologist with the New York Department of Environmental Conservation, "Your chance of getting cancer from eating a weekly eight-ounce meal of trout caught in Lake Ontario is about the same as your risk of being murdered in the United States today -- about one in two hundred." [575]

---

[569] Easterbrook, Gregg. "Cleaning Up". _Newsweek_. Vol. CXIV. No. 4, (July 24, 1989): p. 28.

[570] Ibid. p. 16.

[571] Ibid.

[572] Hanson, David. "Hazardous Waste Management: Planning To Avoid Future Problems". _Chemical and Engineering News_. Vol. 67, No. 31, (July 31, 1989): p. 11.]

[573] Hocker, Philip and Stewart Udal. "What's Mined Is Theirs". _Sierra_. Vol. 74, No. 5 (Sept./Oct. 1989): p. 20.

[574] Hanson, David. "Hazardous Waste Management: Planning To Avoid Future Problems". _Chemical and Engineering News_. Vol. 67, No. 31, (July 31, 1989): p. 11.

[575] Lefferts, Lisa Y. "Something Fishy". _New Age Journal_. Vol. 6, No. 4, (July/August 1989): p. 30.

Although numerous toxic materials can concentrate in food chains, some chemicals appear to be more pervasive. Polychlorinated biphenyls (PCB) still can be found in high concentrations in fish and wildlife even though it was banned in the U.S. in 1979. [576]

The use of DDT was banned in 1972 but it was still found in 334 of the 386 samples of domestic fish tested by the Food and Drug Administration in 1983. [577] Another contaminant frequently found in fish is chlordane, used to control termites and an EPA designated "probable" cause of cancer in humans. [578] Chlordane also persists where it is applied. Data submitted to the EPA by Velsicol Chemical Corporation of Rosemont, Illinois, the sole manufacturer of chlordane and heptachlor (also used to control termites), indicated detectable levels of these pesticides were found in the air of homes one year after they were treated. After reviewing the Velsicol data, the EPA estimated these levels of contamination "pose a lifetime cancer risk as high as 3.3 extra cases per one thousand adults exposed." [579]

Dioxins, associated with the production of paper, have also been found in fish. In September of 1990 the EPA "urged consumers . . . to avoid eating fish caught near 20 paper mills, including two in California, because of the cancer risk resulting from high levels of dioxin in the water." [580] According to the EPA, eating a regular diet of fish caught near the worst plant in Georgetown South Carolina, "would give a person a 1 in 50 chance of getting cancer". [581]

In some aquatic environments, toxic chemicals are so concentrated that even the fish that live there are getting cancer. In an article published in Forbes magazine in 1986 it was reported that "Up to a quarter of the English sole in 20 areas in Puget Sound are diseased." [582] Almost all the sauger perch taken from Michigan's Torch Lake are diseased. "Tumor-laden catfish" are also common in Ohio's Black River. [583] In all, "cancerous fish have surfaced in epidemic proportions in at least ten fresh and saltwater shorefronts and estuaries around the country." [584]

Since humans are at the high end of the food chain, pollutants can reach high concentrations in people who eat contaminated animal products. "Mother's milk in several east-coast states tests so high in PCB contamination that, if it were cow's milk, it could not be sold for human consumption." [585] This is certainly cause for concern. Infants are one step higher on the food chain than their mothers and are even more affected by pollutants during the first few years of their development than when they are older.

---

[576] *Ibid.*

[577] *Ibid.*

[578] *Ibid. p. 113.*

[579] *Cox, Caroline. "Chlordane's Slow Death: Why Does It Take So Long?" The Journal of Pesticide Reform. Vol. 7, No. 3, (Fall 1987): p. 26.*

[580] *Savage, David G. "Fish Taken Near 20 Paper Mills Tied to Cancer Risk." Los Angeles Times - San Diego Edition.(Sept. 25, 1990): p. A-3.*

[581] *Ibid.*

[582] *Lappen, Alyssa A. "On The Waterfront". Forbes. Vol. 137, No. 8, (April 21, 1986): p. 124.*

[583] *Ibid.*

[584] *Ibid.*

[585] *Horton, Paul B. et al. The Sociology of Social Problems, Eighth Edition. Prentice Hall Inc., Englewood Cliffs, New Jersey, (1985): p. 412.*

The bioaccumulation of toxins like the pesticides DDT and DDE and a class of industrial chemicals called PCBs has also been linked to breast cancer. One "study by Frank Falck, Jr., and colleagues in New York and Connecticut involved 40 Caucasian women who had breast lumps removed at Connecticut's Hartford Hospital from May through September 1987. Falck's group analyzed fatty tissue from the breasts of 20 women with cancerous lumps and 20 whose lumps were benign. In the breast-fat tissue of the women with cancer, Falck found significantly higher levels of DDT, DDE, and PCBs." [586]

Because of the small sampling, critics have suggested caution in drawing hard and fast conclusions from Falck's research. Falck counters that view by pointing out that the levels of chemicals found in the cancerous lumps were very high -- so high in fact that even if the researchers had "found considerably lower levels," they would have been "statistically significant" using standard statistical testing. [587]

"The National Cancer Institute agrees that Falck's data warrants concern, and is planning to begin an international investigation of toxic chemicals in breast fat and their relation to breast-cancer". [588]

Heavy metals, which come from a number of industrial sources, are another health problem concern. "Excessive exposure to toxic metals can cause health problems including kidney damage (chromium), impaired mental development (lead), and cancer (arsenic). [589] Methyl mercury attacks human nerve cells and causes numbness and loss of coordination, as well as hearing and visual problems. [590]

"Three-quarters of the 930 tons of mercury drifting in the atmosphere at any given moment is '"anthropogenic,"'or human-caused, most of it coming from the combustion of coal and trash." [591] Other sources include batteries and latex paint, which contained mercury until 1991. "Even Crematoria contribute their share, volatilizing the mercury in tooth fillings." [592]

Some Good Efforts
To Reduce the Production And Use Of Toxic Materials

Although they are still more the exception than the rule, business and industry across the board are adopting more eco-nomically sound methods of production and operation. An important result of such efforts is eliminating or minimizing the use and creation of toxic or otherwise ecologically harmful materials that could pollute the watersheds on our planet.

---

[586] Castleman, Michael. "Telltale Tissue". *Sierra*. Vol. 77, No. 6, (Nov./Dec. 1992): p. 24. (Also see discussion of increased incidences of leukemia in children related to house and garden use of pesticides in the True-Cost-Pricing section.)

[587] Ibid.

[588] Ibid.

[589] Wolverton, B. C. and Rebcca C. MacDonald. "Bioaccumulation and Detection of Trace Levels of Cadmium in Aquatic Systems by Eichhornia crassipes." *Environmental Health Perspectives*. Vol. 27, (1978): p. 161

[590] Lefferts, Lisa Y. "Something Fishy". *New Age Journal*. Vol. 6, No. 4, (July/August 1989): p. 113.

[591] Ranber, Paul. "Mercury Madness". *Sierra*. Vol. 77, No. 6, (Nov./Dec. 1992): p. 38.

[592] Ibid.

Is it possible to eliminate all toxic emissions from industry? Monsanto, a large chemical company, must believe that it is. Monsanto "has already committed itself to zero" emissions. [593] In 1991 Monsanto's CEO "Richard Mahoney committed about $100 million to reducing air pollution an average of 90% at Monsanto's plants around the world by the end of 1992." [594] A press release by Monsanto on July 19, 1993 announced that Monsanto had reached this goal by changes in company operations on many levels. Monsanto reported that these changes "will eliminate 56 million pounds per year of toxic air emissions worldwide, including 16 million pounds per year in the United States, compared with those reported by the company in 1987." [595] Du Pont has also "endorsed the concept" of zero emissions. [596]

Another example of progress in reducing the production and use of toxics in industry is 3M Company. Through its "Pollution Prevention Pays" program, 3M has been able to reduce its use and creation of toxic chemicals and increase profitability at the same time. To avoid the use and production of toxic materials, 3M Company has changed production processes and product designs. Profitability has resulted primarily from using resources more efficiently and avoiding the cost of having to manage toxic materials. As reported in 1987, "3M, which started its own Pollution Prevention Pays program in 1975, claims a 50 percent reduction in all wastes over ten years for a savings of $300 million and is still working hard at it." [597]

Since 1987 3M's Pollution Prevention Pays program continues to chalk up savings. To date, 3M's efforts have "eliminated more than 500,000 tons of waste and pollutants" for a total savings of $482 million. 3M has saved another $650 million through more efficient energy use. [598]

Like Monsanto and 3M, Cleo Wrap, the world leader in the production of gift wrapping paper, is making progress in eliminating toxic materials in its operations. Since it implemented its waste reduction program, Cleo Wrap has saved $35,000 a year in waste disposal costs. In the process the Memphis, Tennessee based firm has nearly eliminated its generation of hazardous wastes by switching from solvent-based to water-based inks in its printing process. Additionally, the company has reduced its fire insurance costs because it no longer stores combustible solvents. Cleo Wrap saved even more money by eliminating its underground solvent storage tanks, thus also avoiding the high costs of complying with new federal regulations governing such tanks. [599]

---

[593] *Easterbrook, Gregg. "Everything You Know About The Environment Is Wrong."* The New Republic. *Vol. 202, No. 18, (April 30, 1990): p. 27.*

[594] *Rice, Faye. "Next Steps For The Environment".* Fortune. *(October 19, 1992): p. 99.*

[595] *Barton, Gary F. "Monsanto Reduces Emissions, Achieves 90 Percent Air Goal."* News Release. *Public Relations Department, Monsanto Co., St Louis, Mo. (July 19, 1993): p. 1.*

[596] *Easterbrook, Gregg. "Everything You Know About The Environment Is Wrong."* The New Republic. *Vol. 202, No. 18, (April 30, 1990): p. 27.*

[597] *Oldenburg, Kristen U. and Joel S. Hirschorn. "Waste Reduction".* Environment. *Vol. 29, No. 2, (March 1987): p. 43., Also see Huising, Donald and Vicki. Editors,* Making Pollution Prevention Pay. *Pergamon Press, New York, New York, (1982): p. 12., and Royston, Michael G. "Thinking Ahead: Making Pollution Prevention Pay".* Harvard Business Review. *(Nov./Dec. 1980).*

[598] *Romm, Joseph J.* The Once and Future Superpower. *William Morrow and Company, (1992): p. 171.*

[599] *Oldenburg, Kristen U. and Joel S. Hirschorn. "Waste Reduction".* Environment. *Vol. 29, No. 2, (March 1987): p. 16.*

The Borden Chemical Company in Fremont, California is another example. Borden Chemical has reduced pollution by changing how it cleans its filters and tanks. Borden has also changed how urea and phenol resins are pumped from tanks and how materials are transferred from tank cars to storage tanks. With these improvements the company has been able to reduce the organics in its wastewater by 93% since 1981. These changes have also saved Borden the expense of maintaining an on-site wastewater treatment facility. [600]

Although it may not be true in every case, it appears that even without true-cost-pricing most firms benefit economically when they implement waste reduction programs. An EPA study found 93% of the companies that invested in waste reduction strategies had a payback on their investment of less than four years. For over half the firms the payback was less than one year. [601] These paybacks do not include the potential savings of pollution control for society. Just in the area of health, "one estimate puts medical bills avoided by pollution control at $40 billion per year." [602]

In spite of obvious advantages of toxic materials reduction, toxic waste management has attracted the lion's share of financial support from federal and state governments. Unlike reduction which eliminates hazardous wastes altogether, waste management only moves the problem around or causes new problems when toxic materials are incinerated. Nevertheless, "of the $16 billion spent each year by local, state, and federal governments, only $4 million was spent on waste reduction in 1986. Or as a report by the U.S. Office of Technology Assessment put it, pollution control measures "receive more than 4,000 times the amount of state and federal funding as do efforts directed at waste reduction." [603] The rest was allocated to programs designed to control and manage the waste once it was produced." [604]

In addition to implementing true-cost-pricing, reducing the use and creation of toxic materials at their source could be greatly accelerated if government policies were modified to encourage toxic waste reducti on instead of just its management. [605]

The Economic Impact Of Environmental Protection

Some people have argued that environmental protection hurts the economy, even though the examples just cited contradict this notion. This is not to say that all environmental regulations make sense from the perspective of eco-nomic security. But even with less than perfect rules, environmental protection seems to make economic sense. "Indeed, some of the leaders in global economic competition, such as Japan and Germany, have some of the most restrictive environmental

---

[600] *Ibid.*

[601] *Ibid.*

[602] *Easterbrook, Gregg. "Cleaning Up". Newsweek. Vol. CXIV. No. 4, (July 24, 1989): p. 33.*

[603] *Belliveau, Michael. "Pollution Prevention -- An Idea Whose Time Has Come". CBE Environmental Review. (Summer 1987): p. 6.*

[604] *Hirschhorn, Joel S. and Kirsten U. Olderburg. "From Facility Citing To Waste Reduction". Forum For Applied Research And Public Policy. Vol. 2, No. 3, (Fall 1987): p. 98.*

[605] *Ibid. p. 7.*

rules." [606]

In Germany, stricter environmental regulations have had the added bonus of catapulting Germany into the global lead in the patenting and exportation of air-pollution control equipment and other environmental technologies. "In contrast, about 70 percent of the air-pollution control equipment sold in the United States is produced by foreign companies." [607]

Efficiency and Renewable Energy:
Developing A Watershed Friendly Energy Plan

The pollution of watersheds can be greatly reduced by becoming more energy efficient and switching to renewable energy resources. The conventional energy sector of our economy (fossil fuels and nuclear power) is a substantial watershed polluter. Pollution from fossil fuels includes:

1.   Acid deposition, (ie. acid rain, fog, dew, snow, and dry deposition).

2.   Volatile hydrocarbons and ozone (ozone, though not a direct fossil fuel pollutant, results when the energy of sunlight causes an ozone producing reaction between gaseous hydrocarbons and atmospheric oxygen.) Low atmosphere ozone and acid deposition as separate agents and in combination, "are the main contributors to forest death along the East and West Coasts and to about $5 billion in crop losses in the Midwest". [608]

3.   Smokestack particulates (i.e., soot, ash, heavy metals, etc.), acids and heavy metals that leach from coal mines and coal mine tailings, and drilling mud and other residues associated with drilling for oil and natural gas and oil spills themselves.

The petroleum industry alone accounts for 3 percent of the hazardous solid wastes generated in the U.S. each year. [609]

Pollution related to the nuclear power industry includes wind and water borne radioactive residues that result from uranium mining, ore milling, and the improper handling of uranium mine tailings, the release of radioactive materials during fuel processing, and from power plant operation and waste storage. [610]

The most important aspect of a watershed friendly energy policy is efficient energy use. If energy is used efficiently, less energy related pollution is created. Using energy more efficiently does not mean having less energy services such as having a warm, well lighted home and working environment. It means providing these services in ways that use energy more intelligently. For example, a well insulated, weatherized home equipped with day-lighting features and state-of-the-art

---

[606]   Flavin, Christopher and John E. Young. "Will Clinton Give Industry A Green Edge", *World Watch*. Vol. 6, No. 1, (Jan./Feb. 1993): pp. 27-28. Also see Romm, Joseph J.. *The Once and Future Superpower*. William Morrow and Company, (1992): p. 172.

[607]   Romm, Joseph J.. *The Once and Future Superpower*. William Morrow and Company, (1992): p. 173.

[608]   Pearlman, Nancy, Ed. "Air Pollution and Trees". *The Compendium Newsletter*. Vol. 17, No. 2, (March-April 1989): p. 9.

[609]   Sarokin, David J., et al. "Cutting Chemical Wastes". *An INFORM Report*. INFORM, Inc., New York, New York, (1985): p. 20.

[610]   Gyorgy, Anna. *No Nukes*. South End Press, Boston, Mass. (1979): pp. 100 - 103.

electric lighting can provide all the comforts we desire while using a fraction of the energy used by the typical energy wasteful house.

After energy efficiency, switching to more ecologically benign renewable energy resources is the next most important step we can take to protect watersheds from energy related pollution. Other than constructing and maintaining the equipment for capturing it, the use of solar energy does not cause pollution or waste products. If solar collectors are designed properly, even the impact of building and maintaining such equipment can be almost eliminated.

Watershed Restoration

The restoration of watersheds that have already been damaged is another important aspect of increasing water security. Watershed restoration is a relatively new science and much research in this area is still needed. Nevertheless, some success in re-establishing ecologically stable watershed systems has been achieved. [611]

Watersheds are made up of complex relationships between plants and animals and their restoration requires much more than just planting trees and ground covers. Restoration requires a deep understanding of how specific biological communities evolve and how different species of plants and animals colonize a particular environment.

For example, after a fire, seeds from pioneering plants are carried by wind, water and animals from locations not affected by the fire to the burnt-over area. The seeds of some plants, like the Jack Pine, actually depend on fires to complete their reproductive cycle. Their cones will not open to release their seeds unless they are heated by fire. [612] As these pioneering plants grow they provide shade which is conducive to the development of under-story plants as well as providing cover and habitat for forest animals.

As with nature, human assisted restoration requires strategies that recognize the complex relationships between plant and animal communities and the environment they inhabit. Such strategies largely consist of letting nature be the guide while looking for opportunities to enhance the natural processes involved.

One strategy that has been used successfully in the Feliz Creek area in Oregon has simply been to increase the survivability of seedlings that sprout naturally by installing curtain fencing around them to keep browsers like deer from destroying the young trees. [613] Once these trees are tall enough to escape damage, the curtain fencing is removed. This approach can be enhanced further by replacing soil nutrients lost to erosion and by planting pioneer community plants to aid the natural reseeding process.

Strategies to correct other types of watershed damage are also being developed. A firm in Montana has developed a vacuuming technique that sucks up the eroded material which covers the pebbled spawning beds that are essential for the reproduction of many species of fish. To complete the process the recovered silt and other debris must be returned to the newly forested areas where

---

[611] Berger, John J., Editor. *Environmental Restoration*. Island Press, Covelo, California, (1990): p. 123.

[612] Clark, Mary. *Contemporary Biology*. W. B. Saunders Company, Philadelphia, London, Toronto, (1979): p. 496.

[613] Berger, John J., Editor. *Environmental Restoration*. Island Press, Covelo, California, (1990): p. 123.

it originated. This vacuuming technique can also be used to remove toxic mining sediments from stream beds. Obviously, such contaminated materials should not be spread on the land. One possible solution would be to seal it up inside played-out mines.

Re-establishing The Beaver

Another watershed enhancement strategy is to reintroduce beaver into damaged forest areas where forests have not been clear-cut or as newly restored forests are maturing. Beaver dams prevent erosion by checking the flow of spring runoff. This checking process also aids groundwater recharge by allowing more time for water to be absorbed into aquifers.

Beaver ponds also form the foundation of a cyclical process that supports a rich variety of plant and animal communities. New beaver ponds provide homes for "otters, muskrat, mink, ducks, fish, turtles, frogs, wading birds -- and continue to do so for as long as it is surrounded by a substantial number of the beaver's preferred food trees. When these are used up, the (beaver) colony moves on, its forsaken dams break, and the pond drains." [614]

"The rich mucky bottoms of what once were beaver waterworks give rise to an entirely different type of vegetation. Meadow plants take root and grow and these support a new array of animals, deer and voles and rabbits, which in turn, become the food base for land predators, foxes, bobcats, coyotes, weasels, hawks." [615]

With the passage of time the meadow "is colonized by trees, the first to pioneer being willow, birch, and aspen -- species the beaver relish. As the forest matures, beavers once again return and turn the place into a pond. First they dam what water trickles through the wooded tract, thus drowning a certain number of trees." [616]

These trees, in turn, serve yet another succession of creatures. "Woodpeckers, owls, kingbirds, and flying squirrels find nesting sites in their decaying trunks. Nuthatches, chickadees, and brown creepers feed on the insect life that proliferates in the rotting wood. Great blue herons construct huge nests on the forked tops of these forest relics. The big gangling birds, whose eight-foot wingspans prohibit flight through dense canopies, now enjoy plenty of clearance to take off and land on the towering eries (nests) they construct. And at the base of these huge nests, crayfish and other aquatic creatures breed in the rising water, providing the herons plenty of food for their chicks." [617] Finally, "the drowned trees become so weakened by decay that they topple into the water," where continued decay releases nutrients that settle "on the pond bottom, enriching it for that future day when the site will once again explode with meadow plants." [618]

The complexity of watershed communities and the difficulties and costs involved in restoring them once they are damaged, underlines the importance of protecting existing watersheds from damage in the first place.

---

[614] Ryden, Hope. _Lily Pond: Four Years With a Family of Beavers_. *Harper Collins, New York, New York, (1990): p. 22.*

[615] *Ibid.*

[616] *Ibid.* pp. 22-23.

[617] *Ibid.* p. 23.

[618] *Ibid.*

Groundwater Management

Groundwater is becoming an increasingly important aspect in maintaining and enhancing water security. The two principal considerations in groundwater management are to keep water extraction rates below the rate of natural recharge and to prohibit the release of toxic materials in watersheds. If toxic materials are released in a watershed they can easily percolate into groundwater deposits. In addition to not exceeding natural recharge rates, groundwater use rates should be reduced to less than 80% of the aquifer's natural recharge rate, where groundwater has been depleted, until historic groundwater levels have been restored. In some cases groundwater deposits can be overdrawn without causing problems like the collapse of water holding deposits or salt water intrusion but these are particular situations that should not be taken as a general rule.[619] The potential to artificially recharge groundwater storage basins with recycled sewage water is another option.

Protecting Groundwater From Pollution

One of the most important aspects of protecting groundwater from pollution is restricting the use of toxic chemicals in any area where their use could result in the contamination of groundwater supplies. Pollutants in groundwater disperse very slowly. The flow rates of aquifers may "vary from five feet per day in rainy areas to five feet per year in deserts." [620] Most aquifers do eventually empty into an ocean but this process can take from tens to thousands of years and ocean pollution is certainly not desirable. Land locked aquifers have no way to clean themselves if they are polluted.

Even more or less non-toxic materials can cause serious groundwater problems. Chemical fertilizers and organic pollutants like feed lot runoff are two examples. Chemical fertilizers are highly water soluble. They can easily become groundwater contaminants as the water they are dissolved in percolates into groundwater supplies. One effect of this kind of contamination is nitrite poisoning which occurs when infants drink "well water contaminated with the nitrate ion (NO_3-) from artificial fertilizers." [621]

Adult digestive systems can metabolize NO_3- safely, but "the digestive tracts of young children contain bacteria capable of converting NO_3- to NO_2". [622] When NO_2 is absorbed into the blood it chemically binds up hemoglobin (red blood cells). With less hemoglobin available to absorb oxygen when red blood cells pass through their lungs, children become anemic. This affliction, which is called methemoglobinemia, or the blue baby syndrome, can reduce an infant's resistance to disease and cause retardation and death in extreme cases. [623] Studies have also "suggested that elevated nitrate concentrations in drinking water may be associated with other health problems

---

[619] *State of California, Department of Water Resources. California's Groundwater. Bulletin No. 118, State of California, Department of Water Resources, (September 1975): pp. 86-93.*

[620] *Clark, Mary E. Ariadne's Thread. St. Martin's Press, New York, (1989): p. 106.*

[621] *Clark, Mary E. Contemporary Biology. W. B. Saunders Company, Philadelphia, London, Toronto, (1979) pp. 223-224.*

[622] *Ibid.*

[623] *Ibid. Also see O'Brian, Mary. "Big Spring Iowa Studies: A Groundwater Warning," The Journal of Pesticide Reform. Vol. 7, No. 3, (Fall 1987): p. 11.*

ranging from hypertension in children to gastric cancer in adults and fetal malformations." [624]

Organic pollutants like the runoff from feed lots present a special problem in aquifers. Unlike surface waters, the absorption of oxygen by groundwater is at best minimal. Without oxygen to support the growth of decomposing bacteria it can take hundreds or even thousands of years for organic pollutants in groundwater to decompose.

Another important aspect of groundwater management is the protection of groundwater recharge areas. In general groundwater recharge takes place where surface materials are porous such as in river valleys. Sand and gravel, carved out by swift running tributaries, settle out when rivers slow down in flat valley areas. This settling out process forms alluvial deposits which absorb and store rainwater that would have otherwise drained into the oceans. The voids between the individual pieces of sand and gravel in an alluvial deposit provide both openings for absorbing water and space for storage.

To protect these deposits, activities that decrease groundwater recharge rates or ground water storage capacity should be carefully controlled. This would include restricting gravel and sand mining in ground water storage basins. Mining alluvial deposits reduces the storage capacity of ground water storage basins. Restrictions should also limit development on ground water recharge areas. Buildings and their associated parking lots and roads speed runoff and block water from being absorbed into groundwater systems. Agriculture on alluvial deposits should be designed to maximize watershed function. (See index for more entries.)

A third groundwater issue is keeping the groundwater use rate well within its recharge rate. If groundwater is extracted faster than it is naturally recharged, the void or drop in the fresh water table can cause salt water intrusion. Salt water intrusion general occurs near the ocean but groundwater can be contaminated by brackish prehistoric water if such waters underlie or lie close to the alluvial deposit from which water is being extracted. [625]

A related issue to groundwater depletion is land subsidence. In the San Joaquin Valley in California, the depletion of groundwater supplies has caused the ground to sink "nearly thirty feet in some places." [626] Land subsidence can be damaging to roads, irrigation canals, wells, buildings, etc. [627] Land subsidence can be particularly damaging to water treatment facilities which are particularly "sensitive to changes in elevation. [628]

Improving Water Infrastructure Security

Implementing more eco-nomically secure water collection, storage, and delivery infrastructures is another way to increase water security. Currently, most water infrastructures are very vulnerable. This vulnerability exists on two fronts: vulnerability to natural phenomenon like earthquakes and vulnerability to human threats like sabotage. This is particularly true of water

---

[624] O'Brian, Mary. "Big Spring Iowa Studies: A Groundwater Warning," *The Journal of Pesticide Reform*. Vol. 7, No. 3, (Fall 1987): p. 11.

[625] *California's Ground Water*. Bulletin No. 118, State of California Department Of Water Resources, (September 1975): pp. 115-117.

[626] Clark, Mary E. *Ariadne's Thread*. St. Martin's Press, New York, (1989): p. 107.

[627] Ibid.

[628] *California's Ground Water*. Bulletin No. 118, State of California Department Of Water Resources, (September 1975): p. 118.

infrastructures that are dependent on aqueduct systems that deliver water from distant sources. Though the weaknesses inherent in any specific water infrastructure may vary, they primarily fall into the following categories.

Dams

Dams, used to collect and store rainwater and snow melt runoff, are vulnerable to earthquakes and sabotage. A "study at the University of California at Los Angeles revealed that the failure of certain dams in the U.S. could cause tens of thousands of deaths and one of them could cause between 125,000 and 200,000 fatalities." [629]

Compounding this problem is the fact that large dams can cause earthquakes themselves. This is because the weight of the water they contain puts pressure on the geological formations which lie under the storage area.

Even if dams were failure-proof, their useful lives are limited because they eventually fill up with silt. Where the watershed that drains into a reservoir has been severely impacted by deforestation, animal grazing, and watershed damaging agricultural practices, this process can be very rapid.

"The Tehri Dam in India, the sixth-highest in the world, recently saw its projected useful life reduced from one hundred to thirty years due to horrific deforestation in the Himalaya foothills. In the Dominican Republic, the eighty-thousand-kilowatt Tavera Hydroelectric Project, the country's largest, was completed in 1973; by 1984, silt behind the dam had reached a depth of eighteen meters and storage capacity (of the dam) had been reduced by 40 percent." [630] A more extreme example is the Sanmexia Reservoir in China. Commissioned in 1960 the Sanmexia Reservoir was completely silted up by 1964. [631]

In the U.S., siltation, caused by ill-conceived forestry, grazing, agricultural, and development practices, is also a mounting problem. For example, "in thirty-five years, Lake Mead was filled with more acre-feet of silt than 98 percent of the reservoirs in the United States are filled with acre-feet of water." [632]

Since 1963 the rate of siltation in Lake Mead has decreased but the reduction of reservoir capacity on the Colorado River has if anything speeded up. The silt that was formerly filling up Lake Mead "is now building up behind the Flaming Gorge, Blue Mesa, and Glen Canyon dams," which are upstream of Lake Mead. [633]

Depending on watershed conditions and whether a dam is protected from silt by upstream reservoirs, the rate of siltation can vary widely. During the ten year period from 1963 to 1973 the Black Butte Receiver in California lost 8.2 percent of its capacity. [634] In a 28 year period the Alamagordo Reservoir, on the Pacos River, lost 30 percent of its capacity, over one percent of its

---

[629] Beckmann, Petr. *The Health Hazards of Not Going Nuclear*. The Golem Press, Boulder Colorado, (1976): p. 95.

[630] Reisner, Marc. *Cadillac Desert*. Penguin Books, New York, New York, (1987): p. 490.

[631] Ibid.

[632] Ibid.

[633] Ibid.

[634] Ibid. pp. 491-492. *Calculations based on the numbers provided on these pages.*

capacity each year. [635] The loss of capacity in Lake Waco on the Brazos river in Texas over a thirty-four year period was 61 percent or almost 2 percent per year. [636]

Strategies For Reducing The Problem Of Siltation

The problem of siltation can be greatly reduced if watershed friendly methods of forestry, agriculture, and development replace their watershed damaging counterparts. It is much less expensive to protect a watershed's function in the first place and very expensive to repair it once damaged. A deforested watershed in Costa Rica "has greatly shortened the life of an expensive hydroelectric dam" and to save the capacity that is left the government is considering reforestation. [637] According to the Costa Rican Minister of Industry, Energy, and Mines, the watershed that serves the dam "might have been protected 20 years ago for a cost of $5 million. Now the government must reforest the watershed at ten times that price." [638]

Even under the best conditions dams will eventually silt up. [639] As Raphael Kazmann, one of the most respected hydrologists in the world, puts it, "dams are wasting assets. When they silt up, that's it." When asked about the possibility of removing silt from them, he replied, "Sure, but where are you going to put it? It will wash right back in unless you truck it out to sea. The cost of removing it is so prohibitive anyway that I can't imagine it being done. Do you understand how many coal trains it would take to haul away the Colorado River's annual production of silt? How would you get it out of the canyons? You can design dams to flush out the silts nearest to the dam, but all you get rid of is a narrow profile. You create a little short canyon in a vast plateau of mud. Most of the stuff stays no matter what you do." [640]

In a attempt to lengthen the useful life of some of its small retention reservoirs, Los Angeles California spent $29.1 million dollars to remove 23.7 million cubic yards of mud that had accumulated in them. At this rate of $1.23 per cubic yard, "it would cost more than a billion and a half dollars, in modern money, to remove the silt that has accumulated in Lake Mead, over thirty years -- if one could find a place to put it." [641]

The True-Cost Of Hydropower

Potential dam failure, siltation, flooding of agricultural soils and wildlife habitats, and the dislocation of people are just some of the costs that should be included in a true-cost-pricing analysis to determine whether a dam should be built or not.

This is the opinion of Bill Robertson, an engineer and a member of the Global Environment and Technology Foundation and the Army Corps. According to Robertson, "A dam may be built with a design life of 100 years," but its "life-cycle consequences could go on for 300 or 400 years. So in the process of thinking through whether we want a dam, there needs to be that kind of reflection on life-cycle consequences. And the bigger the project, the greater the consequences and the

---

[635] *Ibid.*

[636] *Ibid.*

[637] Linden, Eugene. *"The Death of Birth"*. Time. *Vol. 133, No. 1, (Jan. 2, 1989): p. 34.*

[638] *Ibid.*

[639] Reisner, Marc. *Cadillac Desert*. *Penguin Books, New York, New York, (1987): p. 490.*

[640] *Ibid. p. 492.*

[641] *Ibid. p. 493.*

greater the thought." [642]

   The Aswan High Dam in Egypt is a classic example of how the lack of attention to a broad lifecycle analysis can lead to costly problems. The Aswan High Dam was built to store water for irrigation, to control flooding, and to provide hydroelectric power. Although the project achieved these goals to some extent, its construction caused a myriad of other problems, which had all been predicted by an eminent Egyptian hydrologist prior to the dam's construction. [643]

   As predicted, the dam failed to provide the quantity of irrigation water predicted. Some of the water was lost because of excessive seepage. More was lost because the large open water lake created by the dam facilitated wind flows that accelerate evaporation. [644]

   Added to this, silt, which had historically been deposited in the lower Nile Valley during flooding, is now trapped behind the dam. Nile Valley farmers now have to buy expensive imported fertilizers which are inferior to the silt that has been cut off. [645]

   Below the dam, the now silt-free river has proven to be more erosive than in the past and it is under cutting river banks, bridge abutments, and dikes more rapidly than before the dam was built. [646]

   The dam is also keeping nutrient-rich silt laden water from flowing into the Eastern Mediterranean Sea. This has reduced the production of marine life. Since the dam was built the sardine catch "has dropped by 18,000 tons a year." [647]

   The lack of spring floods has also led to a 20 percent increase in the parasitic disease bilharzia (schistosomiasis). One stage in the life cycle of the bilharzia parasite takes place in the body of an aquatic snail. Historically, spring floods washed a large number of these snails out to sea, interrupting the parasites life cycle and reducing the number of snail hosts. [648]

   Even using the water impounded by the dam for irrigation has caused problems. When water from the dam's reservoir is used to irrigate hot arid land, it evaporates quickly. The minerals left behind cause soil salinity to increase rapidly. Drainage systems to control this problem can be installed but will ultimately cost as much as the original dam. [649]

   Given that desilting is cost-prohibitive and that new dam sites are scarce, a more water efficient future is vital to our water security. Likewise, energy efficiency and a switch over to more permanent renewable energy resources is also in order. As silt builds up in our nation's and the world's reservoirs, their capacity to store water and produce hydro-electric power will also be reduced

---

[642] *Cherrington, Mark. "Engineers Salvage the Future". Earthwatch. Vol. XII, No. IV, (May/June 1993): pp. 16-17.*

[643] *Horton, Paul B. et al. The Sociology of Social Problems, Eighth Edition. Prentice-Hall, Inc. Englewood Cliffs, New Jersey, (1985): p. 417.*

[644] *Ibid.*

[645] *Ibid.*

[646] *Ibid.*

[647] *Ibid.*

[648] *Ibid.*

[649] *Ibid.*

and eventually eliminated altogether.

Water Storage Problems

In addition to the problems previously discussed, water stored in open reservoirs is subject to evaporation. As much as 100 percent of the water stored in reservoirs less than 10 feet deep in arid areas can be lost to evaporation. [650] These evaporation losses also reduce the quality of the water that does not evaporate because the minerals left behind in storage become more concentrated.

Beyond natural phenomena like earthquakes, siltation, and evaporation, dams are vulnerable to sabotage. Water stored behind dams can be easily contaminated, either directly or by contaminating rivers or streams that feed into them. The recent accidental herbicide spill into the Sacramento River in California is tragic testimony to how easily such contaminations can take place. Characterized as a "Biological Hiroshima" [651], the spill contaminated 45 miles of the upper Sacramento River and the water stored behind the Shasta Dam. [652]

Dams are also vulnerable to sabotage with explosives. Using explosives to destroy dams is a relatively easy way to cause hardship to a society during periods of conflict. Not only does it eliminate a water supply, it is a weapon that destroys anything downstream of the rushing water that a failed dam releases. If the terrorists who exploded a bomb in the World Trade Center had used the bomb to destroy a major dam instead, one can only imagine the loss of life and property damage that would have occurred.

Aqueducts are even more vulnerable than dams to earthquakes and sabotage. Aqueduct delivery systems consist of open water channels, pipe lines, pumping stations, and in-transit reservoir storage. Aqueducts are especially vulnerable because they often cross or lie in close proximity to earthquake faults and other hazards. They can also be damaged by sabotage at almost any place along their route. Since many aqueduct systems require substantial amounts of electrical power to pump water over obstacles like mountain passes, water delivery can be interrupted by knocking out power plants or transmission lines that are distant from the pumping stations they supply. Even without dramatic events like earthquakes and sabotage, aqueduct systems can fail. Aqueduct failures have been caused by flash floods, rock slides, and pipe failures.

Improving The Eco-nomic Security Of Water Infrastructures

Improving the security of our water infrastructures needs to be addressed on two levels. First, water security can be improved by reducing the dependency of urban and agricultural areas on imported water. Second, make better use of local water resources. In both cases, this can be accomplished by using water more efficiently and through the protection and sustainable management of local watersheds and groundwater storage areas.

Using water efficiently helps reduce the need to import water by getting more work out of

---

[650] *Author's calculations based on data from - State of California, Department of Water Resources. Evaporation From Water Surfaces In California. Bulletin No. 73-1, State of California, (May 1974).*

[651] *Mott, Lawrie and Reisner, Marc. "Biological Hiroshima on the River", Los Angeles Times. The Times Mirror Company, (July 18, 1991): p. B-9.*

[652] *Warren, Jenifer. "Sacramento River Spill Killed Aquatic Ecosystem". Los Angeles Times. Times Mirror Company, (July 28, 1991): p. A-20.*

local water resources. Efficient water use helps to extend the life of local water supplies if imported water supplies are interrupted by infrastructural failures or during periods of drought.

Protecting watersheds and groundwater storage basins allows a region to make the most of any local precipitation by increasing the amount of water available for collection and storage. Even though watersheds and groundwater storage areas are not part of the human constructed infrastructure their protection and sustainable management is vital to minimizing an area's dependence on imported water. **(See Section on Watershed Function.)**

Sustainably managed watersheds and groundwater storage areas are also vital to the longevity and effectiveness of human created infrastructure which extracts water from them. A healthy watershed can greatly extend the useful life of reservoirs by reducing the rate of siltation.

On a second level, water security can be increased by reducing the vulnerability of water infrastructures to natural and human created hazards. High on this list is protecting watersheds from pollution. Though it cannot eliminate intentional contamination, protecting watersheds from agricultural and industrial pollution helps to keep the water collected from a watershed from being contaminated by pesticides, mine wastes, and other pollutants related to human activities. **(See index - watershed pollution from Industry and Agriculture for Details.)**

Another way to reduce water infrastructure vulnerability is to replace open reservoir storage with underground tanks. The technology for the construction of such tanks is already well established. Though such a tank system would be applicable for most water infrastructure storage requirements, it would be most relevant in urban settings. Since the typical urban environment is made up of numerous smaller community units one or more tanks would be located in each of these communities.

The number of tanks, their capacities, and their locations would depend on a community's geology, topography, population and population distribution. Since tank covers are supported structurally by columns, the areas over them can be used as parks for picnicking and for recreational activities like tennis, basketball, baseball, and soccer.

Covered underground tank storage has numerous advantages over open reservoir storage. Covered underground tanks are less vulnerable to earthquakes than are dams. Large impoundment dams are very tall, some over 300 feet, and must be able to totally support the water stored behind them. [653] Tank walls are shorter, usually less than 50 feet.

The cylindrical shape of tanks also makes them very strong. Additionally, the walls of underground tanks get extra support from the earth that is packed in around them after they are completed. Because they hold smaller quantities of water, storage tanks put less pressure on the geologic formations which underlie them than do large dams. Thus underground tanks are less likely to cause earthquakes than are large reservoirs.

A second consideration is the destruction that occurs if a dam fails. Unless a dam is remote, its failure usually results in a substantial loss of property and life, caused by the rapid release of a large quantity of water. [654] If an underground tank fails, the water in storage would be contained by the surrounding earth. At worst, the released water would slowly seep away. This would give

---

[653] Mermel, T. W. *Register of Dams In The United States.* McGraw Hill Book Company Inc., New York, London, Toronto, (1958): P. 10.

[654] Beckmann, Petr. *The Health Hazards of Not Going Nuclear.* The Golem Press, Boulder Colorado, (1976): p. 95.

plenty of time to pump the escaping water to another storage facility or to dissipate it safely.

Unlike dams which must be built in waterways, covered underground storage tanks can be built away from such hazards. They also do not require the flooding of large areas of wildlife habitat, agricultural soils, and human communities to do their jobs.

Ideally, underground tanks should be constructed in the communities where the water they store will be used. Reservoirs formed by dams are often considerable distances from population centers they serve. Even if a dam survives a severe earthquake, it is quite likely that the piping system from the dam to where the water is needed would fail.

An earthquake damaged delivery system is less of a threat to water security if water is stored in community based underground tanks. Even if piping systems are severely damaged, water can still be pumped out of storage tanks and distributed through temporary pipes and fire hoses until normal delivery systems were repaired. Since fires often accompany earthquakes, community-based water storage would also aid in their control. An added bonus of having community-based tanks could be a reduction in fire insurance premiums.

An urban network of underground tanks would be less vulnerable to sabotage than the typical open storage system. If a tank or even several tanks were damaged or contaminated, the impact on water security would be less than if a single large reservoir was contaminated or if its containment dam failed. It would require many tanks to store the same quantity of water as is stored in one large open reservoir. Thus it would require the contamination or failure of many tanks to reduce water security to the degree that the failure or contamination of one large reservoir would cause. Their number, distribution, and the fact that they would be covered also reduces the potential for large scale water supply contamination, either intentionally or accidentally.

Covered storage tanks would also protect water from evaporation. In dry windy areas 10 feet or more water can evaporate from the open surface of reservoirs each year.[655]

To fill tanks, water would be extracted from groundwater reservoirs or taken from streams and rivers. In some cases this would require the construction of small reservoirs along stream or river channels. Unlike the typical reservoir of today, which completely blocks the flow of a water way, these reservoirs would be designed to divert a part of the water flow into pumping reservoirs. These reservoirs would be sited at valley perimeters out of floodplains. As the water rose in these reservoirs, float activated pumps would deliver water to the appropriate storage tanks.

If properly designed, a covered underground storage tank can actually collect water even when precipitation is absent. Since the earth below ground level is relatively cool (usually around 55 degrees Fahrenheit in temperate climates), underground tanks and the water they contain will also remain close to that temperature. During periods of high humidity, warm humid air can be drawn into cool tank environments. As the humid air cools, some of the water it contains will condense and thereby increase the amount of water in storage.

While the quantity of water that can be collected in this way is not large, if combined with the water not lost to evaporation, the net gain is substantial. The addition of condensed water to storage would also improve water quality. Water condensed out of the air contains no minerals and thus, would improve the quality of the water in storage by diluting its mineral concentration.

---

[655]   *State of California, Department of Water Resources. <u>Evaporation From Water Surfaces in California</u>. Bulletin No. 73-1, State of California, (May 1974): pp. 26-169.*

Quick Fixes Verses ·A Whole System Approach

When most people think about issues like water security, they tend to focus on quick fix solutions -- "Let's dam another river, extend aqueducts, desalinate sea water, or tow icebergs to areas that need water!" [656] Unfortunately, as some of the preceding discussion has revealed, quick fixes or <u>any</u> fix that is not consistent with ecological principles will ultimately cause more problems than the one it was designed to solve. To achieve permanent water security, we must take a whole system approach, aimed at meeting our needs in the present in ways that do not undercut the possibility of meeting those needs in the future.

---

[656] *Author's quote.*

Chapter X

ECO-NOMIC SECURITY AND AGRICULTURE

Synopsis

Preserving and replenishing agricultural soils is essential to our eco-nomic security. Worldwide, agricultural soils are being lost to development and erosion. It is therefore imperative that we do everything we can to prohibit the further development of agricultural soils and adopt agricultural methods that build soil fertility instead of causing it to erode away.

Beyond protecting our soils from development and erosion, we need to develop agricultural methods that are eco-nomically sustainable. Fortunately, a number of agricultural systems are approaching eco-nomic sustainablity and their applications are growing in sophistication rapidly. In their book, <u>Alternative Agriculture</u>, the (U.S.) National Academy of Science highlighted a number of economically successful farms in the United States that practice organic/soil-building methods of agriculture. One 280 hector (700 acres) organic farm in Ohio has operated profitably for 15 years. In addition to having higher crop yields than any other farms in its county, its cost of production per hector is 40 percent less than the areas average.

Food Security And Population

Preserving agricultural soils and switching to organic agriculture is another way to increase eco-nomic security. After a sustainable supply of breathable air and drinkable water, having a secure supply of nutritious food is the most vital element necessary for our well-being. Whether we look globally or just at the United States, our food sustainability is in question.

If distributed equitably, there is enough food being produced to feed everyone living on our planet today. [657] Yet, even at our present level of population, researchers from the World Hunger Project at Brown University question whether we can feed a world population of 5.5 billion sustainably, considering current agro-know-how and food consumption patterns. They estimate we could feed 5.5 billion people sustainability, but only if we all adopted a vegetarian diet and food was distributed equitably. [658]

At U.S. consumption levels, of which 25 percent is animal products, the number of people that could be fed sustainably drops to just 2.8 billion according to the World Hunger Project Study. [659] This is because it takes much more land, water, and energy to grow a given quantity of meat than it does to grow an equal amount of edible plant material. It takes ten pounds of grain to produce one pound of beef.

Added to our present situation is the fact that our population is still growing steadily. "Of the 13.4 billion hectares of land area in the world, only about 11% or 1.5 billion hectares (3.7 billion acres) is considered suitable for cultivation." [660] This is less than seven-tenths of an acre per

---

[657] Lappe', Francis Moore and Joseph Collins et al. <u>Food First</u>. Houghton Mifflin Company, Boston, Mass. (1977): p. 1.

[658] Myers, Norman. "The Big Squeeze". <u>EarthWatch</u>. Vol. XII, No. VII, (Nov./Dec.): p. 27.

[659] Ibid.

[660] Pimental, David, Editor. <u>World Food, Pest Losses, and the Environment</u>. Westview Press, Inc. Boulder Colorado, (1978): p. 9.

person for a world population of 5.5 billion people. If world population continues to increase at its present rate of 92 million more people per year, the nearly 8 billion person world population in the year 2020 will have less than half of an acre of quality agricultural soils per capita to grow food on. [661] This is assuming that we protect the agricultural soils we still have, something we have not done very well up to now.

Soil Erosion

In addition to population, a number of problems threaten our food security. One of the most pervasive threats to food security is the loss of agricultural soils to erosion. In parts of the midwest (U.S.), as much as an inch of topsoil is lost to erosion every 20 years. As a whole, 2.7 to 3.1 billion tons of topsoil is lost to wind and water erosion in the U.S. each year. [662]

If a loss of 3 billion tons of topsoil per year were to continue and was uniform and continuous, all the topsoil on U.S. croplands would be washed away in less than 150 years. [663] One result of topsoil loss is that it causes crop yields to drop. Starting with a topsoil depth of 12 inches, the average per acre loss in yields per inch of soil loss is 4 bushels for corn, 2 to 4 bushels for oats, 1.6 bushels for wheat, and 2.6 bushels for soybeans. [664]

To date, energy inputs, primarily from fossil fuels, have masked the negative impact that soil erosion is having on crop production. Fossil fuels have powered a "ninefold increase in fertilizer use and the near tripling of the world's irrigated cropland since mid-century". [665]

In their book World Resources 1992-93, the World Resources Institute reported that a land area "equal to China and India combined -- has become gravely degraded since World War II". In other words, "roughly 11 percent of the planet's vegetative surface has become so damaged" from "overgrazing, agriculture, deforestation, and other human uses," --- "that restoration will be costly or impossible". [666]

It should be noted that in addition to the 3.7 billion acres of good agricultural soil on our planet, there are approximately 3.7 billion additional acres of lower quality soil that could be potentially used for agriculture. [667] But, even under the best conditions, most of these soils will only be marginally productive unless large imputes of energy are applied to them, in the form of intense fertilization, pumped irrigation water, and erosion control.

[661] *State of the World 1992*. p. 3. Also see Brown, Lester, et al. "Earth Day 2030". *World Watch*. Vol.3, No. 2, (March/April 1990): p. 18.

[662] *Committee on the Role of Alternative Farming Methods in Modern Production Agriculture. Alternative Agriculture*. National Academy Press, Washington D.C., (1989): pp. 116-117.

[663] *Author's calculations based on figures taken from Sampson, R. Soil Erosion, Farmland or Wasteland - A Time to Choose*. Rodale Press, (1981): p. 111.

[664] *Jackson, Wes et al. Meeting the Expectations of the Land*. North Point Press, (1984): p. 72.

[665] *Brown, Lester and Edward C. Wolf. "Global Prospects" Not Man Apart. (April/March 1885): p. 13. Also see Borrelli, Peter. "Reinventing Agriculture", The Amicus Journal. (Spring 1984): p. 23.*

[666] *"Study Reveals Alarming Worldwide Erosion", Earth Watch, Vol. XII, No. II, (Jan./Feb. 1993): p. 6.*

[667] *Myers, Norman, Editor. Gaia: Atlas of Planet Management. Anchor Press, Doubleday and Company Inc., Garden City, New York, (1984): pp. 24 & 26.*

Erosion control on marginal soils is also difficult. Even if good management strategies are used, most soils are subject to some erosion but erosion control is a particular problem on marginal soils. In addition to being thin, these soils are often classified marginal because they are steeply sloped. A Nigerian study, which measured soil erosion, showed that it is more difficult to keep soil losses below levels that are sustainable when steeper slopes are cultivated. "Cassava planted on land of a 1 percent slope lost an average of 3 metric tons (3.3 U.S. tons) of soil per hectare (a hector is approximately 2.5 acres) each year, comfortably below the maximize accepted rate of soil loss tolerance of 12.5 tons per hector. [668]   On a 5 percent slope, however, land planted to cassava eroded at a rate of 87 tons per hectare annually--a rate at which a topsoil layer of six inches would disappear entirely within a generation. Cassava planted on a 15 percent slope led to an annual erosion rate of 221 tons per hectare, which would remove all topsoil within a decade." [669]

"Worldwide, an estimated 25 billion tons of topsoil is being lost from cropland each year, roughly the amount that covers Australia's wheat lands." [670]   Under good conditions, five tons of soil loss per acre per year or 12.5 tons per hector per year is considered the maximum soil loss that can be sustained if the plant wastes produced on the soil are returned to it. Unfortunately, this assessment is probably optimistic. Some "scientists estimate that, under agricultural management, around one inch of new topsoil will be formed every 100 to 1,000 years." [671]   At a rate of one inch per 100 years, about 1.5 tons of new topsoil would be added per acre each year. [672] If this is true, the maximum loss of topsoil that can be sustained indefinitely is 1.5 tons per acre or 3.75 tons per hector per year.

Where conditions are less than ideal, the formation of soil is much slower. In areas where moisture is limited and/or growing seasons short, it may take 10,000 years for an inch of soil to form. [673]

Along with the special care and energy inputs needed to keep marginal soils productive, the cultivation of these soils would greatly increase the destruction of the wildlife communities that now inhabit these areas and the watershed function that these wild communities serve.

In addition to losing the productivity of our soils, soil erosion causes other problems. Of the up to 4 billion tons of soil reaching U.S. streams annually, "about one billion tons reach the ocean, while the other three-fourths of the sediment remains in streams, rivers, reservoirs, and lakes." [674]

Whether in coastal estuaries or fresh water environments, silt and sediment can damage spawning beds by covering vegetation or gravel beds needed by fish for egg laying and egg incubation. Other erosion-related impacts include increased flood damage which results when silt and sediment deposits restrict the flow of water in rivers and streams. Sediment laden water also makes potable water treatment more difficult and reduces water related recreational opportunities.

---

[668] Sampson, R. *Soil Erosion, Farmland or Wasteland - A Time to Choose*. Rodale Press, (1981): p. 125.

[669] Brown, Lester R. and Edward C. Wolf. *World Watch Paper 60*. Worldwatch Institute, Washington D.C., (September 1984): p. 10.

[670] Brown, Lester R. "The Grain Drain". *The Futurist*. Vol. XXIII, No. 4, (July/August 1989): p. 15.

[671] Sampson, R. *Soil Erosion, Farmland or Wasteland - A Time to Choose*. Rodale Press, (1981): p. 124.

[672] Ibid.

[673] Ibid., page 126.

[674] Ibid., page 122.

Silt and sediment deposits cause additional damage when they bury aquatic and terrestrial plant life.

Soil particles also carry pesticide residues and nutrients. If concentrated, pesticides can kill aquatic organisms and/or accumulate in aquatic food chains. **(See index for more information on biomagnification.)** Extra nutrients in soil particles can cause excessive aquatic plant growth which can lead to oxygen depletion or eutrophication. **(See index for more information on eutrophication.)** The decomposition of organic soil particles also uses up the dissolved oxygen needed by fish. Stream borne soil can also effect water temperature. Sunlight heats up soil colored water faster than it heats clear water. Additionally, water-borne soil reduces the water depth that sunlight can penetrate. This reduces the production of the aquatic plants which form part of a waterway's food chain base. [675]

Even without including the cost of mitigating the problems just discussed, the non-agricultural production costs caused by erosion are considerable. A 1975 report by the Council for Agricultural Science and Technology (CAST) "estimated that soil erosion cost $83 million for dredging channels and harbors, $50 million for floodplain overwash and reservoir sedimentation, and $25 million for added water treatment costs and system maintenance in municipal and industrial water systems. The CAST report also estimated that, based on 1974 prices, it would cost some $1.2 billion to replace the plant nutrients lost through soil erosion that year." [676]

Beyond these expenses, soil erosion causes other significant maintenance costs. Soil erosion deposits must be periodically cleaned out of roadside ditches, gutters, and culverts. Roads, railroad tracks, fences, and even buildings can be buried by wind blown soil. Airborne dust can also aggravate respiratory ailments. [677]

The Development Of Agricultural Soils

Development is also taking its toll on agricultural soils. Urban fringe areas in the U.S. are home to some of that nation's most productive soils. These same soils also suffer from the fastest farmland-to-development conversion rates in the United States. [678] Currently in the U.S., a million or more acres of agricultural soil are converted to tract houses, shopping malls, and roads each year. [679] Put another way, "every 15 seconds another 45 people arrive on the planet; during the same 15 seconds, the planet's stock of arable land declines by one hectare (2.48 acres)." [680]

Though population is a factor in development of agricultural soils, it is only one cause. A study titled "A Strategic Plan for Land Resources Management", released by the Northeastern Illinois Planning Commission, illustrates this point quite clearly. According to the study, "between 1970 and 1990 the greater Chicagoland area's population increased by only 4 percent, while land in residential use increased by 46 percent. The region's non-farm commercial and industrial land expanded by

---

[675]   *Ibid.*

[676]   *Ibid.*, pages 122 & 123.

[677]   *Ibid.*, page 124.

[678]   Berton, Valerie. "A Landmark Election". *American Farmland. The Magazine of American Farmland Trust*, (Winter 1993): p. 10.

[679]   Clark, Mary E. *Contemporary Biology*. W. B. Saunders Company, Philadelphia, London, Toronto, (1979): p. 152.

[680]   Myers, Norman. "The Big Squeeze". *EarthWatch*. Vol. XII, No. VII, (Nov./Dec.): p. 27.

a whopping 74 percent" and most of this expansion was suburban. [681]

Dependence On Non-renewable Energy Resources

Another agricultural security problem is conventional agriculture's dependence on fossil fuels. The energy inputs used by farmers up until early in the 20th Century consisted of their own labor and the labor of animals. This energy was renewable, since it was supplied by the renewable food energy that farmers and their animals consumed. But starting around 1910, non-renewable fossil fuel energy began to be used in food production in the industrialized world.

Since 1910 the amount of non-renewable energy consumed in agriculture has grown steadily. In the contemporary U.S.food system, 8 to 20 units of fossil fuel are consumed for every unit of food energy that ends up on someone's table. [682] Almost half of this energy, close to 4 percent of all the energy used in the U.S. annually, is expended in food packaging. [683]

Energy consumed in the production of meat is even higher. Ten to 88 units of non-renewable energy are consumed for every unit of animal protein produced. [684] In total, the U.S. food system consumes approximately the same amount of energy contained in 320 gallons of gasoline to feed one person for a year. [685] Three hundred and twenty gallons of gasoline can propel a car averaging 32 MPG over 10,000 miles. [686]

About 4% (3.3 quads) of our national energy budget is consumed on the farm to grow food "while 10 to 13 percent (8.2 to 10.7 quads) is needed to put it on our plates." [687] In all, U.S. "agriculture uses more petroleum products than any other industry in the nation. [688]

With the passage of time, our dependence on fossil fuels to produce food has increased as our agricultural system has become less efficient. "Between 1950 and 1970 off farm energy use (excluding home cooking and refrigeration) increased by 85%, while total food consumption ... rose less than 40 percent." [689] An agricultural system dependent on non-renewable energy resources

---

[681] Riggle, James D. "Suburban Sprawl In The Heartland," *American Farmland*. (Summer 1992): p. 12.

[682] Jackson, Wes et al. *Meeting the Expectations of the Land*. North Point Press, San Francisco, California, (1984): p. 68. Also see *Energy Primer*. Portola Institute, Menlo Park, California, (1974): pp. 115-116. and Steinhart, John S. and Carol E. Steinhart. "Energy Use in the U.S. Food System". *Science*. Vol. 184, (April 1974): p. 311, 312.

[683] During, Alan B. "Junk Food, Food Junk". *World Watch*. Vol. 4, No. 5, (Sept./Oct. 1991): p. 7.

[684] Pimental, David. "Energy Inputs and U.S. Food Security." *Food Security in the United States*. Westview Press, Boulder, London, (1984): p. 106.

[685] Pimental, David, Editor. World Food, Pest Losses, and the Environment. Westview Press, Inc. Boulder Colorado, (1978): p. 12.

[686] Author's calculations.

[687] Gever, John, et.al.. *Beyond Oil*. A Project of Carrying Capacity, Inc., Balinger Publishing Company, Massachusetts, (1986): p. 172.

[688] Jackson, Wes et al. *Meeting the Expectations of the Land*. North Point Press, San Francisco, California, (1984): p. 73.

[689] Gever, John, et.al. *Beyond Oil*. A Project of Carrying Capacity, Inc., Balinger Publishing Company, Massachusetts, (1986): p. 172.

is clearly not sustainable.

Just the use of fossil fuels cuts into agricultural productivity. "A U.S. Environmental Protection Agency (EPA) study estimates that ground-level ozone spawned by fossil-fuel burning is reducing the U.S. corn, wheat, soybean and peanut harvests by at least 5 percent. [690] "Walter Heck, the U.S. Department of Agriculture representative on the EPA study panel, estimates that cutting ground-level ozone by half would cut (yearly) crop losses by up to $5 billion." [691] In addition to ground level ozone, acid deposition, particularly as rain, fog, and dry particulates, also causes crop damage.

Data generated by the World Watch Institute projects that, if present practices continue, there will be a 19 percent loss in the amount of cropland globally between 1984 and the year 2000. Their study also indicates that if the current rate of soil erosion continues, the per capita amount of topsoil on our planet will decline by 32 percent during that same period. [692]

Figures for the U.S. show a similar pattern. In addition to losing around 1 million acres of farmland to development each year, [693] the erosion of U.S. topsoil "exceeds tolerable levels on some 44 percent of the (U.S.) cropland." [694]

Maintaining Genetic Diversity Of Crop Plants

Another aspect of eco-nomically sustainable agriculture is the importance of preserving the gene pool of crop plants. Until recently, the genetic characteristics of plant seeds of the same species grown in different parts of the world varied considerably. If a pest or disease develops in one strain, other strains were likely to be less susceptible or not susceptible at all to the particular pest or disease. The advent of high yield grains has been a blow to plant diversity. "In India, which once had 30,000 varieties of rice, more than 75 percent of total production comes from fewer than ten varieties." [695] Wheat cultivation in the United States is in much the same situation. [696] Cultivating vast acres of a single crop variety makes a region's or country's food supply vulnerable to the development of a rapidly reproducing disease or pest that could potentially wipe out most of a year's crop. "The decreasing genetic diversity of many major U.S. crops and livestock species ... increases the potential for sudden widespread economic losses from disease." [697]

---

[690] Brown, Lester R. *"Feeding Six Billion".* <u>World-Watch</u>. *Vol. 2, No. 5, Sept./Oct. 1989): p. 34.*

[691] *Ibid.*

[692] Brown, Lester R. and Wolf, Edward C. <u>World Watch Paper 60</u>. *World Watch Institute, (1984): pp. 7-8.*

[693] Clark, Mary E. <u>Contemporary Biology</u>. *W. B. Saunders Company, Philadelphia, London, Toronto, (1979): p. 152.*

[694] Brown, Lester R. and Edward C. Wolf. <u>World Watch Paper 60</u>. *Worldwatch Institute, Washington D.C., (September 1994): p. 6.*

[695] Rhoades, Robert E. *"The World's Food Supply At Risk."* <u>National Geographic</u>. *(April 1991): p. 83.*

[696] Feldman, Moshe and Ernest R. Sears. *"The Wild Gene Resources of Wheat."* <u>Scientific American</u>. *(January 1981): p. 102.*

[697] Committee on the Role of Alternative Farming Methods in Modern Production Agriculture. <u>Alternative Agriculture</u>. *National Academy Press, Washington D.C., (1989): p. 7.*

Strategies for Creating An Eco-nomically Sustainable Agricultural System

There are many ways to reduce soil erosion related to agricultural practices. (See Index for other entries.)

Organic Agriculture

In addition to protecting soils from erosion and development, food security is dependent on adopting ecologically sustainable agricultural practices. In other words, we must adopt agricultural systems that increase soil fertility, are non-polluting or health threatening, and that are not dependent non-renewable energy resources. Fortunately, organic agricultural, regenerative agriculture, low input/sustainable agriculture (LISA), and integrated pest management (IPM) agriculture have developed some of the potential to meet these requirements.

From the perspective of ecological sustainability, organic and regenerative agriculture are more desirable methods of growing food than LISA and IPM. Organic and regenerative agriculture expressly exclude the use of petrochemical pesticides and manufactured fertilizers. IPM and LISA take advantage of organic farming strategies but may also use inputs of chemical fertilizers and pesticides. But unlike standard petrochemical strategies, IPM does not use scheduled applications of pesticides. Instead it uses pesticides only if a problem actually exists and treats only the area being attacked by pests. [698] IPM also tries to use the least toxic pesticide available to get the job done. While IPM methods introduce some pollutants into the environment, they are less polluting than more petrochemically-oriented methods of farming. [699] Nevertheless, when these inputs are used, sustainability is reduced. Because of this liability, organic and regenerative agriculture will be the focus of the following discussion. Since the aims of organic and regenerative agriculture are very close, the term organic agriculture will be used to encompass the meaning of both terms.

As currently practiced, even organic agriculture is not eco-nomically sustainable. Organic agriculture will not be completely sustainable until the machinery and materials used in cultivating, transporting, and processing food are manufactured and delivered in ways that are eco-nomically sustainable. And to be sustainable, our whole food production system will have to be powered by renewable energy resources. (**See the sections on true-cost-pricing and the potential of renewable energy resources for more details.**)

Organic agriculture is a food producing system that avoids the use of toxic pesticides and manufactured fertilizers. Instead it uses biological controls for pests, and plant and animal wastes for fertilizer. Although it was largely supplanted in recent years, various forms of organic agricultural have been practiced for some 10,000 years. [700]

If our aim is eco-nomic sustainability, organic farming methods are obviously the best way to grow food. Detractors, however, argue that this would be impractical since an across the board shift to organic farming methods would result in substantially lower crop yields and ultimately food shortages.

---

[698] Olkowski, William et al. "What is Integrated Pest Management," *The IPM Practitioner*. Vol. XIII, No. 11/12, (Nov./Dec. 1991): p. 1.

[699] *Ibid.*

[700] Leonard, Jonathan Norton and the Editors of Time-Life Books. *The First Farmers*. Time-Life Books, New York, (1979): p. 53.

Contrary to this widespread notion, organic farming has in many instances proven to be just as productive and sometimes more so than petrochemical methods. [701]   The Spray Brother's certified organic farm in Knox County, Ohio is a case in point. Rex and Glen Spray have been farming a little over 700 acres of land organically for fifteen years. In addition to having higher crop yields per acre than their county's average, their cost of production per acre is less.[702] Excluding land charges, the cost incurred by the Spray brothers to put in a crop of corn or soybeans is 20 to 30 percent less than the Ohio state average. [703] Simultaneously, Spray Brother Farm per acre corn yields "exceed the county averages by 32 percent, soybeans by 40 percent, wheat by 5 percent, and oats by 22 percent." [704]

The Carl Lee farm in Cairo, Georgia is another example. Though his farm is not totally organic Lee uses no herbicides or pesticides. In 1981 Lee "won the national Class A dry-farm corn yield title sponsored by the National Corn Growers Association." [705] The following year, he had the third highest dry-land corn yield nationally and was number one in his state.[706]

In addition to being competitive to petrochemical agriculture in yield, organic farming has also proven to be a profitable way for farmers to grow food as well. Even though organic farming tends to require more labor, this extra expense is usually less than the cost of chemical inputs organic farmers avoid. [707]

Organic agriculture also tends to do better economically when conditions like weather are less than ideal. When rainfall is low, soils rich in organic materials are good at absorbing and storing whatever water is available. [708] If chemical fertilizers are used in lieu of adding organic material to soils, the absorption and storage of water in the soil is limited. If rainfall is excessive the tunneling of soil organisms help to keep plants from dying from a lack of oxygen in their root zones.

Adding organic materials to the soil and growing cover crops also protects against soil erosion whether from wind or water. [709] These advantages keep the yields and thus profits from organic agriculture high, even when weather conditions are less than favorable.

---

[701]   *Committee on the Role of Alternative Farming Methods in Modern Production Agriculture. Alternative Agriculture. National Academy Press, Washington D.C., (1989): pp. 262, 309.*

[702]   *Ibid. pp. 255, 265.*

[703]   *Ibid., p. 264.*

[704]   *Ibid., p. 255.*

[705]   *Borrelli, Peter. "Reinventing Agriculture", The Amicus Journal. (Spring 1984), p. 30.*

[706]   *Ibid.*

[707]   *Lockeretz, William, et al. "Organic Farming in the Corn Belt," Science. Vol. 211, (Feb. 6, 1981): p. 544.*

[708]   *Schaller, Neill., Program Director, Low-Input Sustainable Agriculture Research and Education cooperative State Research Service, U.S. Dept. of Agriculture, Washington D.C., "A Look At Low-Input Sustainable Agriculture", Published remarks for Oklahoma Agricultural Policy 1989 Conference, Oklahoma City, Oklahoma, (March 28, 1989): p. 5.*

[709]   *Ibid. (Neill Schaller is the Program Director for the Low-Input Sustainable Agriculture Research and Education Program Cooperative State Research Service, U.S. Department of Agriculture, Washington D.C.).*

In short, farmers using organic, low-input, and regenerative methods "report that their costs of production are lower than those of their conventional-method neighbors. Some farmers report somewhat lower yields than their neighbors, but the yield sacrifice is frequently more than offset by cost reductions." [710]

An analysis of earlier studies appears to substantiate this observation. During periods when weather and other conditions are favorable, "yields on conventionally managed fields were generally higher than those on the organic farms". [711] When farming conditions were less favorable, "yields from organic fields came closer to or even exceeded those of the conventional fields." [712] The reduced production costs enjoyed by organic farmers are graphically illustrated by comparing the fossil fuel inputs required for organic farming versus conventional farming. Over the 5-year period, 1974 through 1978, "organic farms required about two-fifths as much fossil energy to produce one dollar's worth of crop" as conventional methods. [713]

Agricultural Eco-nomics

Organic farming's economic edge over petrochemical methods is actually larger than the figures just stated indicate. If all the eco-nomic costs, like the cleanup of pesticide and chemical fertilizers from groundwater and treating pesticide related health problems, were included in the price of petrochemically grown crops, the economic edge of organic over petrochemical would be even more striking. In a 1979 article, David Pimentel estimated that the environmental and social costs of just using pesticides totaled $840 million per year in the United States. [714] If other costs associated with conventional agriculture, like soil lost to erosion and the pollution of surface and groundwater with chemical fertilizers, were included in the accounting, organic agriculture's economic edge will be even greater. (See index for more entries.)

Added to the absence of true-cost-pricing in agriculture are the numerous government subsidies that tend to keep farmers on the petrochemical treadmill. Currently, "many federal policies discourage adoption of alternative (agricultural) practices and systems by economically penalizing those who adopt rotations, apply certain soil conservation systems, or attempt to reduce pesticide applications." [715] If these subsidies were removed, the adoption of organic agriculture would be accelerated.

Even though organic agriculture is competing against such subsidies and the lack of true-cost-pricing, organic agriculture is still holding its own in yield and profitability. This fact is even more remarkable considering that almost all the funding for agricultural research conducted over the last

---

[710] Madden, Patrick. *"Can Sustainable Agriculture Be Profitable?"* Environment. Vol. 29, No. 4,(May 1987): p. 33.

[711] Lockeretz, William, et al. *"Organic Farming in the Corn Belt,"* Science. Vol. 211, (Feb. 6, 1981): p. 543.

[712] Ibid. p. 544.

[713] Ibid.

[714] Dahlsten, Donald L. *"Pesticides in an Era of Integrated Pest Management.* Environment. Vol. 20, No. 10, December 1983, pp. 49.

[715] Committee on the Role of Alternative Farming Methods in Modern Production Agriculture. *Alternative Agriculture.* National Academy Press, Washington D.C., (1989): p. 10.

50 years has been directed at improving the yields of petrochemically-supported agriculture. [716]

In recent years, agricultural colleges have made modest shifts in the direction of increasing the effectiveness of organic farming methods. But it wasn't until 1987 that "the world's first Sustainable Agricultural chair" was "established at the University of Minnesota." [717]

In spite of the myth of petrochemical agriculture's superiority, the last 25 years has seen organic farming practitioners grow in number and improve their methods. To a great extent, this growth has been driven by the public's increasing concern over the environmental and health consequences of using toxic pesticides and other petrochemicals on the food they eat. This concern, in turn, has led to a growing demand for organic produce. Up through 1987 the organic market "was expanding at a rate four times faster than that of conventional produce," and this rate of growth appears to be continuing if not increasing. [718]

"In 1987 two separate studies estimated that 40 to 50 million dollars worth of organically grown produce was sold in California alone." [719] A 1988 article in The Progressive stated that "Organic food, once relegated to health-food stores and campus areas, has become a $3-billion-a-year-and growing mainstream market as consumer concerns about pesticides increases." [720] In recent years, the adoption of organic agricultural methods has continued to accelerate. One illustration of this continued growth is the fact that, most of the wine grapes grown in California are now grown organically. And these grapes are grown organically because it works and it is a cheaper way to grow grapes.

With increased demand for organically grown food, concern has also grown related to how "organic" a product is, if it carries an organic lable. "Oregon passed the first organic labeling law in 1973. Since then 13 other states have passed similar laws, and another dozen states have such laws pending." These laws specify the growing and handling requirements for food sold in their states that is labelled "Organically Grown". [721] In some states it also requires membership in statewide certification organization which do periodic soil and plant tissue testing to insure that any food labeled grown organically is actually grown organically.

Organic Agriculture In The Future

Compared with the research dollars that have been devoted to improving the yields of petrochemical agriculture, formal research in organic methods has been almost non-existent. It therefore follows that as research in organic agriculture expands, crop yields on organic farms will undoubtedly increase beyond present levels. Indeed, continued research in this direction holds the

---

[716] Dahlsten, Donald L. "Pesticides in an Era of Integrated Pest Management. *Environment*. Vol. 20, No. 10, December 1983, p. 51.

[717] O'Brien, Mary, Editor. "Sustainable Agriculture Gains a Toehold in Minnesota Legislature, University," *The Journal of Pesticide Reform*. Vol. 7, No. 2, (Summer 1987): p. 33.

[718] Wollan, Otis. "Organic Marketplace: Still a Long Bright Row to Hoe", *Journal of Pesticide Reform*. Vol. 9, No. 1, (Spring 1989): p. 22.

[719] Ibid.

[720] DeMarco, Susan. "A Fresh Crop of Ideas". *The Progressive*. The Progressive Inc., 409 E. Main St. Madison, Wisconsin 53703, Vol. 53, No. 1, (1989): p. 29.

[721] Popkin, Roy. "A Future for Pesticide-Free Foods?" *EPA Journal*. United States Environmental Protection Agency Office of Communications and Public Affairs, Vol. 16, No. 3, (May/June 1990), Chart on p. 33.

promise of ushering in a new era of even higher yielding organic agricultural systems that will be more productive than any past or present method of agricultural production.

As in other areas, the computer will play an important role in the design and maintenance of new food production strategies. With the computer's capacity to evaluate and organize large bodies of information comes the potential to develop symbiotic multi-species agricultural associations designed to mimic the productivity and stability of naturally occurring ecologies.

Presently, most crops, even when grown organically, are grown as monocultures, one crop grown over a large area. Monocultures provide the ideal habitat for the pest that eats a particular crop and eliminates the habitat for predators that would feed on that pest. [722]

Integrated multi-species agriculture would differ from monocultures in that they would be designed to maximize the habitats of pest predators while minimizing pest habitats. Breeding and nesting places for insect eating birds, lizards, frogs, and bats would be designed into agricultural arrangements. Tall trees would anchor windbreaks and provide nesting and roosting places for hawks and owls to control rodents.

Plants, in such systems, would also be arranged to maximize the availability of sunlight. Large trees would be spaced far enough apart so that smaller trees, bushes, and annual plants could be grown among them and still receive sufficient sunlight to prosper. Shade loving plants would be grown under the canopies of appropriate plants. Deciduous (plants that lose their leaves in winter) trees and smaller plants would be interspersed with evergreens to minimize evergreens shading each other when the winter sun was low in the sky. With this arrangement, sunlight that passed through the leafless canopies of deciduous trees and smaller plants would maximize evergreen plant growth in the winter.

The integration of trees, bushes, vines, and annuals would create a multi-story or three dimensional agricultural system. In such a system, food and other products would be produced at various levels, starting at ground level with a mix of annual plants and small perineals and ending in the tops of tall trees, depending on the plants involved. Intermediate level crop production would take place in smaller trees, bushes, or vines. Multi-level productivity would increase overall yields when compared to monocultures. The productivity of monocultures, which feature a single crop growing to a uniform height, tends to be two dimensional with all the crop maturing at, more or less, the same time. In a multi-level system, the crops of different plants would be maturing at various times throughout the growing season. In mild climate areas, one crop or another would be maturing year round.

A less sophisticated form of this kind of agriculture is already beginning to emerge. "In many tropical and subtropical regions, agroforestry (the incorporation of trees and field crops into a single farming system) is proving to be highly productive. Trees can provide food, forage, fuel, organic matter in the form of leaf drop, and, if they are nitrogen fixing, nitrogen for the crops grown in the immediate vicinity." [723]

Though integrated multi-dimensional agricultural systems would tend to keep the populations of crop damaging pests low, other control agents would undoubtedly have to be used from time to time. But just as conventional agriculture draws on a variety of toxic chemical weapons in the attempt to control pests, there are an increasing number of non-toxic pest specific remedies available

---

[722]   Horton, Paul B. et al. *The Sociology of Social Problems*, Eighth Edition. Prentice-Hall, Inc. Englewood Cliffs, New Jersey, (1985): p. 417.

[723]   Brown, Lester R. "The Grain Drain". *The Futurist*. Vol. XXIII, No. 4, (July/August 1989): p. 14.

if the need arises. Just as poisons can be sprayed at ground level or from helicopters and airplanes, predatory insects, biocides, and other non-toxic control ingredients can be distributed in similar ways.

Organic Agriculture: Current Technologies

In recent years the science of controlling pests without using toxic agents or using them only sparingly has expanded rapidly. To explore to any depth the growing literature on this subject would require a book, if not volumes, devoted to this topic alone. What is offered here is only a snapshot of the many bio-control strategies and products that are now commercially available and some of the ongoing research being conducted in this area.

The first line of defense in controlling pests organically is the maintenance of healthy soils. Healthy soil fosters the growth of healthy plants. Like us, healthy plants are resistant to diseases and to attack by pests. With organic agriculture, soil health is maintained by using methods of cultivation which minimize the loss of soil and nutrients. These methods include mulching, covercrops, alternative tillage methods, and windbreaks. (See index for additional entries.)

Additional pest control is achieved through the use of crop rotation strategies which make it harder for pests to feed and breed. [724] Growing the same crop in the same location year after year provides a continuous supply of food for the pest population that attacks that crop. Crop rotation breaks the cycle by periodically replacing a crop that pests like, with one which will not support the pest's life cycle.

Pests can also be controlled by providing habitat for their natural enemies. Such habitats can be integrated with wildlife areas and windbreaks that provide breeding and nesting areas for pest consuming birds, frogs, lizards, and snakes. While various species of frogs, toads, birds, and lizards consume insects, snakes, weasels, hawks, and owls focus on rodents. There are also many insects that eat pests directly or kill pests by laying eggs on them or in them. When these eggs hatch into larva, they grow to maturity by eating their host.

If provided with the appropriate habitat, these organisms are very helpful in controlling pests. For example, China has been inter-planting cotton with other crops to attract cotton pest predators. Although, pesticides are still used in this system, their application has been reduced to one-fifth of what would have normally been used and the income earned by the interplanted fields averaged 22 percent more than from cotton fields grown without interplanting. [725]

Though research in the area has been scant, the success record of biological control measures is impressive. "According to Dr. Ken Hagan of the University of California Berkeley's Division of Biological Control, introduction of natural enemies has brought 60 major pests under complete biological control, another 60 under substantial control, and 40 under partial control." [726] By comparison, "crop losses from insect damage have increased from 7% in the 1940's to 13% at present despite a ten-fold increase in insecticide use." [727]

---

[724] *Committee on the Role of Alternative Farming Methods In Modern Production Agriculture. Alternative Agriculture. National Academy Press. Washington D.C., (1989): p. 259-260, 263.*

[725] *Darr, Sheila et al. Editors. "Intercrops that Encourage Beneficial Insects in Cotton,", The IPM Practitioner. Vol. XV, No. 3, (March 1993): p. 5.*

[726] *Olkowski, William. "Biological Control: A Century of Success". The IPM Practitioner. Vol. XI, No. 1, (Jan. 1989): pp. 1.*

[727] *Ibid.*

In addition to being homegrown, a number of factory grown predatory insects and parasites can be purchased and applied like pesticides. By 1989 the public demand for pesticide free food had spawned an estimated $25 million industry worldwide to supply beneficial pest fighting organisms. Actually the amount of money involved in the use of beneficial organisms is much higher than $25 million. China and the former Soviet Union produce large numbers of beneficial organisms. But the capital resource involved in their programs is not public information and is not included in the $25 million estimate. [728] Since 1989, the beneficial organism industry has continued to grow, to keep pace with the switch to non-toxic pest control methods.

Use and improvement of the many strategies and controls discussed here will usher in an agriculture of the future that will work in harmony with nature on every level. And, like nature, it will be extremely productive. As in other economic sectors, the implementation of true-cost-pricing is an important aspect of accelerating the development of sustainable agricultural systems and their adoption around the globe.

Agricultural Appendix

This section is for those who would like a more in depth look at some of the organic methods currently being used in agriculture and a few of the new tools being developed. It will also take a more detailed look at the numerous problems presented by our current petrochemically based agricultural system.

Biocides are just one class of organisms currently produced by the beneficial organism industry for use in agriculture. Biocides are naturally occurring bacteria, fungal, and viral agents that attack various agricultural pests and diseases. "Organisms used for biocontrol of soilborne pathogens are generally either soil bacteria or fungi." [729] "Bacteria such as B. subtilis are popular for seed treatment because they form spores that are stable and easy to apply." [730] The effectiveness of B. subtilis in controlling soilborne pathogens is reflected in increased yield. "After treatment yields of carrots have increased by 48%, oats by 33%, and peanuts by 37%." [731] Bacillus thuringiensis or BT is mixed with water and sprayed on plant foliage. As insect larvae eat foliage, they ingest BT which causes them to sicken and die. BT kills tomato hornworms, cabbage worms, and other butterfly family larvae.

Bacillus Popilus, another commercially available organism, is fatal to the grub larvae of the Japanese beetle, another crop damaging insect. [732] The biocide B. bassiana, a fungal pathogen, is used to control "sweetpotato" whiteflies. This pathogen attacks the sweetpotato whitefly at every stage of its life cycle "from egg to adult on cotton, vegetables, and ornamentals." [733]

---

[728]   La Ganga, Maria L. "Bug Busters", *Los Angeles Times Business Section*. San Diego County Edition, (Sunday, Oct. 1, 1989): Part IV, p 5.

[729]   Quarles, William. "Alternatives to Methyl Bromide: Trichoderma Seed Treatments,", *The IPM Practitioner*. Vol. XV, No. 9, (Sept. 1993): p. 2.

[730]   Ibid.

[731]   Ibid.

[732]   Wood, Marcia. "Microbe Blows Those Hornworms Away". *Agricultural Research*. (mag.) Vol. 4, No. 6, (June 1992): p. 4.

[733]   Grossman, Joel. "Entomological Society of America's 1992 Annual Meeting - Part I." *The IPM Practitioner*. Vol. XV, No. 2, (Feb. 1993): p. 13.

Sometimes biocides work in concert. "Entomophora grylli (a complex of more than one species) is being used to control grasshoppers." [734]   Biocides can even be used to protect agricultural products from decay after they have been harvested. To reduce spoilage, "antagonistic" bacteria, yeasts, and fungi "compete with pathogens for nutrients, or attack them directly with secretions of antibiotics, enzymes, and other substances." [735]   From 12 to 23 percent of fresh fruit and vegetables are lost to spoilage after harvest. Losses are as high as 50 percent without refrigeration or other measures. [736]

Still in the research stage is the celery looper virus. This virus, which is naturally occurring, could be commercially available in the next five years. While the use of biocides to control pests is becoming increasingly common "the celery looper virus stands out from others because of an impressively broad array of destructive insects it kills." [737]   Pests susceptible to the virus include: the pale-green celery looper, the cabbage looper, the tomato and tobacco hornworm, the cotton bollworm (a.k.a. corn earworm and tomato fruitworm), the pink bollworm, the tobacco budworm, and a number of other wormlike pests. [738]

Nematodes, small wormlike organisms which live in the soil, can also be used to control pests. Insect-attacking nematodes have been used in the U.S. to control pests on "citrus, cranberries, turf, figs, hops, mint, strawberries, sweet potatoes, and rhododendrons." [739]   "Nematodes are also being used successfully against fly larvae in poultry and dairy operations." [740]   The first commercially available insect-attacking nematodes developed in the U.S. were used to control mosquitos in the 1970s. Current research is exploring the use of beneficial nematodes to control wireworms, cutworms, cabbage root maggots, onion maggots, white fringe beetles, cornworms, black vine weevils, flea beetles, and the sweet potato weevil. [741]

Pheromones, which are powerful hormones emitted by insects to attract mates, are another tool available to organic farmers to thwart pests. Pheromones can be used to reduce pests by confusing them during breeding periods, so they are less successful at breeding, or to lure them into traps. [742]

Recent research in pheromone use has focused on controlling nematodes. While many nematodes are beneficial, some of the transparent eel-shaped worms damage plant roots while they

---

[734]   Grossman, Joel. "Horticultural Oils: New Summer Uses on Ornamental Plant Pests". *The IPM Practitioner*. Vol. XII, No. 8, (Aug. 1990): p. 13.

[735]   Quarles, William. "Biological Control of Postharvested Fruit Disease", *The IPM Practitioner*. Vol. XV, No. 5/6, (May/June 1993): p. 3.

[736]   Ibid., page 2.

[737]   Wood, Marcia. "Microbe Blows Those Hornworms Away". *Agricultural Research*. (mag.) Vol. 4, No. 6, (June 1992): p. 4.

[738]   Ibid.

[739]   Olkowski, William and Sheila Darr. "Update: Chinese Use Insect-Attacking Nematodes Against Major Pests", *The IPM Practitioner*. Vol. XI, No. 11/12, (Nov./Dec. 1989): p. 1.

[740]   Ibid.

[741]   Ibid. pp. 6-7.

[742]   Grossman, Joel. "Conference Notes: Entomological Society of America's Annual Meeting - Part Seven". *The IPM Practitioner*. Vol. XIII, No. 9, (Sept. 1991): p. 9. Also See Vol. XIII, No. 3, p.12, - Vol. XIII, No. 4, pp. 2, 4, - Vol. XIII, No. 5/6, pp. 19-20, - Vol. XIII, No. 7, p. 10.

drain nutrients from them. "Scientists estimated that the soybean Cyst nematode, Hererodera glycine, costs (soybean) growers $420 million a year in crop losses." [743] Historically, nematodes have been controlledby applying nemacides to the soil. This is costly and groundwater contamination is a concern. Now, scientists are testing pheromones as a nematode control agent. In the quest for a pheromone solution, pheromones were first isolated from female nematodes by Robin L. Huettel andthen approximated (close enough to the real thing to fool the target pest) by chemist Albert B. DeMilo. At the beginning of their life-cycle, hatching young nematodes attach themselves to soybean roots with "a needlelike mouthpart called a stylet". "When a male nematode matures, he leaves the root to seek a mate, drawn by the female's pheromone." The strength of the pheromone signal tells the male nematode when a female is near, which triggers "a dance like rite--coiling and uncoiling--in an effort to mate." When the pheromone substitute is applied to the soil, the chemical "noise"confuses the male nematode so that he can't find a mate. To the degree that this happens, less nematode eggs are fertilized. [744]

Beyond the growing arsenal of beneficial organisms, several other pest control measures are available to organic farmers. Oils, for example, have been used to control pests for thousands of years. Various petroleum derived oils are advertised with names like "dormant," "summer," "superior," "supreme oil," and other designations. While these oils are more or less non-toxic and effective as pest control agents they are still made from a non-renewable resource.

Renewable plant oils are also being used to control pests and "rank with petroleum oils in killing aphids, whiteflies and spider mites on cotton and vegetable plants." [745] A common way to apply oils is to mix them with a detergent in water and spray them on plants. To keep the oil/detergent blend uniformly distributed in the water medium, it is necessary to keep the spray container constantly agitated. [746]

Insecticidal soaps are also used to control pests by them selves. In experiments to test the effectiveness of insecticidal soaps, "mite reproduction rates were reduced by 8-fold" compared with controls. [747] Additionally, "there was 100% mite mortality with oleic acid and a 75% mortality from cis-linoleic acid." These are ingredients in the Safer brand insecticidal soap. "After one fatty acid treatment, plants showed none of the yellow pin-prick symptoms of mite feeding even after 30 days of monitoring." [748]

Mixing insecticidal soap with oil has also proven to be effective against pests on which soap alone had little effect. In studies on controlling the pear rust mite in Michigan it was found that Safer soap had no measurable effect. But "a concentrated spray of 2% Safer soap plus 2% Ultrafine oil was as good as (the toxic chemical controls) avermectin, kelthane, dithane and Mitac@." [749]

---

[743] De Quattro, Jim. "Micro-Pests Inflict Macro-Headaches". *Agricultural Research*. Vol. 40, No. 5, (May 1992): p. 10.

[744] Ibid.

[745] Grossman, Joel. "Horticultural Oils: New Summer Uses on Ornamental Plant Pests". *The IPM Practitioner*. Vol. XII, No. 8, (Aug. 1990): p. 3.

[746] Ibid.

[747] Grossman, Joel. "Entomological Society of America's 1989 Annual Meeting IPM Highlight -- Part Five", *The IPM Practitioner*. Vol. XII, No. 7, (July 1990): p. 8.

[748] Ibid. p. 8.

[749] Ibid. p. 9.

As discussed earlier, maintaining the genetic diversity of crop plants is very important. Insects that attack plants are constantly mutating. Greenbugs, aphids "that injects a toxin into seedlings as they feed," are especially adept at hybridizing or forming new races or biotypes if "suppressed by pesticides or host plant resistance." [750]

In an average year, greenbugs will "inflict a $67 million loss on U.S. wheat farmers". In a bad year, the state of Oklahoma alone can sustain damage in the $150 million range. [751]

To counter this damage, plant geneticist David Porter is working on cutting into greenbug related wheat losses by using 5 breeding lines of wheat, developed by the geneticist Emil Sebesta. These lines are resistant to "the three most prevalent and destructive biotypes of greenbug -- B, C, and E, plus a new and particularly destructive biotype, G." Porter is now involved in "crossing several breeding lines to combine the desired resistance genes. [752]

Genetic breeding also promises to be a valuable tool in protecting crops against rust-causing fungi. Rust is one of the most damaging diseases of the bean plant. According to plant pathologist Rennei Stavely, "in a bad year, it (rust) can cost $250 million in (beans) losses nationwide." [753] Through his work Stavely discovered that "nature gave a few P. vulgaris plants -- and related species -- the genetic know-how for stopping rust from taking hold, or bowing so slightly to it that there's little or no loss in bean yield or quality." [754] "Stavely and colleagues are putting those genes into breeding lines that commercial breeders are turning into market varieties. Since 1984, the scientists have released 53 lines of beans resistant to all 55 rust races." [755] Porter's and Stavely's work, and that of plant geneticists in general, highlights the need to protect the genetic diversity of plants. If we let gene pools shrink, the possibility of breeding pest resistance into plants will be greatly hampered.

Although rust-causing fungi and other fungal species can cause crop damage, scientists are using some species of fungi to protect crops. A mutated strain of the fungus, Verticillium lecanii is being used to prevent the eggs of soybean cyst nematodes from hatching. In one test, "nematode populations were 70 percent less on soybean plots protected by the fungus than on plots where nematicide was mixed into the soil." When fungus was used in conjunction with pheromone compounds, the reductions were 86 percent. [756] As attractants, pheromones can be used to attract organisms into traps or broadcasted into the general environment to confuse pests seeking to mate.

Fungi are also being used against each other. When peanuts are infected by the fungi Aspergillus parasiticus and A. flavus, "they can produce a natural toxin known as aflatoxin which

---

[750] Hardin, Ben. "*Overcoming Greenbugs in Wheat*". <u>Agricultural Research</u>. Vol. 40, No. 2, (February 1992): p. 21.

[751] Ibid.

[752] Ibid.

[753] De Quattro, Jim. "*Rust-No-More Beans*". <u>Agricultural Research</u>. Vol. 40, No. 2, (February 1992): p. 12.

[754] Ibid., pp. 12-13.

[755] Ibid.

[756] Ibid.

means financial losses to peanut growers." [757]   If aflatoxin is found in peanuts in concentrations of more than 20 parts per billion, the U.S. Food and Drug Administration prohibits their use for human or animal feed in most instances. Twenty parts per billion is less than 20 drops in 10,000 gallons of liquid. According to the Peanut Advisory Board, aflatoxin contamination cost U.S. "peanut growers an estimated $25 million annually." Through ongoing work begun in 1980, scientists have isolated a parent fungi strain and developed a mutant fungi that are "very effective in controlling aflatoxin in peanuts." Not only are both the parent strain and mutant "highly competitive in the soil" at displacing the toxin producing fungi, they do it without increasing the soil's overall fungal population. [758]

Petrochemical Agriculture:
Why It Is Not Eco-nomically Sustainable

With the advent of petrochemical farming in the 1930's, organic farming was largely supplanted in the industrialized world. This resulted from the fact that petrochemical imputes like pesticides and chemical fertilizers had the effect of increasing crop yields dramatically over the average crop yields of the period. Although, as the material previously discussed has shown, scientifically applied organic farming methods in use today can meet or even exceed the yields and profits of petrochemical practices.

One of the most important ingredients in the petrochemical regimen is pesticides. When pesticides were first introduced, they were hailed as scientific miracles. Pesticides were the magic wand that promised to end the age old struggle between humanity and the myriad of pests which prey on us and our crops. Unfortunately, this promise was not to be fulfilled.

One reason for this failure is that pesticide use triggers a process that results in the selection of pest populations that are pesticide-resistant. [759]   When pesticides are used, they kill the members of a particular pest population that are most susceptible to them. This leaves a residual population of pesticide-resistant pests, which reproduce and pass on their resistant genes to their offspring.

Pesticide resistance was documented as early as 1914 when it was discovered that San Jose scale was resistant to lime sulfur sprays. [760]   Since that early discovery, the number of resistant pests have grown. To date, according to the National Resource Council, "more than 440 insect and mite species and more than 70 fungus species are now known to be resistant to some pesticide." [761]

With increasing pesticide use this selection process seems to be accelerating. Between 1970 and 1980, "the number of insects resistant to insecticides nearly doubled." [762]   Some pests

---

[757]   Kinzel, Bruce. "Pitting Fungus Against Fungus". *Agricultural Research*. Vol. 40, No. 5, (May 1992): p. 9.

[758]   Ibid.

[759]   Dahlsten, Donald L. "Pesticides in an Era of Integrated Pest Management. *Environment*. Vol. 20, No. 10, December 1983, pp. 46-47.

[760]   Ibid.

[761]   Committee on the Role of Alternative Farming Methods in Modern Production   [761]12 Agriculture. *Alternative Agriculture*. National Academy Press, Washington D.C., (1989): p. 124.

[762]   Mott, Lawrie, and Karen Snyder. "Pesticide Alert". *The Amicus Journal*. (Spring 1988): p. 23.

have even developed resistance to multiple pesticides. As of 1983, "at least 25 species (of pests) can resist the four principal classes of insecticides: DDT, cyclodienes, phosphates, and Carbamates." [763] As many as "10 insects have already developed resistance to a new class of insecticides, the synthetic pyrethroids." [764]

In all, the amount of crop damage caused by pests since pesticides were first introduced has doubled, even though the amount of pesticides used nationally and their toxicity level has increased many-fold. [765] "In the 1940's when little insecticide was applied to corn, 3.5 percent of the crop was lost to pests. Though insecticide use has since gone up 1,000 fold, losses (are) up to 12 percent." [766]

By 1975 the annual pesticide use in the United States had risen to "an estimated 1.1 billion pounds of pesticides, or about 5 pounds per person". [767] Of this 1.1 billion pounds, "about 700 million lbs. of pesticides--of which about 38% are insecticides, 52% herbicides, and 10% fungicides-are applied to crops and farm lands." [768] By 1988 pesticide use in the U.S. had risen to around 2.6 billion pounds, almost 2.4 times the 1.1 billion pounds used just 13 years earlier. [769]

Pesticides amplify the problem of pest damage further by harming animals, like birds and insects, that eat pests. Since the life-cycle of predator organisms is often longer than the pest they eat, it takes longer for them to develop a pesticide resistant population. This means that as pests develop resistance to pesticides there are less natural predators to take up the slack. With natural predator populations down, there is a resurgence of resistant pests, which triggers still more pesticide application -- these further debilitating predator populations just when they are recovering from the initial pesticide application. [770]

This "'pesticide treadmill'" is further aggravated because pest predators, like birds, may pick up a debilitating or even lethal dose of pesticides by eating a quantity of pests that are pesticide contaminated, even though the pesticide does not affect the resistant target pest.

The use of pesticides, especially broad spectrum pesticides has also been associated with the "creation of secondary pests." [771] Secondary pests are created when the natural enemy of a non-problem pest is debilitated by pesticides being used to control a target pest. Even though the pesticide application may control the target pest, it may unleash another pest whose population

---

[763] Dahlsten, Donald L. *"Pesticides in an Era of Integrated Pest Management.* Environment. *Vol. 20, No. 10, December 1983, pp. 47.*

[764] *Ibid.*

[765] Olkowski, William. *"Biological Control: A Century of Success".* The IPM Practitioner. *Bio-Integral Resource Center, Berkeley, California, Vol. XI, No. 1, (January 1989): p. 1.*

[766] Brody, Jane. *"Using Fewer Pesticides Is Seen as Beneficial".* The New York Times. *The Environment Section, (April 2, 1991): p. C4.*

[767] Pimentel, David et al., *"Pesticides, Insects in Foods, and Cosmetic Standards".* BioScience. *Vol. 27, No. 3, (March 1977): p. 178.*

[768] *Ibid., p. 180.*

[769] *Ibid., p. 22.*

[770] Dahlsten, Donald L. *"Pesticides in an Era of Integrated Pest Management.* Environment. *Vol. 20, No. 10, December 1983, pp. 47.*

[771] *Ibid.*

growth had previously been held in check by natural predators.

There are numerous examples of this phenomenon. Mites, for example, "have only become important pests since the introduction of broad-spectrum insecticides." Another example occurred in Peru. When insecticides were used to control pests attacking Peruvian cotton in 1949 the initial result was "a dramatic increase" in yield. But with the passage of time, the pesticide induced ecological disruption led to an increase in the number of cotton pests from 6 to 16. "This eventually resulted in the lowest yields ever during the 1955-56 season, and necessitated the development of a new approach to pest control." [772]

In 1970, 25 species of insects in California caused at least one million dollars worth of damage to agriculture. "Of these 25 insects, 17 species were resistant to one or more pesticides, and 24 of the pests were the result of secondary pest outbreaks or resurgences." [773]

The use of pesticides also kills other beneficial organisms like the honey bee. "Honey bees and wild bees are vital to the production of about $20 billion worth of fruit, vegetables, and forage crops." [774] It has been estimated that "the loss of honey, and reduced crop yields" resulting from pesticide-caused honey bee deaths "accounts for at least $135 million in losses (in the U.S. each year (Pimentel et al. 1980). [775]

The Effect Of Pesticides On People

As early as 1974 the U.S. EPA estimated that up to "'14,000 people may have been nonfatally poisoned by pesticides in a given year, 6,000 seriously enough to require hospitalization". [776] Annually, there are about 200 deaths from pesticide exposure in the United States. [777]

Although a large percentage of the poisonings cited above were of people working in agriculture, consumers of food grown with pesticides are also at risk. "In the summer of 1985, nearly 1,000 people in several western states and Canada were poisoned by residues of the pesticide Temik in watermelons. Within two to twelve hours after eating the contaminated watermelons, people experienced nausea, vomiting, blurred vision, muscle weakness, and other symptoms." [778] Although no person died, symptoms "included grand mal seizures, cardiac irregularities, a number of hospitalizations, and at least two stillbirths following maternal illness." [779]

A 1987 report by the National Academy of Sciences "concluded that pesticides in our food

---

[772] *Ibid, (all citations in this paragraph).*

[773] *Ibid.*

[774] *Committee on the Role of Alternative Farming Methodl in Modern Production Agriculture. Alternative Agriculture. National Academy Press, Washington D.C. (1989): p. 122.*

[775] *Ibid., Pimental et al. 1980.*

[776] *Pimentel, David et al., "Pesticides, Insects in Foods, and Cosmetic Standards". BioScience. Vol. 27, No. 3, (March 1977): p. 181.*

[777] *Ibid.*

[778] *Mott, Lawrie, and Karen Snyder. "Pesticide Alert". The Amicus Journal. (Spring 1988): p. 20.*

[779] *Ibid.*

may cause more than 1 million additional cases of cancer in the United States over our lifetimes." [780] An analysis by the Natural Resources Defence Council of fruits and vegetables from San Francisco supermarkets "found that 44% of the produce contained measurable residues of pesticides; 42% of the samples with residues contained more than one chemical," and "some had as many as 4 different pesticides present." [781]

An EPA report, entitled Unfinished Business, published in the same year, "ranked pesticides in food as one of the nation's most serious health and environmental problems." [782]   As of 1988 the EPA had "identified fifty-five pesticides that could leave residues in food as being carcinogens." [783] This number is probably conservative considering that "a 1982 congressional report estimated that between 82 percent and 85 percent of pesticides registered for use had not been adequately tested for their ability to cause cancer; the figure was 60 percent to 70 percent for birth defects, and 90 percent to 93 percent for genetic mutations." [784] "In 1987 Consumers Union surveyed 50 common pesticide ingredients and found that only one had been properly tested for neurotoxicity." [785]

Herbicides: Deja Vu All Over Again

Though weed killing pesticides or herbicides are late entries in the pesticide arsenal they have been found to carry liabilities similar to those that emerged with the use of other pesticides. Herbicides were first used commercially in the late 1940s. According to a report by the U.S. Dept. of Agriculture Economic Research Service published in 1988, herbicides were used in the cultivation of 95% percent of the soybeans and corn grown in the U.S in 1987 and in 60% of the wheat farming operations. [786]

"Herbicides now account for 50 to 60% of synthetic pesticide production at the 330 U.S. pesticide (production) plants" (30% are insecticides and miscellaneous pesticides and 20% are fungicides). [787] The principal attractiveness of herbicides is their capacity to eliminate undesirable plants with a minimum amount of labor.

Recently, concerns about the potential side effects of herbicide use have been raised in light of suggestive evidence linking herbicide use to birth defects in unborn humans and other animals. [788] Although it is only one element in the herbicide controversy, dioxin and in particular the dioxin

---

[780]   *Ibid.*

[781]   Mott, Lawrie. *"Regulations Breaks Down, But Pesticides Linger On"*. Los Angeles Times. *Part II, (Monday, Aug. 12, 1985): p. 7j.*

[782]   Mott, Lawrie, and Karen Snyder. *"Pesticide Alert"*. The Amicus Journal. *(Spring 1988): p. 24.*

[783]   *Ibid.*

[784]   *Ibid.*

[785]   Pearlman, Nancy - Editor. *"Harmful Impacts of Chemical Pesticides"*. The Compendium Newsletter. *Vol. 20, No. 4, (July/August 1992): p. 13.*

[786]   Darr, Sheila, Helga Olkowski, William Olkowski, editors. *"Update, Box A. Weed Resistance Builds as Herbicide Use Soars"*, The IPM Practitioner. *Bio Integral Resource Center, (BRIC), Vol. XI, No. 6/7, (June/July 1889): p. 2.*

[787]   *Ibid.*

[788]   Clark, Mary E. Contemporary Biology. *Second Edition, W. B. Saunders Company, Philadelphia, London, Toronto, p. 588.*

compound known as TCDD or 2,3,7,8-tetrachlorodibenzxo-p-dioxin has drawn the most fire.

TCDD, an unavoidable byproduct of herbicide manufacture, is one of at least 75 dioxin compounds. "Little information is available about the toxicity of most of these dioxins - either separately or in combination - but it is known that TCDD is a fetus-deforming agent 100,000 times more potent than thalidomide, and that (it) is toxic at any level of exposure measurable, down to parts per trillion." [789] Thalidomide is a tranquilizer that was prescribed in the 1960s to "alleviate the psychological and physiological symptoms often accompanying early pregnancy".[790] During the three-to -four year period that the drug was prescribed, "thousands of severely deformed babies were born." [791]

Herbicides have also been implicated in the development of serious health problems in workers who are exposed to them. "A 1986 study by the National Cancer Institute found that Kansas farm workers who were exposed to herbicides for more than 20 days per year had a 6 times higher risk of developing Non-Hodgkin's lymphomas (NHL) than non-farm workers." [792]

Liabilities like those described above are even more alarming considering that the long-term use of herbicides may actually make the problem of controlling weeds more difficult than it was before herbicides were introduced. Like insects that have become resistant to pesticides, some "super weeds" are showing a similar capacity. Since this phenomenon was first cited in 1970, "at least 54 weed species, a 450% increase since 1980," have developed a resistance to herbicides. [793]

Specialists in chemical weed control have expressed confidence that they can answer this challenge by attacking weeds with a rotating barrage of herbicides from different classes. Even if this were true, the health and environmental risks are probably not worth it -- particularly considering that there are many physical and biological options available for weed control that have few if any health or environmental liabilities.

Non-toxic Weed Control

Although a safe weed control product has not yet been marketed, there are many methods for controlling weeds that do not require toxic materials. Ever since the dawn of agriculture, people have strived to overcome weeds that competed for nutrients, water, and sunlight with their crops. Many of the methods they pioneered, like pulling weeds, plowing or hoeing them under, covering them with mulch, growing aggressive cover crops to squeeze weeds out, and turning an assortment

---

[789] Miller, Fred. *Coalition Coordinator, Northwest Coalition for Alternatives to Pesticides,* "Exposure", *The Monthly Journal of the Waste and Toxic Substance Project.* *Environmental Action Foundation, Washington D.C., (July/August 1983): p. 3.*

[790] Clark, Mary. *Contemporary Biology.* Second Edition, W.B. Saunders Company, Philadelphia, London, Toronto, (1979): p. 464.

[791] *Ibid.*

[792] Committee on the Role Alternative Farming Methods in Modern Production Agriculture. *Alternative Agriculture. National Academy Press, Washington D.C. (1989): p. 121. (For a complete treatment of this study see Sheila K. Hoar et al. "Agricultural Herbicide Use and Risk of Lymphoma and Soft-Tissue Sarcoma". JAMA. Vol. 256, No. 9, (September 5, 1988): pp. 1141-1147.*

[793] *The IPM Practitioner. Bio-Integral Resource Center, (BRIC), Vol. XI, No. 6/7, (June/July 1889): p. 2. Also see Kloppenburg, Jr., Jack. "Biopesticides and Economic Democracy", Global Pesticide Campaigner. Vol. 1, No 2, (Jan. 1991): p. 7.*

of geese, goats and other animals loose on them are still effective strategies.

Modern biological weed control made its accidental debut around 200 years ago. Aiming to break the lucrative Spanish red dye monopoly in Mexico, the British imported the Brazilian Scale insect into Northern India. But instead of importing the cochineal species associated with red dye production they mistakenly imported a Brazilian relative. Though the Brazilian species was not good for the production of dye it did attack and finally eliminate the undesirable South American weedy prickly pear which had spread unchecked throughout India after its introduction. [794]

Since the accidental introduction of the Brazilian scale into India 200 years ago, many other biological control organisms have been introduced around the world to control undesirable plants. In addition to being more ecologically benign and non-health threatening, biological control methods are also economical.

During the 1940s the Klamath beetle was introduced into a two million acre area in California to control the Klamath weed. The Klamath weed which is also known as St. John's-wort, crowds out nutritious forage plants and is poisonous to sheep and cattle. Within a decade of its introduction the Klamath beetle had eliminated 99% of the Klamath weed in the control area. The savings, over other control methods, continues to range in the millions of dollar per year. Just during the years from 1953 to 1959 the savings amounted to 20 million dollars. [795]

The U.S. Department of Agriculture's Agricultural Research Service (USDA/ARS), the agency responsible for bio-control research, estimates "that its four complete successes against weeds since 1944 (i.e., Klamath weed, alligatorweed, Alternanthera Philoxeroides, puncturevine, Tribulus terrestris, and Tansy ragwort, Senecio jacoboea) results in annual benefits of $155.6 million per year." [796]

Given that the "total ARS biocontrol research budget was only $21.5 million in 1988,", "the cost effectiveness of biological control technology (for weed control) is hard to deny (USDA/ARS 1989)." [797] If peripheral costs like the avoidance of water pollution and health problems associated with use of chemical controls are added, the savings would be considerably higher. By replacing expensive herbicides, biocontrols also reduce overhead costs by several hundred million dollars each year.

Developing plants with built-in weed control systems is a new nontoxic way to keep weeds at bay. In the mid-1980s plant geneticist Robert Dilday noticed that ducksalad, an invasive weed that plagues rice farmers, "would grow right up to some rice plants, but other rice plants didn't have any of the weed around them." [798]

This discovery led Dilday on a research quest to isolate rice varieties that had allelopathic (growth inhibiting) properties against ducksalad. In 1988 and 1989 Dilday and fellow researchers, Roy J. Smith and Palo Nastasi of the University of Arkansas "evaluated some 10,000 rice accessions

---

[794] *The IPM Practitioner.* Bio-Integral Resource Center, (BRIC), Vol. XI, No. 6/7, (June/July 1889): pp. 1-2.

[795] *Ibid.,* p. 3.

[796] *Ibid.,* p. 5.

[797] *Ibid.*

[798] Hays, Sandy M.. "Victims No One Mourns". *Agricultural Research.* Vol. 40, No. 2, (February 1992): p. 10.

(varieties)" for allelopathic properties. [799] Their work resulted in the discovery of 347 rice varieties "with allelopathic activities against ducksalad." They also "identified 132 rice varieties that repelled redstem, another aquatic weed, and six that looked promising for resistance to broadleaf signalgrass." [800]

Dilday believes the information he and his colleagues have uncovered can be used in at least two ways. One would be to breed allelopathic characteristics into commercial rice varieties. Preliminary work in this direction looks promising. He also sees the possibility identifying the chemical that the allelopathic plants produce. If these chemicals can be identified, they might be able to be produced commercially.

Another difficulty with many pesticides, herbicides included, is that they do not degrade easily. In both agricultural and landscaped settings, pesticide residues that do not break down in soil and water can be absorbed by plants or ingested by herbivore (plant eating) animals and insects.

Although biological methods for controlling all weed problems have not been developed, it is definitely an area where more research would be valuable. But even today, current biological control methods in combination with other non-toxic weed control strategies are sufficient to eliminate the use of most if not all chemical controls.

Biological Magnification

Through a process called **biological magnification,** many pesticides like DDT and its relatives "accumulate in the fatty tissues of organisms, especially those at the high end of the food chain." [801] When these organisms or their products (like milk and eggs) are eaten, pesticide residues further concentrate in the body of the animal or person who eats them.

In general, such concentrations increase around 10 times with each step up the food chain. One four level food chain study traced the biological magnification of DDT from plankton to silversides (a small plankton eating fish) to needlefish, to the osprey. At the osprey end of this food chain DDT was 345 times more concentrated than it had been in the original plankton. [802]

Animals like bald eagles, ospreys, bears, and humans that consume animals and animal products from the high end of the food chain are exposed to the highest concentrations of food chain pesticides. Such concentrations have been linked with a decline in the reproduction of predatory birds. [803] An Environmental Protection Agency study released in 1983 stated that 99% of all Americans have some pesticide residues in their tissue.

The contamination of breast milk is one of the more frightening aspects of food chain contamination. Pesticide-contaminated breast milk has shown up in areas as widespread as Montana, New York, Virginia, Michigan, and Hawaii.

---

[799]   *Ibid.*

[800]   *Ibid.*

[801]   *Clark, Mary E. Contemporary Biology. W. B. Saunders Company, Philadelphia, London, Toronto, (1979): p. 10, Also see Sheeline, Leonora and Barbara Bramble. "Silent Spring Rerun: Pesticides in the Global Environment". The Journal of Pesticide reform. Northwest Coalition for Alternatives to Pesticides, Vol. 6, No. 1, (Spring 1986): p. 30.*

[802]   *Ibid.*

[803]   *Ibid.*

Studies conducted over the last 30 years to detect DDT in human milk have not shown a decline even though DDT was banned in 1972. "E.J. Calabrese comments there does not seem to be a downward trend in DDT levels in human milk over the 30 years since the original reports. He notes that despite the differences between studies, all reported that breast milk had such high levels of DDT that substantial percentages of nursing infants were ingesting more DDT than was considered acceptable by the World Health Organization. Calabrese states that cow's milk containing the average level of DDT found in human milk would have been banned by the Federal Department of Agriculture." [804]

Additionally, pesticide residues carried by wind and runoff can contaminate waterways and can leach into groundwater supplies. "Pesticides have been detected in the groundwater of 26 states as a result of normal agricultural practices." [805] These contaminants include 30 herbicides and 7 insecticides. [806]

Chemical Fertilizers

Like pesticides, chemical fertilizers seemed to be an answer to the farmer's dreams. Like a magic potion, the application of chemical fertilizers increased crop yields dramatically. Initially the use of chemical fertilizers seemed to have no drawbacks but as time passed a number of problems emerged.

"Soils are the natural, living systems where the root systems of most higher plants live, along with millions of microorganisms that carry out essential functions of converting minerals, dead plant and animal remains, water, and air into compounds that nourish the plants in a continuous cycle of life." [807] While petrochemical fertilizers provide nutrients for plants, they do not provide food for soil organisms. If concentrated, petrochemical fertilizers can even be toxic to them. Soil organisms die without food. This coupled with the lack of organic material, leaves soil less able to absorb moisture which makes soils more vulnerable to wind and water erosion.

Research has also shown that nitrogen fertilizer also diminishes the uptake of methene gas by soil microbes. [808] With less uptake, more greenhouse potent methane gas is being released into the atmosphere. "Now a soil scientist has added vitamin C depletion to the list of drawbacks" associated with the use of nitrogen fertilizers. [809] Studies conducted by Sharon B. Hornick of the USDA's Agricultural Research Service showed that "too much nitrogen" from any source reduced the vitamin C content by close to 30 percent in chard. Hornick's work also showed that excessive nitrogen also reduced the vitamin C content "in green beans and kale." [810]

---

[804] *Heifetz, Ruth M. and Sharon S. Taylor. "Mother's Milk or Mother's Poison? Pesticides in Breast Milk". Journal of Pesticide Reform. Northwest Coalition for Alternatives to Pesticides, Vol. 9, No. 3., (Fall 1989): p. 15.*

[805] *Committee on the Role Alternative Farming Methods in Modern Production Agriculture. Alternative Agriculture. National Academy Press, Washington D.C..(1989): p. 105.*

[806] *Ibid., p. 106.*

[807] *Sampson, R. Soil Erosion, Farmland or Wasteland - A Time to Choose. Rodale Press, (1981): p. 111.*

[808] *Science News Staff. Science News. 9/30/89.*

[809] *Science News Staff. Science News. Vol. 136, No. 16, (Oct. 16, 1989): p. 255.*

[810] *Ibid.*

Although it appears that excessive nitrogen, in any form, can diminish the vitamin C content in at least some plants, this is less likely in healthy soils. In healthy soils, abundant soil organisms release the nitrogen bound up in organic materials at rates that can be more fully utilized by plants.

Petrochemical fertilizers are also more likely to cause water pollution problems than are plant residues and manure. When petrochemical fertilizers are applied, more nutrients are often available than plants can readily use. The excess is carried off by runoff or leaches into the soil beyond plant root zones and eventually into groundwater supplies where it is a harmful contaminate. When children drink contaminated well water, nitrate ions (NO_3-) from artificial fertilizers are converted by intestinal bacteria in children into nitrite ions (NO_2-). The reaction of NO_2- with blood hemoglobin causes anemia in children which is debilitating and in extreme cases can be fatal.

In contrast, as soil organisms break down organic materials found in plant residues and manure, plant nutrients are slowly released. This slow release allows plants to absorb nutrients with a minimum of nutrient loss. Organic materials in the soil also help to hold water and keep nutrients from leaching away before plants can absorb them. In short, adding "organic matter improves soil quality by granulation, water infiltration, nutrient content, soil biota (soil organisms) activity, and soil fertility and productivity." [811]

Agriculture in the future will work in harmony with nature on every level. And, like nature, it will be extremely productive. As in other economic sectors, true-cost-pricing will accelerate the development of sustainable agricultural systems and their adoption on a global scale.

---

[811] *Committee on the Role of Alternative Farming Methods in Modern Production Agriculture. Alternative Agriculture. National Academy Press, Washington D.C., (1989): p. 119.*

PART FIVE

TOWARD A SUSTAINABLE FUTURE

Chapter XI

THE ROLES OF SOCIETY

Synopsis

The preceding chapters have explored many of the ways that eco-nomic security can be enhanced and why doing so is in everyone's interest. The material that follows will focus on how we as individuals, groups, and institutions, can actively participate in the process of getting us from where we are now to a more eco-nomically sustainable future.

Things We Can All Do

Whether we are talking about individuals, business, government, or other organizations, some general things can be done at each of these levels to improve eco-nomic security.

1. At every level, using resources like energy and water more efficiently will help improve eco-nomic security. It will also lessen the environmental damage associated with resource procurement and use. Plus, saving resources will almost always save money.

2. Resources can be saved, in general, by following the maxim: **reduce, reuse, recycle**. Avoid unnecessary purchases, try to purchase things that are durable, reusable, or at least recyclable or compostable. Try to avoid purchasing things that will end up in landfills.

3. Health and environmental problems can be reduced by not using toxic materials. If the use of such materials is unavoidable, make sure they are recycled or otherwise neutralized after use.

    Note: Even "proper disposal" of toxic materials is problematic. Unless a toxic material is recycled or neutralized its "proper disposal" is bound to emerge as another problem, eventually. (See index for more entries.)

4. Negative ecological impacts can be reduced if potential purchases are evaluated from a true-cost-pricing or total cost perspective. For example:

    □   Where did the raw materials in a product come from and what kind of damage was sustained in its procurement?

    □   What kind of damage was sustained when this raw material was refined and/or used in fabrication?

    □   What are the ecological and social implications of using the refined material or the products made from it?

    □   Finally, is the refined material or the products made from it, easily reused, recycled, and/or composted?

Because some of these questions are only just beginning to be asked, some of the answers have not yet been completely explored. But it is important to ask these questions and for each of us to add our thinking to the process of getting them answered.

Without true-cost-pricing, the product with the least negative impact may not be the least expensive. Nevertheless, eco-nomic security can be enhanced if our purchases are made with total impact in mind. When suitably designed products are not available, let suppliers know that you desire to purchases products with life-cycles that are as ecologically benign as possible.

The Individual And Family:
Voting With Our Dollars

One of the most important statements that individuals and their families can make toward promoting eco-nomic security relates to how they spend their money. When we choose not to buy something or choose one product over another, we send powerful messages to the business community about our vision of the future. Indeed, how we spend our money today has a profound effect on what life will be like in the future.

On a more specific level individuals and families can help create a more sustainable future in the following ways:

1.   If a small parcel of land is available, grow as much of your own food as is practical and grow it organically. With a little skill, even a window box can contribute to your home food supply. When buying food, make an effort to purchase food grown organically and try to eat low on the food chain, i.e., become a vegetarian if possible or at least limit the amount of meat in your diet. If you feel the need to eat meat, try to find suppliers that do not use growth hormones and antibiotics on the animals they raise. Look for suppliers that let their animals "range freely" and that provide them with organically grown feed. Whatever the farming method, producing a pound of meat requires many times more land, water, and energy than producing a pound of vegetables, fruit, or grain. Therefore, all things being equal, a diet that includes meat is more damaging to our eco-nomic security than one that does not.

2.   Purchase clothing made from organically grown fibers whenever possible. Second-hand clothing is also a good option. Even if second-hand clothing is not made of ecologically benign materials, using it longer delays its disposal. Wearing second-hand clothing will also help other clothing last longer and slow the consumption of resources to produce new clothing.

3.   Use household products that are ecologically benign.

4.   Walk, bicycle, or use public transportation where practical. If a car is needed, purchase one that is as efficient as possible and keep it properly maintained.

5.   Make your home more energy and water efficient. Use direct solar energy to heat water and space heat wherever practical. Where it is legal and practical, set up a gray water recycling system. Also, collect and store rain water for later use. Explore the possibility of using solar energy in its various forms to become more energy independent.

6.   In general, avoid wood and fiber products that are not grown, harvested, processed, and transported in ways that are ecologically sustainable. Use domestically produced wood and fiber whenever possible. Many countries have less controls on the cultivation and harvesting of such materials, and thus these methods may be more damaging. Although it is not always the case, moving things long distances often requires a greater expenditure of energy than moving materials shorter distances. Whatever the situation, it is good to be conscious of these issues when we consider purchases.

Educational Institutions

Educational institutions, whether in the United States or abroad, can play a pivotal role in creating a sustainable future on our planet.

Toward this goal, schools and colleges need to broaden their mandates to better address the need to achieve eco-nomic security. More specifically, educational institutions need to develop curricula designed to teach people how to live and make livings on our planet in ways that are economically sustainable. The development of such a curriculum does not mean that subjects currently taught would be replaced. What it does mean is that most of these subjects would be taught from an ecological or biospheric perspective. In other words, students should be encouraged to think critically about how knowledge in a particular subject area relates to our global situation. Further, they should ask how that knowledge can be used to enhance the economic, social, and ecological well being of everyone including the other life forms that share this planet with us.

For example, if an individual's educational goal was to be involved in international trade, the objectives of the curriculum would be:

☐ To develop an individual with the skills and ethics to trade successfully from a profit perspective, but also . . .

☐ in ways that are a "win" for those at the other end of the trade equation and which . . .

☐ protect the ecological foundation that makes possible the economic system within which the trade takes place.

In the area of chemistry, the focus of the curriculum would be on using chemistry in ways that are consistent with achieving eco-nomic security. In this capacity, a chemistry department could, as a partner with the private sector and government, help business and industry develop more ecologically and socially benign ways of producing products and providing services.

New Designs For Educational Institutions

Another aspect of the role of education in promoting eco-nomic security relate to how educational institutions are designed, constructed, and maintained. To be consistent with the goal of enhancing eco-nomic security, learning facilities should be designed or redesigned to reflect that goal. In other words educational institutions should:

☐ Be built and maintained with resources that are mined, harvested, processed, transported, and used in ways that are ecologically sustainable.

☐ Be designed to maximize the efficient use of energy, water, and other resources and put resources like rainfall and solar energy, which the site receives naturally, to work.

☐ Avoid the use of toxic materials in construction or maintenance so that people learning or working in a facility will not be exposed to health-threatening materials during the normal use of the facilities or in the case of fires. (When modern buildings catch fire, most people who die are not burned. They perish from breathing the toxic gases given off by burning plastic and other materials.)

☐ Be built on earthquake-safe geological deposits, in locations not subject to flooding and that do not use up valuable resources like prime agricultural soils or vital habitat areas.

The Business Community

The business community has a major role to play in achieving economic, social, and ecological security. There is a myth in our society that people engaged in business are only interested in profits. While everyone, including people directly engaged in business, is self-interested, business people are not necessarily more mercenary in protecting those interests than anyone else. In fact, examples cited in the preceding text show that many business people, from small businesses to large corporations, are putting extra effort into being ecologically and socially responsible.

Unfortunately, the lack of true-cost-pricing often, though not always, puts such businesses at an economic disadvantage with their less responsible competitors. When all costs are included, more socially and ecologically sustainable business practices are in everyone's eco-nomic interest.

Given that true-cost-pricing is not yet a reality, businesses can still do many things to foster eco-nomic security.

1.   Business and industry should design or retrofit their facilities along the lines previously discussed in the section on **New Designs For Educational Institutions.**

2.   If a business is involved in manufacturing, it should try to use recycled materials instead of virgin materials in production processes. It should also design products and packaging so that they can be easily reused or at least recycled and/or composted.

3.   All businesses should strive to use resources like energy and water as efficiently as possible. In addition to saving resources, efficient use will save a business money by reducing overhead costs.

4.   Businesses should avoid the use of toxic materials in production or maintenance whenever possible and develop production methods that do not produce toxic by-products.

5.   When using virgin materials, businesses should try to purchase materials that were mined, harvested, and processed in ways that are as ecologically benign as possible.

The Government

Federal

As with other sectors of our society, the federal government has an important role to play in moving us toward eco-nomic sustainability. Probably the most important task at the federal level is the implementation of true-cost or full-cost-pricing. This is essential to the process of moving away from our present subsidy-skewed economy to a truly free market system. Toward this aim the federal government can help by:

1.   Establish a true-cost-accounting methodology. Once established, this methodology can be used to find out what the products and services offered in the U.S. market place are really costing us.

2.   Passing legislation to ensure that the true or full costs, to the degree that they can be known, are included in the retail price of the product or service involved.

As was discussed in preceding chapters, at least partial true-cost methodologies are already beginning to emerge. The development of such methodologies could be accelerated by teaming up ecologically knowledgeable economists with the best U.S. accounting firms and the U.S. General Accounting Office for this purpose.

As methodologies and costs emerge from this collaboration, the information could be developed into a comprehensive system for evaluating true or full-cost. As this system evolves, federal legislatures could begin the process of gradually adding the true-cost to the price of products and services. The word "gradual" is used here advisedly. The speed at which the true-cost is added should only be tempered by how rapidly the free market can respond to the leveling of the economic playing field that true-cost-pricing would foster. If the change is too rapid, the market will not have enough time to change over to the production of ecologically benign replacement goods in sufficient quantities at reasonable prices to meet demand.

In addition to the implementation of true-cost-pricing, the federal legislature has another parallel role to play -- to phase out all energy and materials-related subsidies that make non-renewable energy and virgin material prices lower than they actually are. Getting rid of such subsidies would stimulate efficient energy use, the development of renewable energy resources, and the design of reusable and recyclable products and packaging. Eliminating subsidies would also contribute toward strengthening the free market process, in general, by further leveling the economic playing field.

In conjunction with phasing out energy related subsidies, it would be advisable for the federal legislature to set a floor on how low retail energy prices in the U.S. could fall. This is needed for the following reasons.

True-cost energy pricing, coupled with the elimination of tax subsidies for the fossil fuel and nuclear power industries, would greatly stimulate the move to more efficient energy use and the replacement of conventional energy supplies with renewable energy resources. This, in turn, would result in a rapid reduction in the amount of energy consumed in the United States, particularly imported energy. In light of the relatively large change in world energy demand that such a reduction would cause, world oil prices would fall quickly to perhaps $5 per barrel or less. Small improvements in U.S. energy efficiency and over-production by OPEC dropped world oil prices down to $8.50 per barrel for a short time in 1986. [812]

If retail energy prices in the U.S. were allowed to fall with world market prices, the move to efficiency and renewables would be slowed or even reversed. If the demand for oil increased, in response to lower oil prices, world energy prices would rise and we would be back on the same energy see-saw that we are on now.

With an energy price floor, however, lower prices for energy on the world market would not effect retail energy prices in the U.S. Thus, the move to greater efficiency and renewables would not be stifled. If, for some reason energy prices on the world market went higher than the U.S. retail energy price floor, U.S. retail prices would be allowed to rise with them. But as long as the United States continued to reduce consumption, a rise in world energy prices would be very unlikely.

A painless way to set this floor price would be to base it on the price of oil on the world market at the time of its enactment. If this price was $16 per barrel, for example, the retail price of

---

[812] *Copeland, Jeff and Penelope Wang. "Too Much Oil, Too Little Unity." Newsweek. Vol. 108, (October 27, 1986): p. 88. Also see Karmin, Monroe W. et al. "OPEC Searches for Those Good Old Days." U.S. News & World Report. Vol 101, (August 18. 1986): p. 35.*

energy in the U.S. market could fall no lower than $16 for the equivalent amount of energy in a barrel of oil plus any fixed costs and true-costs associated with its procurement, [813] processing, delivery, and use. In the case of electricity, its <u>retail</u> price could fall no lower than what electricity would cost if it was produced by burning $16 a barrel oil plus fixed and true-costs. But unlike its <u>retail</u> cost, the <u>wholesale</u> price of energy in U.S. markets would rise and fall with the world market price.

After setting this floor, the U.S. government should do everything possible, short of providing subsidies, to promote efficient energy use and renewable energy resources. One way to do this would be to provide low interest federal loans to finance energy efficiency improvements and renewable energy projects. These loans would finance projects that have paybacks that exceed by .5 percent plus administration, the interest that the government would be paying on what it borrowed to implement the program. In other words, the loan program would be designed so that the government would earn .5 percent on each loan. Actually, becoming more energy efficient and switching to renewables would happen naturally with true-cost-pricing and the elimination of energy industry subsidies. But setting a price floor and providing loans would make it to happen more rapidly which, after the dust settled, would be to everyone's advantage.

In addition to keeping the U.S. on the efficiency and renewables track, setting an energy price floor would help to reduce our national dept and free up cash to take care of other problems. For example, if the price of a barrel of oil on the world market fell to $5 per barrel while the retail price in the U.S. was based on $16 per barrel energy equivalent, an $11 surplus would be available for every barrel of oil energy equivalent used in the United States. Even if we were only using half the energy we currently use now, an $11 surplus per barrel energy equivalent, would generate over $60 billion each year. [814] This amount is on top of the $100 to $300 billion or more [815] that would be saved by getting rid of direct and hidden energy and material subsidies. [816]

State Governments

Although true or full-cost-pricing should be instituted on national and ultimately global levels, state governments can help the process along in a number of ways. States can set up their own accounting procedures to find out what the products and services offered in the state's economy are really costing the citizens of the state.

Unless products are:

□   made from materials that were mined, harvested, processed and fabricated in way that are ecologically sustainable,

□   designed to be used in ways that are ecologically benign,

□   designed to be easily reused, recycled, or composted at the end of its usefulness,

---

[813]   *The procurement costs levied on imported energy would need to be equal to the U.S. average fixed and true-procurement-cost for the same energy resource.*

[814]   *Author's calculations.*

[815]   *This $100 to $300 billion estimated subsidy only pertains to energy. It does not include the direct and hidden subsidies supporting the virgin materials industry which could be in the billions of dollars itself.*

[816]   *Hubbard, Harold R. Scientific America. Vol. 164, No. 4, (April 1991): p. 37. Also see Romm, Joseph J. The Once and Future Superpower. William Morrow and Company, Inc. New York, (1992): p. 148.*

☐ associated with an in-place, incentive based [817] infrastructure to insure that products are reused, recycled, or composted, as is appropriate, when their usefulness has passed,

the products in question will burden society with hidden costs.

In other words, on one or more of the levels listed above, we as individuals and as taxpayers are going to have to pay something above and beyond what the consumer paid for the product at the retail level. By adding these real costs to the retail price of the product in question, we avoid the public liability associated with them. Since the purchasers of a product are those who assumedly benefit from their purchases, it is only fair that they should pay all the costs connected with the product.

It would also be legitimate and logical to add these same costs to similar products imported into a state. Obviously, the destination state will have to pay for any negative environmental impact caused by the use of a product inside state boundaries. If the product is not designed to be easily recycled and a recycling infrastructure is not in place to handle it, the state will also have to pay for the product's disposal. The destination state will also be on the hook for any negative impacts, like groundwater pollution, that disposal of the product may cause.

Even the negative impacts associated with the creation of products in another state or country and the negative impacts associated with the energy used to transport such products to their retail destination will have a negative economic impact on the state where they are sold. For example, ecological or health problems sustained in one state affect every other state. Even if the costs associated with mitigating such problems are paid by the state where a product is produced, it creates a strain on that state's revenues. This increases the possibility that there will be less money to deal with other problems, such as providing homes for the homeless, public assistance for the poor, better education for youth, and better trained police. If a product's destination state has a superior public assistance program, reduced revenues in other states can have an additional effect. Since the people affected by these cutbacks are mobile, they may migrate to other states where services and conditions are better. As recent migration trends have shown, this phenomenon is also happening between nations.

Federal revenue may also be required to take up the slack in any of the areas just discussed to directly pay for cleanups or to pay health costs. For example, it may ultimately cost hundreds of billions of dollars to clean up all the toxic waste dumps in our country. The payment for pollution-related health costs may also run in the hundreds of billions of dollars. The more federal revenues are used up in dealing with these problems, the less there is money available to help states with education and so forth.

Even when ecological and health damages are sustained in other countries, the eco-nomic liabilities sustained will ultimately affect everyone. For example, if a local fishing industry is damaged or destroyed in a politically unstable country by pollution or over-exploitation, it can lead to civil unrest that may even cause governments to be overthrown. Even short of a revolution, such occurrences would have cost implications for the U.S. on at least two levels. Militarily, this could lead or contribute to expenditures like those we are currently paying to blockade Haiti or keep the peace in Somalia. Although it has not been widely publicized, the environmental degradation of Haiti and Somalia has been a contributing factor to the devastating problems experienced in those

---

[817]   *Incentive based: Either the discarded product or residue is valuable enough, in itself, to insure that it is recycled and/or returned to the ecology in a way that is ecologically benign, or its purchase includes a sufficient returnable deposit to achieve the same aim.*

countries.

Local Government

Since these same issues apply to the local level, local governments can also play a role in implementing true-cost-pricing. One area where local true-cost-pricing could be applied is in the disposal sector. Any product residue or product packaging that is not designed to be easily reused or recycled is going to cost something to dispose. At a minimum, these disposal costs include getting the residue or package to the disposal site and the cost of replacing the landfill volume the packaging or residue will use up. If the packaging or residue results in the release of air or water pollution, additional costs would be sustained. If the product residue or its packaging is toxic or partially toxic, even more costs, like cleaning up groundwater pollution, will be involved.

Under California State law, a $1 can of spray paint, with paint residue in it, costs about $20 to dispose legally. [818] With local true-cost-pricing, the can of spray paint would cost at least $21. Of course no one would buy it, which would quickly lead to the development of spray paint cans designed to be reused or at least recycled which would contain non-toxic paints and ecologically benign solvents.

In addition to disposal costs, the use of toxic materials has health cost implications to local governments. If the use of a material causes health problems, these costs should be added to the cost of the material involved. Leveling the economic playing field in these ways, would foster the development of non-toxic replacement products that would avoid such liabilities.

The Media

The media can be another important player in achieving eco-nomic sustainability. Probably the most important contribution the media can make is to do a better job of reporting on ecological issues. It is not so much that more time needs to be devoted to these topics, but that better research needs to go into its reporting.

When the Alaskan oil spill occurred, the media missed a great opportunity to broaden public awareness of the issue in ways that could lead to the avoidance of such problems in the future. Over and over, it was reported that although the spill was a tragedy, the only options available to us were to resign ourselves to similar disasters, from time to time, or we would have to stop driving our cars or accept freezing in the dark during the winter and roasting in the summer.

In the reporting, there was almost no mention, and certainly none in detail, of the many ways to avoid the use of fossil fuels altogether by using energy more efficiently and switching to renewable energy resources. Nor was the fact highlighted that if we pursued this course, many more jobs would be created than if we continue on our present energy path. Additionally, the reporting made no mention of the many other ways, economically and environmentally, we would benefit from, by becoming more energy efficient and switching to renewables. (See index for more entries.)

Another example of the need for improved media coverage is in the area of recycling. Although the media is largely sympathetic to the idea of recycling, much of the reporting on it ends by concluding that the expansion of recycling is hampered by the lack of markets for recycled materials.

The question never explored by reporters and editors is: **why aren't the markets there?** Even a cursory look into the subject reveals that using recycled materials in industry instead of virgin

---

[818] *Conversation with Gary Stepheny, the Director of Health, San Diego County, California, USA.*

materials saves large amounts of energy. Melting down a piece of refined metal and forming it into a new product takes much less energy than mining and processing virgin ores to make a product.

A little deeper look would uncover the direct tax subsidies that support the mining and harvesting of virgin materials. Further research would expose a long list of hidden costs related to our throw-away society which are ultimately paid by taxpayers. These costs range from the ecological damage caused during the procurement and processing of virgin materials to the landfill space that throwaway objects use up. Research like this would disclose that the "limited market" for recycled materials is completely artificial. Further, it would suggest that, if we truly had a free-market economy, industries needing raw materials would always purchase recycled materials first. Why? Because in a free market this would be the most cost-effective thing for them to do.

The Artist

Historically, consciously or unconsciously, the artist has served as a kind of beacon for the rest of humanity, pointing out new things or new ways of seeing the familiar. The artist has also played the role of a heightened sensory receptor for society at large, sensing some threat, challenge, or opportunity as yet unrecognized by the rest of us, then using art to bring it to our attention. Today the artist has a new challenge -- the challenge to imagine an ecologically sustainable future and use art to create that future. As an artist/designer I am of this camp and I encourage all artists to join in.

But even before launching oneself on such a daunting task, the artist can contribute to this future by using non-toxic ecologically benign media whenever possible. Many of the materials used by artists today are harmful to the artist and the environment. Yet, some of the most enduring art like cave paintings and pictographs were made with natural materials. Even the paintings by the masters were made using hand-ground pigments fixed in egg yolk, linseed oil, and bee's wax.

The Scientific and Engineering Community

The scientific and engineering community has a very important role in the development of an eco-nomically secure future. Historically, artists, scientists, and engineers were one. It is that shared heritage that the scientific and engineering community needs to embrace. Whether working as an individual or as part of a team, try to spend as little time as is needed figuring out why things will not work, or analyzing the things we are doing as a species to weaken our life support system.

Instead, spend your most creative energy discovering how we can live, as the modern beings that we are, in ways that protect our planet's life support system sufficiently to ensure its and our own future well being.

Even though the solutions discussed in this book are on the right track, none of them could be described as totally eco-nomically sustainable. Sooner or later, the contradiction inherent in these technologies will have to be worked out by scientists and engineers.

In addition to the technologies discussed in this book, there is one research direction that I would like to suggest to researchers.

Bioluminescence - This is the light that is generated by fireflies, glow worms, and other organisms. Compared even to fluorescent lighting which converts about 25 percent of the energy delivered to it into light, bioluminescence, which is virtually "light without heat", converts close to 100 percent of the energy consumed to create it into light. [819] If a practical bioluminescent light could be developed it could be many times more efficient than today's best lighting technology.

The Religious And Spiritual Community

Whatever religious, spiritual, or philosophic path we follow, we honor the creation of the universe and its creator when we strive to live on our planet in ways that are eco-nomically sustainable. Not only is protecting our planet's life support system in our own interest, it is also totally consistent with the precepts of doing unto others as we would have them do unto us, and loving thy neighbor as thyself.

When we conduct our affairs in ways that preserve the quality of the air, the purity of our water, and the health of the soil, we contribute to the well being of each other and all life. Toward this goal, there are a number of practical activities that religious and spiritually-directed individuals and groups can undertake:

❑ If your religious and spiritual path is practiced in a building or other facility, it should be designed or redesigned to be energy, water, and in general resource- efficient. Facilities should also be maintained using ecologically benign strategies and products.

❑ If your path involves education, people in general and our youth in particular need to know how to be responsible astronauts on Spaceship Earth. They need to know how our planet's life support system works and how we as individuals and a species can provide ourselves with the things we need and want in ways that are sustainable. This can be accomplished through regular lecture and classroom formats and through hands-on projects like putting in an organic garden, recycling, wildlife study camping trips, etc.

If your organization purchases food, try to purchase organically grown food. For a time, this may be more expensive than buying the typical petrochemically grown fare, but in reality organically grown food is healthier to eat, and it protects farm workers, wildlife, and water supplies from pesticides and chemical fertilizers. It also gives farmers an economic incentive to convert to sustainable agricultural practices.

More ecologically sound consumption choices can be made on other levels as well. In general, all purchases, be they kitchen towels or dish washing liquid, or materials for a major construction project, should be made on the basis of total-cost and ecological sustainability.

We are at a turning point. How we conduct ourselves over the next few years will greatly determine the future of our children. As expressed by a Kenyan proverb, "Treat the earth well. It was not given to you by your parents . . . . it was lent to you by your children". How our children remember us in the future will have a great deal to do with the wisdom of our acts in the present. [820]

---

[819] *Harvey, Newton E. Bioluminescence. Academic Press Inc. New York (1952): p. v.*

[820] *Larson Geanne and Madge Mecheels-Cyrus. Seeds Of Peace. New Society Publishers, (1987): p. 118.*

Chapter XII

ACHIEVING ECO-NOMIC SECURITY THE SAN DIEGO/TIJUANA REGION

A CASE STUDY

Note: *Although the material presented here focusses on the San Diego/Tijuana region the principals it is based on can be applied to any region on our planet.*

Synopsis

This five part chapter explores the possibility of creating an economically and ecologically (eco-nomically) sustainable economy in the San Diego/Tijuana region.

Part one describes how the region and its economy are vulnerable. The threats discussed range from intentional attacks on key infrastructure elements like aqueducts, electric transmission lines, natural gas and oil pipelines, freeway overpasses and railroad tressels or their damage from natural causes like earthquakes and floods; and how this could effect the flow of basic resources like energy, water and food into the region. Also discussed is how the region is vulnerable economically, from a purely business-as-usual perspective, even if the threats to its security, just discussed, never manifest.

Part two introduces the concept of Eco-nomically Integrated Planning (EIP) and how it can be used to strengthen the region's economy while making it and the communities that make it up less vulnerable to the threats described in part one. For example, if floodplains, which are vulnerable to flood and earthquake damage, are not developed, the public at large won't have to bear the economic burden of floodplain clean-up when floods and earthquakes occur.

Part three focuses on how the region's economy can be further strengthened and made more secure by pursuing business and employment opportunities aimed at making it more energy and water efficient and more energy, water and food self-sufficient.

Part four examines the potential for the San Diego/Tijuana region to become more energy and water efficient and energy, water and food self-sufficient -- in ways that meet the test of cost-effectiveness from a purely investment perspective.

Part five is an exploration of the future. It answers the question: If the San Diego/Tijuana region was well on its way to becoming a sustainable economy, what would living in in the region be like?

Vulnerability By Design?

Even if it had been planned intentionally, it would be difficult to create a regional economy that is less sustainable and more vulnerable than our case study.

As it is currently configured, the region's infrastructure could be seriously damaged by a small group of people or even an individual. Power lines, oil pipelines, natural gas pipelines, freeway over-passes, railroad trestles, aqueducts, and dams are all vulnerable to simple explosives that can be home-made or stolen from mining or construction projects.

Water stored in open reservoirs can be easily contaminated by dropping something into them from a plane or by contaminating their upstream watersheds.

Power lines can be knocked out with hunting rifles.

If a terrorist attack was well orchestrated, the region's infrastructure could be damaged so severely that the flow of energy, water and food to the region, for all practical purposes, would be cut off. The loss of key freeway overpasses and rail lines would also make it difficult for people to leave the region to obtain these necessities.

The region's dependence on imported oil makes it vulnerable to political changes, terrorism and war in the countries from which it imports oil. Just the fear of reduced oil imports can affect the regional economy by causing oil and other energy prices to rise. During the recent Gulf War, oil prices on the world market almost doubled even though there was never any real oil shortage. If shortages were to become real, the impact on the regional economy would be doubly traumatic.

The Mexican part of the region is slightly less vulnerable to events in other countries that affect the supply and price of oil in the world market. Unlike the U.S., Mexico currently pumps enough oil out of the ground to meet its domestic demand. Nevertheless, Mexico's economic well-being is affected by the supply and price of oil on the world market.

Beyond the threat of intentional human acts, the region's key infrastructural elements are also vulnerable to earthquakes.

Geologists, who study the region, conclude that there is a high probability that the Tijuana/San Diego Region will experience a serious earthquake sometime in the next 30 years. Additionally, the region's vulnerability to earthquake damage has been aggravated because of extensive development on its valley floors which overlay alluvial deposits.

Structures built on alluvial deposits are more vulnerable to earthquake damage than structures built on most other geological formations. Alluvial deposits are composed of sand and groundwater which tend to liquify if shaken. This well known phenomenon is called liquefaction. Since these deposits usually lie in floodplains, developing them has made the region vulnerable to flooding from excessive rainfall or the loss of upstream dams during earthquakes.

Obviously, if any of the possibilities discussed above occurred singly or in concert, the region's economy would be seriously damaged. The clean-up and repair costs associated with a serious earthquake or flood, or both, where valley floors have been developed could range in the hundreds of millions of dollars or more.

Even if the damage was insured, the economic impact would be devastating. Insurance never covers everything, and when faced with catastrophic losses, insurance companies have gone broke. To avoid going under, insurance companies would almost certainly raise rates for everyone else. To the degree that the losses were not covered by insurance, federal, state, and local tax revenues would be tapped. Whatever the case, the public ends up footing the bill.

Even if it could be guaranteed that no earthquake or flood will occur, the region's economy is still quite vulnerable from a purely business-as-usual perspective.

There are three principal ways that dollars come into our case study's economy -- through exports, from federal and state governments (on both sides of the border), and from tourism and new residents. All three of these sources are shaky.

Although the region's economy has a substantial export sector, it is probably running at or close to a cash-flow deficit. If there is a broad economic down-turn, the cash flow defficit related to trade could get much worse. When the economy is weak in other parts of the world, the demand for products produced locally declines.

The region's nearly total dependence on imported necessities like water, food and energy is another point of trade vulnerability. When economic times are tight, it's easier for people living outside the region to cut back on purchasing the things that it exports than it is for locals to curtail their purchase of necessities like water, food and energy.

This means that during broad national and global economic slow-downs, the rate that money flows into the region slows down faster than the flow of dollars leaving. If this continues for any substantial period of time, dollars will become scarce, local business will suffer, and economic activity will be stifled.

Another point of economic vulnerability is the region's dependence on federal and state funding.

Changes in policy by the central governments on both sides of the border can severely reduce the amount of cash coming into the region. Although the study region hasn't been hit that hard yet, federal cut-backs and base closures have had a devastating impact on some communities. Whether dollars are lost because of a base closure or for some other reason, federal and state dollars can be taken away at any time. Additionally, the central governments in both countries are in serious debt and looking hard for ways to cut costs. This will be true for some time even under the most optimistic scenario.

Tourism and new residents are a third major way that dollars come into the region's economy. Tourists spend money when they visit and new residents bring assets with them. Like trade, the amount of dollars brought into the region by tourism and new residents is vulnerable to broad national and global economic slowdowns.

The economy is also vulnerable ecologically. Currently, it is almost completely dependent on the use of non-renewable energy resources. It also uses potentially renewable resources in ways that make them non-renewable or difficult to renew. The region's rapidly filling landfills are graphic testimony to this fact. To replace what is buried, our planet is being scoured for a rapidly shrinking supply of virgin resources.

Similarly, the region's agricultural and forest soils are often being used in ways that cause them to erode more rapidly than they can be renewed. These soils are also being used up by urban sprawl. In the U.S., an estimated one million acres of prime agricultural soil are being converted into shopping malls, housing projects and roads each year. Practices in the study region are reflective of this trend.

Groundwater, an important element in a more water-secure future, is being contaminated with pesticides and industrial poisons. Additionally, the development of and damage to the region's forests and grasslands is reducing groundwater recharge rates.

In short, the region's economy is undercutting the ecological resource foundation that makes the creation of a sustainable economy possible. As the ecological resource base shrinks, the region's economic options shrink with it.

Obviously, the picture just painted is not very pretty, but is the current state of regional vulnerability inevitable? Absolutely not.

Developing A Plan

One of the most important aspects of making the San Diego/Tijuana Region more secure is to develop an eco-nomically integrated land-use plan. The aim of this plan would be to reduce the region's vulnerability to terrorism, earthquakes, floods, and potential shortages of water, food and energy while strengthening and diversifying its economy.

An important step in this process is the creation of a set of Eco-nomically Integrated Planning (EIP) maps for the region. The purpose of these maps is to answer a very simple, yet profound, question: If the aim is to create a sustainable economy in this region, where is it appropriate to do what?

Where are the best places to locate intense human activities like cities? What land should be set aside for agriculture and wildlife habitat? What hazards, like floodplains and geologically unstable areas, should be avoided? (For a detailed explanination of ecologically integrated planning and EIP mapping see chapter VI.)

Obviously, floodplains are dangerous places to develop. They are also costly places to repair when floods or earthquakes occur. Considering the eco-nomic vulnerability that floodplain development represents, it would be prudent to adopt a set of regional land-use rules which would:

--- prohibit further development of the region's floodplains,

--- establish a process whereby existing floodplain development can be removed in an orderly and equitable manner, hopefully before the region experiences a major earthquake, flood, or both.

Although prohibiting new floodplain development and, over time, retiring existing floodplain development --- would make the region more eco-nomically secure, doing so will affect some people's economic situation negatively.

Since it would be unfair to penalize people who were playing by the existing rules, these people **must** be fairly compensated for what ever economic loss they sustain under the new land-use regimen.

If the new-land use rules indicate that a property should be used in a way that would produce less income than what would have been possible under the existing rules, the property's owner must be fairly compensated for any financial losses that the rule changes bring about. If a parcel of land should be retired from its present use, the owner must be compensated for any reduction in the value of their investment in the land and the value of any improvements they have made to the land.

Although the details of moving inappropriate development out of floodplains needs to be worked out, the general idea would be to prohibit any further development in floodplains, either on undeveloped sites or existing sites. Businesses already located in floodplains would be allowed to stay where they are and maintain their facilities, but would not be allowed to expand. The newest structures in the floodplains can be maintained, barring a serious flood or earthquake, for around 50 years before maintenance become so costly that it would be more cost-effective for the owner to build a new facility than to repair what they have. As these new replacement facilities are built in safer locations, structures in the floodplains would be removed.

As these areas are reclaimed they can be converted to parks, agriculture, wildlife habitats, and other uses eco-nomically compatible with the conditions and hazards that floodplains present.

In any event, property owners must be compensated for any legitimate losses they sustain because of rule changes. Not only is this the right thing to do, it is the only way that the necessary changes will have a chance to succeed politically.

How would such compensation take place?

Here are just a few ideas.

---- Direct public purchase - While the direct purchase of privately held land may appear to be cost prohibitive, this may not be the case. Although changing land-use rules would make some land less valuable, it would also make other land more valuable. Since this added value would be unearned, a percentage of it could be used to purchase land in floodplains or to compensate land owners whose land became less valuable due to changes in land-use policies. This would be done as land whose value was increased by land-use rule changes is sold, or developed and sold.

---- Selling density rights - It is possible for owners of land in areas that should not be developed to sell density rights to developers that own land in areas appropriate for development.

---- Creative financing - An example of this would be to work out agreements with the landowners to purchace their land by paying them a monthly income for the rest of their lives. This would be an especially good way to keep agricultural soils from being developed. Today, many farmers sell their land to provide for their retirement. A steady income would negate that need. Upon the landowner's death, the land would revert to public ownership. This is similar to the negative equity loans now available to home owners.

Along these same lines, the Trust For Public Land, the Nature Conservancy, and locally, the Cleveland National Forest Foundation, have developed a number of ways that privately owned land can be donated or partially donated to the public in ways that save the private owner as much or more in taxes than they would have made if they had developed their land or sold it on the open market. Once ownership comes under public control, it should not be sold, only leased. Leasing land will provide an income for the public forever. If land is sold, the income stops.

Efficiency and Self-Sufficiency
Pathways To A Secure Future And A Strong Economy

Making the region more resource-efficient and self-sufficient is another way to reduce the chance that natural phenomena, or accidental or intentional human acts, can cut-off water, food and energy supplies upon which the region now depends.

Becoming more energy and water efficient improves security by extending the useful life of imported energy and water supplies stored locally, if imported supplies are cut-off.

Regional security can be improved further by collecting more water and energy locally, and by growing as many crops (food and energy) as can be justified eco-nomically.

Not only will this reduce the threat of energy, water, and food shortages in the future, it will insulates the region from conditions in other parts of the world that might affect the quality, availability and cost of these necessities in the world market. [821] Increasing regional self-sufficiency has the added benefit of increasing the number of times that money circulates in the local economy, thus creating new business and job opportunities across the board.

---

[821]   *On the global level there are a number of conditions that could have an effect on the San Diego/Tijuana region's food security.*

Currently around 90 to 95 percent of the food consumed in the region is imported. [Scott Murry, Faustino Munoz] Continuing population growth coupled with the accelerating loss of agricultural soils to erosion and development, will eventually lead to higher food prices due to increasing competition for food in the world market [Committee on the Role of Alternative Farming methods in Modern Production Agriculture. Alternative Agriculture. National Academy Press, Washington D.C., (1989): pp. 116-117, and Brown, Lester R. et al. Vital Signs 1994. Worldwatch Institute and W.W. Norton and company Inc., New York, London, (1994): p. 20.]

*This situation will likely be further aggravated by the increasing food purchasing power in countries like China. The average per capita income in China rose 26 percent during 1992 and 1993 and is expected to rise another 10 percent in 1994. [Brown, Lester R. "Who Will Feed China," World*Watch. Vol. 7, No. 5 (September/October): p. 12.] Coupled with China's increased purchasing power is the accelerating loss of China' croplands to development. [Brown, Lester R. "Who Will Feed China," World*Watch. Vol. 7, No. 5 (September/October): p. 13.]*

If this trend continues, China's still growing population will be increasingly dependent on the global supermarket for food. With 1.2 billion plus citizens, even a small increase in per capita purchasing power can have a large impact on world food prices and availability. If the region was food self-sufficient or nearly so, it would be much less vulnerable to the powerful forces shaping the global supermarket of the future.

When local people are employed to make the region more energy, water, and food self-sufficient, a good part of the money they earn will be spent there. This spending will help local business, thus creating more local jobs and new business opportunities. Economists call this the multiplier effect. Just saving energy and water puts money in peoples' pockets by reducing their utility bills. This is a benefit that can be enjoyed by individuals and businesses alike.

Obviously, much could be gained by becoming more resource-efficient and self-sufficient, but global competition presents a hurdle.

The region is not an economic island. Therefore, things produced and/or extracted in it must be priced competitively with equivalent imports to be successful. This is true even though such imports are often created in ways that are not eco-nomically sustainable, are subsidized, and are extracted and produced by people earning less than liveable wages,.

While overcoming this hurdle is a problem, it is not impossible.

For example, many strategies to increase energy and water efficiency are already competitive with subsidized imports. Numerous studies backed up by a large amount of real world experience have shown this to be true. Intelligent investments in energy and water efficiency will give a better return on investment than most money-market funds. (Read Chapter VII for details.)

While employing local people to collect energy, and water and grow food and energy crops would create business opportunities and jobs, doing so is less easily justified economically than becoming more energy and water efficient. This is because the cost of developing local resources is more expensive than most ways of saving them. This extra cost makes it more difficult for regionally produced energy, water and food to compete with subsidized imports. Just considering energy, Harold Hubbard, (Scientific American, April 1991), calculated that direct and hidden subsidies for non-renewable energy resources "range between $100 billion and $300 billion per year" in the United States.

If the subsidies supporting non-renewable energy resources, imported water, and imported food were removed, becoming more resource efficient and self-sufficient in the region would be easy. With these subsidies removed, almost any well conceived strategy to increase efficiency and self-sufficiency would be cost competitive with imports.

Unfortunately, these subsidies, which are largely federal, are not likely to be eliminated in the near future. But even with this as a given, there is considerable work that can be accomplished in a cost-effective manner that will help create a stronger and more sustainable regional economy.

The usual way we evaluate cost-effectiveness is to compare prices. Is it cheaper to produce a kwh of electricity by burning imported natural gas, than it is to produce it by manufacturing solar (photvoltaic) cells locally and installing them on the region's roof tops, over parking lots, and other places where shade would be desirable?

If only the over-the-counter cost is included, purchasing the natural gas is still "cheaper", though not by much and probably not for long. Texas Instruments in conjunction with Southern California Edison is planning to have a more competively priced solar cell on the market in the near future.

But is "cheaper" always the best buy? Let's take a closer look.

When money is spent on imported water, food and energy to meet local needs, the lion's share of it ends up in the pockets of people who don't live in the region. Therefore, very little if any of the money they receive will be spent in the region's economy. Thus, local business and job opportunities are lost. When money is invested in making the region more efficient and self-sufficient, most of it will end up in the pockets of people who live there. Because the people earning this money live locally, much of what they earn will be spent locally, which will create even more business and employment opportunities.

From a municipal perspective, this increase in business and employment will save money by reducing welfare and unemployment rolls. A stronger business and employment environment will cause the value of real estate to increase which will increase property tax revenues. It will also invigorate the rental market, and the increase in business in general will generate additional sales tax revenue. Plus, when a municipality makes its own facilities more energy and water efficient, it reduces its own overhead costs.

In other words, when we invest in becoming more efficient and self-sufficient, we reduce municipal costs while increasing revenues.

If a portion of this increase in revenue is allocated to projects designed to increase efficiency and self-sufficiency, such projects will be able to compete more effectively with subsidized imports.

This allocation should not be considered a subsidy because the increased revenue and lower costs would not have come into existence if efficiency and self-sufficiency were not pursued. The fact that the revenue benefit comes after the efficiency or resource development take place, is no different than investing in office buildings or shopping malls. Buildings and malls do not produce revenue until they are completed.

How Efficient And Self-Sufficient
Can The Region Cost-Effectively Become?

Currently, the region exports around $6 billion dollars out of the regional economy each year to pay for imported energy (98%), food (90%), and water (90%). To the degree the region can create business and employment opportunities aimed at developing cost-effective ways to save, collect, and/or produce these necessities locally, these dollars will keep circulating locally. Since the majority of the workers and business people earning this money would live there, most of what they earned would be spent there, strengthening the economy on all fronts.

With good planning, all of the $6 billion dollars currently exported can be reclaimed at a better return on investment than that earned by the typical money market fund. But even if only half of this money could be retained, it would give birth to a thriving regional economy for the next 30 to 40 years. Additionally, it would make the region less vulnerable to the cut off of water, food or energy resulting from accidental or intentional human acts here or abroad (imported oil), or from natural phenomena like earthquakes and floods. Every time a dollar is spent on something produced or grown locally, it generates one to three dollars of additional economic activity. Thus capturing the $6 billion now exported out of the region would translate into $12 to $24 billion of additional economic activity in the region each year.

The potential to save energy and water in the region is substantial. In fact, if the best available technologies and strategies were in place, per capita energy consumption could be cost-effectively reduced to around 20 percent of what it is today, and few if any lifestyle changes would be necessary. (See index for efficient energy use specifics.)

Although the savings potential for water is not as dramatic as with energy, water efficient technologies and strategies could cut local per capita water consumption by 70 percent -- again with little if any lifestyle changes. (See the index for efficient water use specifics.)

Renewable Energy
The Region's Potential

Even without efficiency, our study region has more than twice the renewable energy resources necessary to be completely energy self-sufficient. Indeed, it is so wealthy in these resources that it could be a large energy exporter. More on this later.

Yet in terms of regional security, it would be far more cost-effective and eco-nomically sound to reduce the amount of energy needed by becoming more energy efficient. Up to a point, saving energy through efficiency is generally more cost-effective than producing energy from any source, renewable or otherwise. This is especially true for non-renewable energy sources if the **true-cost** of their extraction, use and waste disposal is included in the accounting. (See chapter III for details on true-cost accounting.)

Even though a solid case can be made that the region could be 5 times more energy efficient than it is today, its renewable energy resources are so plentiful that becoming more energy if efficient is not a requirement for energy self-sufficiency. Even if the region stayed just as inefficient as it is today, all the energy required by 5 million people, using as much energy as the average San Diego county resident uses today, could be produced by installing 548 million square meters of solar cell panels -- on roof tops, and over parking lots and other paved areas. For perspective, 548 million square meters of solar cells divided between 5 million people, equals 110 square meters or 1,183 square feet of solar cell panels per capita. While this is no small amount of cells, their installation is certainly possible.

Completely installed, 548 million square meters of solar cell panels would cover around 8 percent of the land that is projected to be urbanized when the region's population reaches 5 million people, around 2005. This solar array would produce enough electricity to power everything that requires energy. This would include all commercial building services, all transportation services (cars, trucks, trains -- everything but airplanes), and all commercial, industrial and residential needs. Also included is plenty of extra production for storage. When energy is plentiful it could be stored for use at night and during cloudy periods. As clouds thicken, the production of electricity by solar cells declines.

With increased efficiency, the number of square meters of solar cells required can be reduced proportionally. If regional energy consumption was reduced by a conservative 50 percent, it would only require 55 square meters of solar cells per capita to meet the total energy needs of the region. If energy consumption was reduced by 75 percent, only 27.5 square meters or 296 square feet of solar cells per capita would be required. A room 20 feet long and 15 feet wide contains 300 square feet of floor area.

If 55 square meters of solar cells per capita were installed but only required 27.5 square meters per capita were needed to meet local needs, the regional economy could earn a billion or more dollars each year by selling energy to other areas. At current energy prices, a fully developed regional renewable energy system could bring 1 to 5 billion dollars into the local economy each year depending on the level of efficiency that is achieved, the scale of renewable energy development, and the price of energy in the world market.

Efficient Water Use
Strategies And Technologies

Shifting the focus to water --- at present wasteful per capita water consumption levels, our study region can not achieve water self-sufficiency. Nevertheless, the region can be water self-sufficient, if an efficient, integrated water collection, storage, use, and reuse strategy is adopted.

Per capita water consumption could be reduced considerably if better water use and reuse measures were adopted. Some measures are already widely used like low flow toilets and shower heads, and drip irrigation. Other less-used approaches included soil moisture sensors which turn on irrigation equipment when the sensor is triggered by plant needs, drought tolerant landscaping, and water reuse in industry. If widely adopted, these and other related measures could reduce regional per capita water consumption by 70 percent, with little if any life style changes. (See index for more specifics on efficient water use.)

Renewable Water Resources,
The Region's Potential

Given the goal of achieving water self-sufficiency, how much water can be sustainably collected from the region's watersheds each year?

If only 6 percent of the rainfall received by the region in an average rainfall year (half the natural runoff) was collected and stored in underground tanks so it would not evaporate*, it would be enough water to supply a 5 million person regional population with 64 gallons of water per day, per person, for one year.

This 64 gallon figure is based on the assumptions that:

--- The total area encompassed by the Tijuana/San Diego Region's coastal watersheds is 6,220 square miles or 3,980,800 acres.

--- The average rainfall over this whole area is 18 inches per year. (Yearly rainfall in the region ranges from around 10 inches along the coast to 40 inches plus in the higher mountains.)

--- 12 percent of the Region's yearly average rainfall of 18 inches runs off into the ocean or is captured behind dams.

--- Only half of this runoff (6 percent of the Region's total rain fall) can be collected from the 3,980,800 acres that make up the region's coastal watersheds without causing unsustainable trauma to the region's (plant and animal) watershed communities.

In addition to the 64 gallons per capita per day that could be collected from watersheds, another 25 gallons per capita per day of runoff can be collected from impervious surfaces like rooftops, parking lots, paved playgrounds, driveways and patios. When rain falls on these surfaces, close to 100 percent of it can be collected. (This 25 gallon per capita figure is based on impervious surface estimates derived by the author from data published 3/29/94 in SANDAG/SOURCEPOINT taken from "Source: Series 8 Regional Growth Forecast." Note: Road and freeway surfaces are not included in the calculations as potential collection surfaces.)

Obviously, water collected from parking lots and driveways would need to be filtered for most uses. Even water from rooftops, patios, and paved playgrounds would need filtration. Filtering can be expensive, but if coupled with a good watershed education program, its cost can be greatly reduced. A good watershed education program can improve the quality of the water collected from impervious surfaces markedly. As more people come to understand how their activities affect the water they drink, they will be much more conscious about releasing pollutants that will end up in it.

In addition to collecting rainwater from watersheds and impervious surfaces, there is around 100,000 acre feet of water that can be extracted sustainably from the region's groundwater supplies each year. If these resources are developed, it would add another 18 gallons per capita each day for the projected regional population of 5 million people.

Adding these three sources together --- 64 gal. + 25 gal. + 18 gal. equals a water supply of 107 gallons per capita per day for 365 days a year for a 5 million person population.

If 80 percent of this water is recycled after it is used, it would supply another 85 gallons per capita per day for irrigation. This 85 gallons added to the 107 gallons that could be collected, adds up to a total per capita water-use allowance of 192 gallons of water per capita per day. This is close to 90 percent of the per capita water usage in the San Diego part of the region in 1995. The San Diego part of the region currently uses around 214 gallons of water per capita per day for all purposes, (residential, commercial, industrial, and for agriculture).

*(Four to ten feet of water evaporates from the surface of the region's open reservoirs each year.)

Agricultural Resources
The Region's Potential

On the food front, the San Diego/Tijuana Region is very rich in agricultural soils. From the most productive to the least, there are 8 agricultural soil classifications, number "1" being the most versatile for growing crops. The land areas covered in the region by the 4 best soil classifications are estimated to be as follows:

Number 1 soil ----- 153 square miles (396 square kilometers.)

Number 2 soil ----- 145 square miles. (375 square kilometers.)

Number 3 soil ----- 670 square miles. (1,735 square kilometers.)

Number 4 soil ----- 1,221 square miles. (3,162 square kilometers.)

Although there are ample soils to feed many more than 5 million people, regional food production is limited by the availability of water. However, an 85 gallon per capita per day recycled water budget would be enough water to irrigate over 400,000 acres or 625 square miles one foot deep, or all the region's number one and two soils (298 square miles or 190,720 acres or 77,215 hectares) a little over two feet (.6 meters) deep each year. Two acre feet of water used efficiently, combined with the natural rainfall that does not run off, is enough water to grow a wide variety of crops. Average yearly rainfall in the region ranges from just under 12 inches along the coast to up to 4 feet in mountains.

To feed 5 million people by growing food on 190,720 acres (298 square miles) of agricultural soils, each acre would have to feed 27 people, or each person would be fed by growing food on a 1,600 square foot or 148.8 square meter plot of land (a square piece of ground 12.2 meters or 40 feet on a side). This is enough land (190,720 acres) to comfortably feed 5 million people if their average diet is low in land-dependent meat products. Even more food could be grown with the available water if grown in greenhouses designed to recycle the water that evaporates and transpires from the soils and plants they enclose.

In summary, our study region has the resources to supply 5 million people with all the energy they require and still be a large energy exporter. It also has the capacity to be water and food self-sufficient for this same population, even though water is a limiting factor. Additionally, this can be done while maintaining a per capita standard of living that's higher than what is average in the San Diego part of the region today (1995).

This capacity, coupled with Eco-nomically Integrated (land-use) Planning would greatly improve the region's economic future, while reducing its vulnerability to natural phenomenon and to intentional or accidental human acts.

The San Diego/Tijuana Region
A Vision Of A Sustainable Future

If our study region's economy was well on its way to becoming completely sustainable, what would it be like to live there?

Actually, at least on the surface, life would be much the same as it is today, except that the region would be much more park-like in appearance and there would be little if any pollution. If they chose to, people would still have cars and would be able to drive them as far and often as they do now. The difference would be that they would be driving much more efficient cars powered by renewable energy produced locally.

Electric cars would be powered by solar (photovoltaic) cell which would convert the solar energy that now falls on rooftops, parking lots, etc. into electricity. Cars powered by (solar) generated electricity are already considerably more efficient than those powered by fuel. If 100 units of gasoline will allow a car to travel 100 miles, the same car converted to electricity and charged with 100 units of electrical energy could travel 300 miles. This is because engines powered by fuels only convert 16 to 20 percent of the energy they consume into vehicular motion. Electric motors used in cars convert 90 percent plus of the electricity they consume into vehicular motion. Even if losses related to charging and discharging storage systems (batteries, flywheels) are included, electric powered cars convert 60 percent or more of the energy they use into vehicular motion. As far as range goes, American Flywheel Systems Inc. is expecting to have a comercial flywheel storage system on the market in 2 to 3 year and flywheel storage in cars in 1998. Flywheel storage will give an electric car a highway range of 360 miles and be able to accelerate from 0-60 mph in 7.9 seconds. Additionally, a flywheel storage system can be completely recharged in 25 minutes and last for 20 years. [822]

For fuel powered cars, even 100 MPG is not the limit. The Rocky Mountain Institute (RMI) in Colorado calculates that a fuel powered station wagon sized car could be developed that would get 150 MPG, simply by taking advantage of technologies like those demonstrated by the Voyager Aircraft. The Voyager Aircraft flew two people completely around our planet on one tank of gas. Additionally, if these cars were mass produced, they could be sold for an affordable price. Supporting this assertion, RMI reports that "10 manufacturers (including Volvo, Volkswagen, and Renault) have built and tested attractive, low-pollution, prototype cars that get 67 to 138 miles per gallon," and that "better designs and stronger materials make some of these safer than today's cars, as well as more nimble and peppy."

Even though plenty of energy for powering cars and trucks would be available, people probably wouldn't drive nearly as much as they do today. This is because the communities they live in would include various pathways designed for pedestrians, human powered vehicles, and electric carts. Electric carts would be used to move cargo and people needing transport assistance in and around community centers. This arrangement would be facilitated by changing existing community designs to maximize the balance between the availability of homes and apartments, with opportunities for work, education, and recreation. Some people would still commute to jobs and visit other communities, but the opportunity to work and play in one's own community would be optimized. The expanded use of telecommunications would also reduce the need to commute by making it possible for more people to work or be educated at home or at satellite locations in their own communities.

Mass transit between communities would provide a convenient way for people living in different areas to get together. Cars and delivery vehicles coming into community centers would be brought in on underground roads to underground parking and loading docks and/or be kept to the outskirts of smaller community centers.

Buildings would look more or less the same as they do today but would be much better insulated and very resource efficient in all their operations. Some low-cost ($40-$45 per square foot) buildings in Canada are as much as 10 time more energy efficient than are most buildings in our study region today. Even though winter temperatures may drop to as low as minus 60 degrees fahrenheit, some 2,000 square foot homes in Canada have heating bills that are less than $60 per year. (See index for more details on energy efficient building designs.)

In addition to being well insulated, most buildings in the region would get 85 percent of their light during the day from daylight sources. Windows, skylights, electric lighting, wall coloring, etc., would be coordinated to maximize the benefits of natural light to increase the comfort and productivity of each individual.

Electric lighting fixtures would be very efficient and fixture placement would focus on

---

[822] *This and other information about mechanical flywheel systems is available by calling or writing to American Flywheel Systems Inc., P.O. Box 449, Medina, WA 98039, (206) 454-1818.*

delivering light to where tasks requiring it are performed. Light systems would also be controlled by automated motion/heat sensors so that electric lights would turn on when someone entered a room and turn off automatically when the last person left. Light intensity sensors would also dim or turn electric lights off according to the amount of daylight available. The range of light levels in a room would be infinitely adjustable by its occupants. (See index for more on energy efficient lighting.)

Buildings would also be designed or remodeled to avoid external and internal heat gain. This would be accomplished through the thoughtful placement and choice of windows, and by using the most energy efficient machinery and office equipment available. New openable window designs provide as much as 20 times more insulation value as do the single pane windows widely used today. Some computers use a fraction of the energy to do the same work as do others.

Although a building with features like those just described would require very little cooling, cooling would be provided by installing heat-absorbent pipes horizontally below the ground. When cooling is required, air collected in naturally cool places like in the shade of a tree, would be drawn by a fan through the buried pipes. As it passes through the pipes, the air is cooled further by the earth before it is discharged to cool the building. The temperature a few feet below the surface of the earth is usually around 55 degrees fahrenheit. (See the index for more details on efficient energy use for more details.)

In most situations, this system alone would be sufficient to cool thoughtfully designed buildings. Where air conditioning is necessary, earth-cooled air would save energy and money by reducing the amount of cooling the air conditioner would have to provide.

If all costs are considered, direct solar energy is the most cost effective energy source available in the region for heating space, water, and for producing steam and/or drying heat needed for many industrial processes. Selective surface*, flat plate collectors can produce steam even when it is overcast. Concentrating tracking collectors can deliver steam at 600 degrees centigrade (1,112 degrees fahrenheit) or more on clear sunny days. Back-up energy for these processes will be provided by solar generated electricity -- primarily from solar (photovoltaic) cells mounted on roofs, parking areas, and other areas where shade is desirable.

Industries, their machinery, and the electric motors that power them would also be much more efficient than today. Most of this technology is already available, and in most cases, its installation will pay for itself just by saving energy.

Whether industrial, commercial, or residential, new buildings would not be built in areas that are subject to flooding or earthquake damage due to liquefaction. Buildings already located in these areas would not be rebuilt there when they wore out.

Efficient Water Use

Although water consumption per capita cannot be reduced as much as energy, good strategies of efficient water use can cut water consumption substantially without changing lifestyles. In other words, people could shower, bathe, and flush toilets just as often as today, but all the toilets and showerheads installed in the region would be low flow.

Landscaping, to the casual observer would appear to be much the same as today with perhaps a bit less grass. Other plant elements would be drawn from a pallet of luxuriant drought tolerant, useful material, and food-producing ground cover, shrubs and trees.

Where irrigation is desired, it would be supplied by water-efficient irrigation technologies like drip irrigation that would be controlled by moisture sensors installed in the soil. These sensors, called tenseometers, insure that irrigation water is only applied when there is a real need. (See

(*A specially designs surface that is very good at absorbing and converting light energy into heat energy while not letting heat energy escape once it's absorbed.)

index for more details on efficient water use.)

Water Reuse

In addition to efficient water use, water resources would be stretched through water reuse. Homes with yards would be equipped with graywater systems which would filter and disinfect bath, wash and sink water so it can be used for irrigation.

Sewage water, which would no longer be contaminated with industrial chemicals and heavy metals, would be filtered and disinfected, then used to irrigate farms and landscaping. During rainy periods, recycled water would be stored in underground tanks buried under parks and various sports areas like tennis courts.

Water Collection And Storage

Being more water-efficient would also allow the region to reverse its present dependency on imported water. Instead of being dependent on the importation of 90 percent of its water, 90 to 100 percent of its water needs would be supplied by collecting rainwater runoff from local watersheds, roof tops, and through the sustainable use of the region's groundwater supplies. Conservatively, enough water can be sustainably collected from these sources each year to supply 5 million people with 107 gallons per person per day, 365 days per year. If 80 percent of this water was recycled and used for irrigation, the sustainable water budget per person would be 192 gallons per day.

Food

In the sustainable economy of the future, most of the food consumed in the region would be grown locally. If we were to recycle 80 percent of this 107 gallon per person water budget, enough irrigation water could be freed up to irrigate 300 square miles of agricultural soils 2 acre feet deep (24 inches). Three hundred square miles is approximately the amount of number 1 and 2 (prime) agricultural located in the region.

In summary, our study region has a lot to gain economically and otherwise by adopting an economic strategy aimed at sustainability. This is particularly true if the focus is on increasing self-sufficiency to keeps dollars in the economy that would have otherwise been exported. Since the people earning this money would live here, most of what they earn would be spent locally, creating economic pluses on all fronts.

From a municipal perspective, this new employment would reduce unemployment and welfare costs. With more money on average in people's pockets, more people could qualify to purchase a home or business. This would increase property values and property tax revenues. It would also strengthen the rental market and increase individual savings, freeing up investment capital.

In addition to the economic pluses discussed above, using resources more efficiently and developing those available in the region, would provide a number of other benefits:

1. Efficient resource use and regional resource development brings the added security of being less vulnerable to resource delivery cut-offs or politically-generated price fluctuations.

2. Efficiency and resource development would also reduce pollution and ecological damage in general. With less pollution, people are sick less often, happier, and more productive. With less damage to the region's ecology, less money is needed for clean-up and repair.

There is also the aesthetic value of living in a pristine environment where the air and water are clean, the food tasty, nutritious, and pesticide free, and where the landscape is clean, beautiful, and rich in plant and animal life.

Although these benefits are less easy to quantify, their dollar value is at least as great as the economic benefits described earlier.

If considered from an overall quality of life and sustainability perspective, the value of these benefits is infinite.

Conclusion

After I've given a lecture, I am often asked if I think we can make it. By this, the questioner means, "will we make the changes needed to become eco-nomically secure fast enough to avoid some catastrophic decline?" My answer to this question is, I don't know.

Do I think it is possible? Yes, I do. The potential is definitely there. If enough of us decide that this is what we want, there is no question in my mind that we can do it. Obviously, I'm personally committed to this path. I look forward to meeting you and working with you along the way.

Sincerely,

****

Energy Calculations And Assumptions
Photovoltaic (Solar) Cells

Assumptions

1. Each square meter of solar cell, tilted 32 degrees toward the south, converting the sunlight it receives into electricity at 10 percent efficiency, would produce .5 Kwhrs per day on average or 182.5 Kwhrs per year. This is actually a conservative estimate of the solar potential of the region. According to figures in the <u>Solar Radiation Data Manual for Flat-Plate and Concentrating Collectors</u> which was published by the U.S. Department of Energy's National Renewable Energy Laboratory, the actually production of a one square meter solar cell panel would be 208 Kwhrs per year or 13 percent more than the 182.5 Kwhr figure being used for these calculations. Additionally, the monitoring station where this data was collected is located on the east side of San Diego Bay, which experiences considerably more cloud cover than the regional average. [823]

2. When the region's population reaches 5 million people, the per capita energy use in Tijuana and San Diego will be:

---- the same as it is in the San Diego part of the region in 1995,

---- fifty percent less than it is in the San Diego part of the region in 1995,

---- seventy five percent less than it is in the San Diego part of the region in 1995.

3. All cars, trucks, buses and trains in the region would be converted to, or replaced by, vehicles powered by solar generated electricity. Aircraft would still be powered by liquid fuels which would be derived from plants grown in the region. Storage systems are still too heavy for electricity to be a practical energy source for aircraft.

4. A given amount of electrical energy is 30 percent more efficient at heating a given quantity of

---

[823] Marion, William and Stephen Wilcox. *Solar Radiation Data Manual for Flat-Plate and Concentrating Collectors*. National Renewable Energy Laboratory, Golden Colorado, 1994: p. 42.

space or water than the same amount of energy in the form of natural gas. Natural gas heats water or space externally; therefore, around thirty percent of the energy in the gas goes out the stack with the combustion gases. When electricity is used to heat water or space, it is heated from the inside out; therefore, all the energy applied to the task is converted into the work of heating space or water.

5. A given amount of electricity is 3 times more efficient at moving a comparably-sized, electric-powered vehicle a given distance, than is using the same amount of energy in the form of gasoline or diesel, to move the same sized, internal combustion engine powered vehicle the same distance. The electric motors used to power electric cars convert 90 to 95 percent of the energy they consume into motion. When losses associated with charging and discharging batteries are included in the calculations, an electric powered vehicle converts 60 percent of the electricity used to charge the vehicles batteries into vehicular motion. By comparison, only 20 percent of the energy in a given amount of gasoline is actually converted into the motion of a vehicle. This is due to the inherent inefficiency of the fuel-powered internal combustion engines.

Note: Except for the requirement that devices designed to convert renewable energy resources into electricity need to produce several times as much electricity as is required to:

1. produce the devise in the first place,

2. maintain it during its working life,

3. and recycle it when it wears out,

the issue of the conversion (thermodynamic) efficiency of solar energy into electricity can be largely ignored.

As long as a solar device achieves the requirements stated above, the efficiency of conversion, within limits, is not relevant. This is because, for all practical purposes, our solar energy supply is infinite, and the solar energy that is intercepted by our planet is constantly being dissipated into space whether or not we convert it to electricity or some other form of useable energy.

Based on these assumptions: How much electricity will be needed to power a Tijuana/San Diego Regional economy with a population of 5 million people if:

1. The average level of energy service enjoyed throughout the region is the same as is now enjoyed by the average person living in the San Diego part of the region.

2. And the efficiency of energy use will be the same throughout the region as it is in the San Diego part of the region in 1995, when the population reaches 5 million people?

Calculations

Currently, there are approximately 47 trillion Btu of electricity [SANDAG (revised) Draft Regional Energy Plan Volume 2, 10/1/93, p. 7] or 13.8 billion Kwhrs of electricity used in the San Diego part of the region for all residential, commercial, and industrial purposes. 47 trillion Btu electricity x 2.93 x 10 -4 = 13.8 billion Kwhrs. (2.93 X 10 -4 is the conversion constant for converting Btu into Kwhrs.) This means that the average per capita electricity use per year in San Diego is 5,053 Kwhrs or just under 14 Kwhrs per day. One Kwhr of electricity is enough energy to keep a 100 watt bulb lit for 10 hours. 13.8 billion Kwhrs divided by the 2,730,995 people living in the San Diego part of the region in 1995 = 5,053 Kwhrs per person each year. 5,053 Kwhrs divided by 365 days = 14 Kwhrs per day.

An additional 50 trillion Btu in the form of natural gas are used in the San Diego portion of the region each year, primarily for space and water heating and for providing heat for industrial processes. [SANDAG (revised) Draft Regional Energy Plan Volume 2, 10/1/93, p. 7] If solar produced electricity was used to replace this natural gas it would require 30 percent less energy than is required to do the job with gas or 35 trillion Btu of electricity. 49.6 trillion Btu natural gas X .7 = 35 trillion Btu electricity. This is because there are no combustion gas losses with electricity. (See assumption #4 above for a more detailed explanation.) Thirty-five trillion Btu electricity equals 10.3 billion Kwhrs of electricity or 10.2 Kwhrs per capita per day. (35 trillion Btu electricity X 2.93 X 10 -4 = 10.3 billion Kwhrs --- 10.3 billion Kwhrs divided by 2,730,995 people = 3,772 Kwhrs per person per year --- 3,772 Kwhrs per year divided by 365 days per year = 10.3 Kwhrs per person each day.

Residents in the San Diego part of the region also use 111 trillion Btu in the form of gasoline and diesel fuel to power its cars, trucks and trains. [SANDAG (revised) <u>Draft Regional Energy Plan Volume 2</u>, 10/1/93, p. 7] But, internal combustion engines only convert 20 percent of the energy they consume into the work of moving a vehicle. By comparison, electric powered vehicles, even including charging and discharging losses, convert 60 percent of the electricity they use into vehicular motion. 111 trillion Btu X 20 percent = 22.2 trillion Btu. 22.2 trillion Btu is the portion of the fuel that actually gets converted to work. 22.2 trillion Btu = .6y, y = 37 trillion Btu electricity. Instead of needing 111 trillion Btu to power the region's vehicles, they could be powered by only 37 trillion Btu of electricity if they were all converted to electricity.

Electric motors used to power electric cars are 90 to 95 percent efficient at converting electrical energy into vehicular motion. But since electric powered vehicles use up energy when batteries are charged and discharged, the calculations used to come up with the 37 trillion Btu of electricity are based on a total electric drive train efficiency of 60 percent, instead of the actual efficiency of electric motors - 20/60 reduces to 1/3 X 111 trillion Btu = 37 trillion btu electricity. Converted to Kwhrs 37 trillion btu electricity equals 10.84 billion Kwhrs or 10.9 Kwhrs per person per day. 37 trillion Btu of electricity X 2.93 X 10 -4 = 10.84 billion Kwhrs --- 10.84 billion Kwhrs divided by 2,730,995 people (San Diego County's population in 1995) = 3,969 Kwhrs per capita per year --- 3,969 Kwhrs per capita per year divided by 365 days per year = 10.9 Kwhrs per capita per day.

Therefore, if all the energy needed to run the San Diego part of the region's economy at <u>current levels of efficiency</u> were in the form of electricity, the total per capita energy use would be 35.2 Kwhrs per day. 14 Kwhrs + 10.3 Kwhrs + 10.9 Kwhrs = 35.2 Kwhrs equals the total energy consumption per capita per day in the San Diego part of the region. If this level of per capita energy use is projected onto a 5 million person regional population, the total electrical energy needed to run the economy each year, at current efficiency levels, would be 64.2 billion Kwhrs -- 35.2 Kwhrs per capita per day X 365 days per year X 5 million people = 64.2 billion Kwhrs per year. If we add another 35.8 billion Kwhrs of production capacity to build up storage for night time an cloudy weather periods, the total electrical energy needed to supply all the energy for a population of 5 million people would be 100 billion Kwhrs per year. 35.2 Kwhrs per capita per day X 365 days = 12,848 Kwhrs per capita per year X 5,000,000 people = 64.2 billion Kwhrs per year plus 35.8 billion Kwhrs for storage = 100 billion Kwhrs per year total.

To produce this amount of electricity with solar cells would require 548 million square meters of solar cell panels or 110 square meters of solar cells per capita. 100 billion Kwhrs per year divided by 182.5 Kwhrs produced per year by a fixed 1 square meter solar cell panel, tilted at an angle of 32 degrees from the horizontal, due south = 548 million square meters --- 548 million square meters divided by a 5 million person population = just under 110 square meters or 1,183 square feet per person.

Surface Water Calculations

.06 - the amount of rainfall to be collected X 1.5 feet average rainfall each year = .09 feet of rainfall collected each year, (1.08 inches). .09 feet X 3,980,800 acres = 358,272 acre feet of water. 358,272 acre feet of water divided by 5,000,000 people = .072 acre feet per capita per year. .072 acre feet X 43,560 cubic feet per acre foot = 3,136 cubic feet of water per capita per year. 3,136 cubic feet X 7.48 gallons per cubic foot = 23,457 gallons per year divided by 365 days per year = 64 gallons of water per capita per day.

Collecting Rain Water From Impervious Urban Surfaces

Another 25 gallons per capita per day could be supplied by collecting rainwater runoff from impervious surfaces like rooftops, parking lots, paved playgrounds, driveways, and patios. When rain falls on these surfaces, close to 100 percent of it can be collected. Author's calculations based on figures published 3/29/94 in SANDAG/SOURCEPOINT taken from "Source: Series 8 Regional Growth Forecast," an estimated 183,418 acres of impervious surfaces will exist in the San Diego side of the region by 2005. 183,418 acres divided by 3,274,548 people, the projected population in the San Diego part of the Region in 2005 equals .056 acres pre capita. .056 acres X the 5 million projected Regional population in the year 2005 = 280,000 acres of impervious surface region wide in the year 2005. Assuming that only 6 inches of rainfall can be collected from these surfaces each year, 280,000 acres of impervious surface X .5 feet = 140,000 acre feet of water each year. 140,000 acre feet divided by 5 million people = .028 acre feet per capita. .028 acres per capita per year X 43,560 (the number of cubic feet in an acre foot of water) = 1,220 cu. ft. of water per capita per year X 7.48 gallons per cu. ft. = 9125 gal. per capita per year. 9125 gal. per capita per year divided by 365 days per year = 25 gallons per capita per day. This 25 gallon estimate is conservative considering that it assumes that only 6 inches of rainfall can be collected from the region's impervious surfaces even though 10 to 14 inches of rainfall actually falls on them in an average rainfall year. (Urban areas in the region tend to be relatively close to the ocean where rainfall is actually less that the regional average of 18 inches.) Additionally, the number of impervious acres used in these calculations do not include road or freeway surfaces.

Groundwater Resources

In addition to collecting rainwater from the region's watersheds and impervious surfaces, there is around 100,000 acre feet of water that can be extracted sustainably from groundwater supplies each year. If these resources are developed it would add another 18 gallons per capita each day for the projected population of 5 million people. (100,000 acre feet of water divided by 5 million people = .02 acre feet per capita per year. .02 X 43,560 cu. ft. per acre ft. = 871 cu. ft. X 7.48 gal. per cu. ft. = 6,516 gal per capita per year divided by 365 days per year = 18 gal. per capita per day.)

Adding these three sources together, 64 gal. + 25 gal. + 18 gal. = a water supply of 107 gallons per capita per day for 365 days a year for a 5 million person population.

If 80 percent of this water is recycled after it is used, it would supply another 85 gallons per capita per day for irrigation. (107 gallons per day X .80 = 85 gallons per capita per day.) This 85 gallons added to the 107 gallons just discussed adds up to a total per capita water-use allowance of 192 gallons of water per day per capita. This is close to 90 percent of what is used per capita in 1995 in the San Diego part of the region. The San Diego part of the Region currently uses around 214 gallons of water per capita per day for all purposes, residential, commercial, industrial, and for agriculture.

ELSI Publications

1. **Achieving Eco-nomic Security On Spaceship Earth** by Jim Bell. 185 pages. $16.00, (includes taxes). Add $4.00 for postage and handling.

Quite simply, Achieving Eco-nomic Security On Spaceship Earth is a nuts and bolts, how to, common sense book about how to use free-market-forces to revitalize our national and world economies in ways that are completely ecologically sustainable. Although the book is comprehensive it is written for the average reader. It also has over 800 footnotes for those who want to explore the subjects discussed in the book in more depth.

2. **Achieving Eco-nomic Security: The San Diego/Tijuana Region - A Case Study** by Jim Bell. 21 pages. $5.00 (includes taxes). Add $1.00 for postage and handling.

This paper shows how a specific region can gracefully transform its non-sustainable economy into one that is completely sustainable. It begins by examining how the region's economy and infrastructure are vulnerable to threats ranging from intentional human acts of terrorism and natural phenomena to global economic dynamics beyond regional control. With this as a given, it shows how ecologically integrated economic planning can reduce such threats in ways that increase business and employment opportunities through ecologically based land use planning and by becoming more energy and water efficient and energy, water and food self-sufficient.

3. **If Free Trade Is The Answer, What Is The Question?** by Jim Bell. 14 pages. $4.00, (includes taxes). Add $1.00 for postage and handling.

This paper turns the trade debate on its head by showing that speeding up non-sustainable economies through free trade will only hasten their decline. It also shows how economies can become sustainable and how trade can be expanded in ways that contribute to that goal.

4. **Planning For Water Sufficiency** by Jim Bell. 8 pages. $3.00, (includes taxes). Add $1.00 for postage and handling.

The problem of potential water scarcity has been largely ignored by developers, planners, and the public on the assumption that water can be imported as needed. However, importing leaves the community vulnerable to disruptions in supply and pricing, political decisions that are not locally controlled, and can have a high environmental cost. Planning can minimize these negative effects by using resources, like the rainfall that falls on a community or building sight, cost-effectively.

5. **Ecologically Integrated Planning: A Case Study** by Jim Bell, Lyn Snow, and Donna Vary. 39 pages. $7.00, (includes taxes). Add $3.00 for postage and handling.

This Study focuses on the Otay Ranch Project, located in the San Diego/Tijuana region, which is one of the largest developments ever proposed in modern times, and shows how that development could be more economically successful by adopting an ecologically integrated planning, design, and implementation strategy.

6. **Eco-nomic Sustainability: A Planning Guide For Protecting The Water Quality Of Bays And Lakes - Mission Bay, A Case Study** by Jim Bell. 20 pages. $4.00, includes taxes. Add $1.00 for postage and handling

This paper shows how public education coupled with watershed based ecological planning can improve and protect a lake's or bay's water quality permanently.

Get the complete set and save $7.00. Send $30.00 plus $4 for postage and handling to: ELSI, 2923 East Spruce St., San Diego, CA 92104. Make checks payable to the Green Store.